This For

Male Homosexuality:
A Culture & History Guide

David Ledain

For Jeremy, who needed a book like this.

Also by David Ledain:

Gay Dad – Ten True Stories of Divorced Gay Men With Kids, Living in the UK Today

You can follow David on Facebook & Twitter @DavidLedain and visit his website www.gaydad.co.uk for more information and his blog.

You can also very easily leave a review for *This Forbidden Fruit* here: www.amazon.co.uk/thisforbiddenfruit/createareview

Contents

Introduction

For me, as a gay man, and for many others, these past twenty years have been life-affirming, and yet whilst the changes in our laws have affected so many in the LGBTQ+ community, the majority of the population, often perplexed at the commotion, have remained unaffected, despite the doom-makers' predictions of the collapse of all morals and the demise of decent human behaviour if homosexuals were ever given equal rights. And though the vast proportion of people might feel their lives unchanged by LGBTQ+ legislation, the collective positivity and optimism acquired by the gay community, empowering many to fulfil their lives and dreams, has had a knock-on effect for everyone in numerous good and productive ways. So much so that we now see large corporations and businesses taking up the cause of diversity in the workplace and making their products and services appeal to their LGBTQ+ consumers.

In 2016, I wrote a book called *Gay Dad*: *ten true stories of divorced gay men with kids, living in the UK today*. I wrote it because, as a gay, divorced father myself, I could not find anything that told the stories of other gay men in the same situation as me. There were the celebrity biographies, the sports stars who had written about their 'coming out' experiences, and self-help books, particularly in America, for same-sex couples wishing to adopt, but there was nothing that spoke directly to me. I wanted to read the stories of other gay men who had faced the difficulty of coming out to their wives and children and all the emotional turmoil and practical problems that inevitably brought on the family. I decided to write that book myself.

Through talking to other gay dads, I not only had an insight into the private and often intimate lives of these men but a view of the times in which they grew up, through decades of AIDS, prejudice and mockery, when the UK law discriminated against them. Now these men find themselves riding a wave of hope, where equality and normality have become tangible concepts within their grasp.

Gay Dad is a social document of our times; looking back on childhoods and young adult lives when it was impossible to be who you really were, when the rich history and culture of gay men over hundreds and thousands of years was not open or taught but shut away, secret, taboo and disgusting.

In 2008, my brother, whom I had no idea was gay or even bisexual, died from AIDS. In the five years before, during which his body slowly and painfully fought for survival, and for years after, I fought a personal battle of fear and dread that I would also end up like that. The 1980s had initiated that horror and my brother's illness made it ever more real. The closet seemed the safest place for me to be. What I lacked was any point of reference to help me to see that it didn't have to be that way. Where were the positive gay role models of everyday life? It seemed they didn't exist.

Through my research, writing *Gay Dad*, I was surprised at the depth and permanency of gay history and culture, and I realised that I knew nothing about it, because I was never told it or knew where to find it. Suddenly I was awoken to the fact that I had a heritage; a strong and vibrant culture that could not be denied and without which the world would have been a far less rich and inspiring place. *This Forbidden Fruit* is the story of that rich and diverse culture which every gay man should have at his fingertips and look at with pride and say: 'These are my people. This is what we have achieved. This is what we have given the world'.

In this book I wanted to explore and write about gay culture in a way that addressed some of those unanswered questions gay men have not been given access to, for all sorts of reasons and for far too many years. For instance: what is our heritage? What are the key dates and events that marked our progress through history? How did society evolve from a time when homosexuality was viewed in an entirely different way from the way we think about it today? I also wanted to write a timeline of LGBT history without making it a dull presentation of facts and dates. I have therefore split this book into two parts: Part One – Culture & History; Part Two – Significant Events.

This Forbidden Fruit is a personal commentary; a book that answers many of the questions I didn't even know I needed answering when I was struggling with who I was and where I came from. The research and key events I have included give, I hope, that much required background information but it is not an encyclopaedia of every event that has ever happened to the gay community. In Part One – Culture & History, there are stories of homosexual men who have seen in their lifetimes, in art and literature, in the military and through the dynamism of gay culture, a long revolution that has brought us to where we are now. In Part Two – Significant Events, I have sought to write about the events and changes that have had the biggest impact.

This Forbidden Fruit is about acknowledging our past, but it is also about looking forward and how much better it is for our society when diversity is celebrated, encouraged and endorsed at every level. We have moved from a national position of intolerance and bigotry to one of inclusion and acceptance. However, it is a long road we are on and it is up to us, the gay community, to light the way and do our bit, to show what can be achieved and what we have achieved already. If *Gay Dad* was a snapshot of our times and struggles – a retrospective glance over the shoulder – *This Forbidden Fruit* points to the future.

David Ledain.

Part One

Culture & History

1.
Gays in World History

The earliest art depicting male figures in what could be construed as either a religious initiation, some form of dancing, or acts of male-on-male sex, can be found in Sicilian Mesolithic rock carvings dating back to between 9000 and 5000 BC. George Nash writes in *The Subversive Male: Homosexual & Bestial Images on European Mesolithic Rock Art*:

Images of sexuality within prehistory are not uncommon, while in contrast, scenes depicting homosexuality are rare. However, there are images that deserve comment, not just for what they portray, but also for the underlying socio-cultural set-up that controlled those societies and the artists who executed the images. Assuming these societies were based on heterosexual lineage, what were the consequences of carving such images? It could be argued that such art was a reaction against the norm. However, it could also be that homosexuality, ritual or otherwise, was tolerated. Certainly, within later archaeological records, homosexuality is considered part of the life-cycle experienced mostly by males. Secrecy and persecution, concepts present in our own society, appear, according to the art, not to have been an issue.

The rock art in question is not obvious or straightforward for the layman to interpret, and it is easy to imagine that the carvings might simply have been the scrawling graffiti of lone individuals, indeed 'carried out in secrecy', rather than lewd artforms for a wider audience to 'appreciate'. Whatever the reason, the underlying perception is that sexual exploration was perhaps as much a part of Mesolithic man's lifestyle as it is our own, and we do him an injustice to assume that he lived an existence of merely hunting, gathering and procreating with little time or energy for much else. When we look at our nearest relatives, the chimpanzees, who are adept at utilising sticks and stones as tools, and who have a hierarchy and sophisticated social intercourse, which includes homosexuality, we can see that imagination and an enquiring mind all play a distinct role in primal, yet complex societies. It is not, therefore, unthinkable to imagine our own ancestors living just such multifaceted and inquisitive lives, even before the dawn of recorded history.

In 1964, at the necropolis of the Egyptian Old Kingdom capital of Memphis in Saqqara, thirty kilometres south of Cairo, an archaeologist by the name of Ahmed Moussa discovered a series of tombs and passages cut into an escarpment of rock that faced a causeway leading to the ancient pyramid of the Pharaoh Unas. Entering one of the old tombs, Moussa was surprised to see that there were scenes on the walls depicting two men intimately embracing and touching noses. This was unique. The touching of noses was something only ever portrayed between married couples, a man and a woman, and it had never been seen before portrayed between two men. Some of the stone blocks from the entrance of the tomb had been used in the construction of the causeway leading to Unas' pyramid and when they rebuilt the entrance using these blocks, it was revealed that the tomb was built for two high-ranking male officials, Nyankh-Khnum and Khnum-hotep, who shared the same title, that of Overseer of Manicurists and were royal confidants in the court of Pharaoh Niuserre of the Fifth Dynasty, around 2400BC. The two chief manicurists would have held extremely privileged positions, being among a very select few who could touch the Pharaoh.

Both men, it seems, had wives and families of their own. In one scene, Nyankh-Khnum's wife is depicted sitting behind him at a banqueting table, and in others,

Khnum-hotep occupies a position next to Nyankh-Khnum which would normally be reserved for the spouse. Further evidence of their closeness comes in the hieroglyphs that make up their combined names. When strung together they read as 'joined in life and joined in death'.

There is some speculation about the exact meaning and interpretation of the reliefs, but in Ancient Egypt the depiction of close nose-to-nose touching signified a kiss. Historians and Egyptologists, however, still disagree on what it means in this context. Some say that it shows a clear example of homosexuality between two married men, therefore making their relationship acceptable within the ancient Egyptian society at the time. Others say that they were twins, possibly even conjoined twins (though there is no evidence for this), and that the reliefs show their closeness to one another both in body and spirit. This seems to be clutching at straws to disregard what is otherwise obvious. Whatever the precise detail, these two important men of the royal household were clearly very close and upon their deaths the families carried out their wishes to have them buried together in one tomb.

Nearly two thousand years later, around 630BC, an inscription in Crete is the oldest known record of the institution of pederasty, which involved the ritualised kidnapping of noble boys by aristocratic adult males. With the consent of the boy's father, the upper-class man, known as the *philetor*, 'befriender', took the boy, known as *kleinos*, or 'distinguished', into the wilderness, where they spent two months hunting and feasting with friends. If the boy was satisfied with the conduct of his mentor, he would change his title from *kleinos* to *parastathentes* or 'sidekick', indicating that he had fought in battle alongside his lover and had returned to live in a close, intimate and openly public relationship. The function of the institution, besides teaching the youth adult skills, was to confirm the noble character and deserved respect of both those involved. The man was honoured by being allowed to take the boy, and the boy's honour was increased by being taken. The Greek historian Strabo wrote:

The Cretans have a peculiar custom in regard to love affairs, for they win the objects of their love, not by persuasion, but by abduction; the lover tells the friends of the boy three or four days beforehand, that he is going to make the abduction; but for the friends to conceal the boy, or not to let him go forth the appointed road, is indeed a most disgraceful thing, a confession, as it were, that the boy is unworthy to obtain such a lover; and when they meet, if the abductor is the boy's equal or superior in rank or other respects, the friends pursue him and lay hold of him, though only in a very gentle way, thus satisfying the custom; and after that they cheerfully turn the boy over to him to lead away; if, however, the abductor is unworthy, they take the boy away from him.

The custom, it seems, was highly regarded, and it was considered shameful for a youth not to acquire a male lover. Strabo also wrote:

It is disgraceful for those who are handsome in appearance or descendants of illustrious ancestors to fail to obtain lovers, the presumption being that their character (masculinity) is responsible for such a fate. But the *parastathentes* (those who stand by their lover in battle) receive honours; for in both the dances and the races they have the positions of highest honour, and are allowed to dress in better clothes than the rest, that is, in the habit given them by their lovers; and not then only, but even after they have grown to manhood, they wear a distinctive dress, which is intended to make known the fact that each wearer has become *kleinos*, for they call the loved one *kleinos* (distinguished) and the lover *philetor*.

Recent scholars have suggested that this practise, adopted by the Dorians, spread from Crete to Sparta and then to the rest of Greece.

In Ancient Greece, though marriage between men was not legally recognised, men could, and did, form life-long relationships akin to a 'marriage', in which the older partner would take on the role of mentor to the younger one, much in the same way as the Dorian practice.

We should note here our own, very different and modern connotations around the word 'pederasty' in conjunction with paedophilia. A paedophile, according to the definition in the Concise Oxford Dictionary, is 'a person who is sexually attracted to children'. More than that, it is about the violating act of gratification and the grooming of children to that end. Pederasty derives from the Greek word *paiderastia*, literally meaning *paid* 'boy', and *erastes* 'lover', implying something more than just sexual attraction. In fact, these relationships were entered into only after a negotiated contract was agreed. In the context of the historical period of the ancient world, these adolescent boys were not considered children and documented evidence states that though slave boys could be bought, free boys had to be courted and their father's consent sought first. Such relationships did not replace marriage but coincided with it. The normal practice was for adult men not to have a male mate of an equivalent age, though there were exceptions. Alexander the Great, for instance, and his long-term companion and some say lover Hephaestion, were the same age.

In Greek, the older man was known as the *erastes*, and was the lover to a younger *eromenos* or 'loved one'. It was thought improper for the *eromenos* to feel desire towards the older man, as that would imply un-masculinity. The *erastes*, the older lover and pursuer, could however be driven by desire and admiration, and would devote himself unselfishly to providing all the educational needs his *eromenos* required to thrive in society. These relationships were emotionally, as well as sexually, motivated, and the

17

Greeks believed very much in the power of semen as the source of knowledge and that these relationships served to pass on that wisdom.

Alexander and Hephaestion, who was a general himself in Alexander's army, together conquered most of the then known world, bringing Hellenistic culture and values, including the positive way in which they viewed homosexuality, to millions of people.

Ancient Greece thrived from 800BC-146BC, by which time the Romans had arrived. They had a different temperament from the Greeks, predominantly that of the male psyche to conquer all. This shaped even their views on homosexual practices. For so long as Roman men partook in the dominant and penetrative role, sexual activity between men was socially acceptable. In fact, it was considered quite natural and there was no loss to a man's masculinity or his social standing because of it. To be the submissive partner however, the one giving the pleasure, was regarded as subservient and therefore demeaning. Also, sex between men of equal status was not socially acceptable and was in some cases severely punished, though little evidence of this remains. Sex with young Roman boys was a crime, but with slaves, prostitutes, actors, or anyone else with no social standing, it was perfectly legitimate for the dominant Roman male to take whoever he wanted. It might be said that it is this Roman attitude to homosexuality that has stuck with Western culture ever since – the idea that it is more or less accepted that there are some men who take on the passive, effeminate role of submission (even though submissive/effeminate men are seen as having a lower status and less academically inclined), but it is utterly unacceptable if the roles are reversed, i.e. the dominant male 'flip-flops' and gives himself up for penetration. This stereotyping of homosexuals is none so clearly demonstrated than in the comedy sketch TV programmes of the 1970s, where homosexual men were only ever depicted as whimsical, effete and air-headed, and caricatured by pantomime one-liners. Based on this analogy, it could be interpreted that this was how the Romans also perceived male sexual passive behaviour.

China and Japan both share a long tradition of homosexuality within their cultures, and it wasn't until relatively recently, at the time they came into contact with the Western world, that attitudes changed. During the Qing dynasty in China, AD1644-1912, there was an open acceptance that aristocrats would take male partners as well as having one or more wives (having more than one wife was a sign of wealth and status). All upper-class men were expected to marry and father children to carry on the family line, while their wives, especially those in the harems of the Chinese emperors, were expected to fulfil their duties by keeping their husbands company and rearing their children. Women who were not favourites could lead very lonely lives in the harems, while men enjoyed the freedom to bed whoever they pleased.

In the culture of the Far East there has always been less of a fixation on the 'roles' of same-sex male partners, unlike in Western culture. Art and literature from a thousand years ago often describes sexual intercourse performed between men in flowery terms, such as in the Chinese expressions '*pleasures of the bitten peach*' or '*the cut sleeve*' – this particular reference is from a story from the time of Chinese Emperor Ai of Han (27–1 BC) who ascended the throne at the age of twenty. The story goes that after falling asleep one afternoon with his male consort, Dong Xian, Emperor Ai cut the sleeve of his tunic rather than wake his sleeping lover to free it – a gentle and caring portrayal of what male same-sex love was in the Imperial Court, compared to the power and domination with which the Romans equated sex.

'Countenances of linked jade' and *'they were like Lord Long Yang'*, are other gentle and inoffensive phrases that refer to past manuscript stories. None of these expressions are recognisable in terms of speaking about sexuality to someone who was not familiar with the literal tales and

their meanings, and they were easily slipped into polite conversation without causing offence. The dominant or submissive behaviour in the sexual act is also of little importance, and there is a sense that homosexuality, as a part of everyday life, was well known and accepted. As it would be socially unacceptable to talk about sex in explicit terms in Asian cultures today, an acceptance of it as just being part of life was adopted by the ancient culture too.

In South Asia, particularly in India, the Hijra have a 4,000-year-old tradition of acceptance and even veneration, appearing in ancient texts as bearers of good luck and fertility. Assigned as male at birth, the transgender, or third-gender, Hijra live in communes overseen by a Guru or Hijra elder mother. Some communes offer sanctuary and safety and a strong hierarchical family for the young Hijras. Some, however, are often places of exploitation, and though rejected by their families and facing homophobic discrimination and persecution, the Hijra are, ironically, believed to hold great spiritual powers which are often called upon by the wider community. Singing and dancing and offering prayers at birthing ceremonies can be lucrative means of making money, but frequently the Hijra subsidise a living through the sex trade.

A third, or transgender, sex is not unusual or specific to the Indian Sub-Continent. Among the native tribes of the Americas, the presence of male Two-Spirits was a fundamental institution. Thought to be 'the dusk between the male morning and the female evening', Two-Spirits might be gay, but a gay person might not necessarily be Two-Spirited. Identified during their early life development, their parents were given the choice of which path the child should follow. Like the Hijra, they were revered individuals, often shamans, bestowed with extra powers beyond those of ordinary shamans. Two-Spirits, homosexuals and transgender individuals were also commonly recognised among the many civilizations of

South America, including the Aztecs, Mayans, Quechuas, Zapotecs and the Tupinamba of Brazil.

African culture is no stranger to homosexual tendencies and behaviour either, but the history of it is mostly unwritten, and because of modern Africa's largely hostile treatment towards homosexuals and its anti-gay rhetoric, it is difficult to uncover. Language, however, provides evidence that homosexuality has long existed on the African continent and that it was recognised within the tribes.

The Hausa people of northern Nigeria and those of the surrounding area were among the last African cultures to be subjugated by Europeans. Conquered by the British in 1904, they had experienced very little contact with Europeans prior to that and were subsequently studied in great detail and depth by British ethnographers, into their customs, characteristics and sexual practices, including homosexuality. In northern Nigeria, for example, *van daudu* is a Hausa term used to describe effeminate men, while in Yoruba the word for homosexual is *adofuro*, a slang word meaning someone who has anal sex – a word that is as old as Yoruban culture itself. While the Yoruba word is about behaviour, the Hausa *yan daudu* term is about identity. Both are significant in that they are neutral. There is no intention in either of these phrases to impart hate or repugnance, simply a descriptive. Likewise, in Angola and the Congo, the word *jimbandaa,* meaning 'passive sodomite', came into being after tribesmen who wore loincloths with the ends at the front, left the rear open.

The British anthropologist, E. E. Evans-Pritchard, published his research into the Azande warriors of the Sudan in 1970. He wrote that before colonialism there was a good deal of fighting between opposing kingdoms in the region and part of the male population of each side was organised into military compounds which were situated away from their villages. These companies were made up of married men and bachelors, and it was customary for the bachelors to take on boy-wives as there was a lack of marriageable women. Young girls were engaged and essentially legally married, at a very young age, sometimes even at birth; and in the days when nobles and rich men kept large harems, available girls for marrying were few. Having adulterous relations with married women was a very dangerous pursuit and if discovered, the fine on the young man's father would be very high – twenty spears plus a woman, or even mutilation and castration. It was therefore expected that a bachelor warrior would select a boy between the ages of 12-20 and request of the boy's parents his hand in marriage. The warrior would pay a bride-price for the boy, which would be in the form of five to ten spears and other goods. The boy-wife's role was to take on all the household duties including fetching water, building a fire and carrying his warriors' shield when travelling. Once married, the warrior referred to the boy's parents as *gbiore* and *negbior*, father-in-law and mother-in-law. He and the boy would address each other as *badiare*, 'my love' or 'my lover'. The two slept together at night, the warrior satisfying his sexual desires between the boy's thighs – intercrural – never anally, as this was considered disgusting. Once the boy-wife had come of age, it was the duty of the warrior husband to give him a spear and shield so that he could then become a warrior himself and take on a boy-wife of his own. The relationship between the two was one of caring companionship, and it was very much in the interests of the warrior to be good to his boy-wife so that the parents might reward him with a woman from the harem or a daughter, once his boy-wife had come of age. After marrying a woman, only heterosexual relations ensued.

The status quo of the mighty Azande could not be further from that depicted by some modern rappers and African governments who claim that homosexuality is not a habit that is natural to Africans or within African culture, and who widely perceive it to be the curse of the West imposed on them by the European Colonialists. This belief that the practice of homosexuality has no roots in Africa is not a recent phenomenon, however. Even during the eighteenth century Europeans thought that overt heterosexuality played a significant part in the make-up of African tribespeople. However, other anthropologists such as Stephen Murray and Will Roscoe have provided wide-ranging evidence to support the fact that throughout Africa's history, 'African homosexuality is neither random nor incidental – it is a consistent and logical feature of African societies and belief systems'. That such behaviour undoubtedly existed prior to European contact is also evidenced in stories that have been handed down from one generation to another. In Zimbabwe, long before Europeans arrived, the San people, ancient hunter-gatherer bushmen, whose territories spanned from Angola to Zimbabwe, and down to South Africa, recorded group anal sexual intercourse in rock art that dates back thousands of years.

In other tribes too, homosexual behaviour among pre-marriage adolescents is still common and not even considered to be sex, since it does not involve procreation. In Cameroon, for example, homosexual acts amongst teenagers up to the age of 17 are deemed innocent and not 'true' sexual relations, and these young men consider themselves to be virgins at marriage, even though they may have considerable homosexual experiences in both dominant and passive roles.

There is an argument that colonialism, particularly British Colonialism, has led to many of the governments and rulers in modern-day Africa taking the position of defending anti-gay colonial laws, effectively outlawing traditional African values of diversity and tolerance. The criminal codes imposed by the British on their territories prohibiting same-sex relations was indeed contrasted by those nations colonised by other European powers. The French, for instance, abolished the offence of sodomy in 1791, consequently the penal code of 1810 did not include it. This then influenced other nations such as The

Netherlands, Belgium, Spain, Portugal and Italy in adopting similar codes in respect to their own colonies.

However, when scrutinising LGBT laws in Africa by each nation, it is by no means as simplistic. Countries such as Burkina Faso, Benin, Central African Republic, Chad, Cote d'Ivoire, Djibouti, Gabon, Madagascar, Mali, and Niger are all former French territories in which there are no laws against same-sex sexual activity, but there are notably no laws recognising same-sex unions or marriage, no anti-discrimination laws, no laws for same-sex couples to adopt, or for LGBT personnel to serve openly in their country's military. It is true that in many of the former British territories it is still illegal for male-to-male sexual activity and has been ever since colonial times, but nations such as Libya, Egypt, and Morocco, where independence was gained in 1951, '53 and '56 respectively, still maintain laws against homosexuality that were not introduced until 1953 in Libya, 2000 in Egypt and 1962 in Morocco, long after independence. There is also little consistency in penalties upon conviction; anything from three years' imprisonment in Morocco and seventeen years in Egypt, or fourteen years to the death penalty, dependant on the state, in Nigeria. In Uganda homosexuality has been illegal since 1894 and those convicted can expect up to a life sentence in prison, but they are more likely to fall foul of vigilante groups who hunt down homosexuals and impart their own penalties which can result in death at the hands of the mob.

It is unfair to blame British colonialism solely for the anti-gay laws of its former colonies or to put nations up against others that do not criminalise homosexuality as if they were paragons of virtue, for those same nations are by no means open and tolerant societies. The exception is South Africa, where laws exist that do not discriminate against homosexuals, where the state does recognise same-sex unions, including marriage, and same-sex couples can adopt. LGBT individuals can also serve openly in the military. It is clear though, that many countries, including some of the Commonwealth, have a way to go yet.

2.
Homophobia

During the Inquisitions – the trials and persecutions of heretics against the Catholic Church, which included Pagans, Witches, blasphemers and free thinkers – sodomy was often cited in evidence against such groups, who were said to indulge in sexual acts at their secret rituals. This idea of the 'unnatural act against nature' was particularly useful to the Inquisitors as propaganda against dissenting sects, such as the Cathars of the Languedoc region of Southern France and later, the Knights Templar.

Sodomy was never an act specific to homosexuals and homosexuality as a concept (as discussed elsewhere) was not something people considered, but the 'unnatural' act of sodomy by anyone was condemned by the Church as something completely abhorrent to nature and hence against the will of God.

There is theological evidence to indicate that the users of early Medieval penitentials, the Christian sacrament of penance, questioned what sins penitents who came to them had committed. The practices reflected in the penitentials show that heterosexuals in the Middle Ages had wide and varied sexual activity. As well as procreative sex in the missionary position, which the church upheld as the only form of sex people should succumb to, they also enjoyed sex with the woman on top and in the 'doggy position', as well as oral sex. Heterosexuals also had anal sex, which seems to have been used as a form of contraception. The thought of what might happen to the soul after death was a very real concern, and the constant preaching against sodomy from the pulpit was probably enough to make most sinners think twice. But the real targets were the sodomites, those who practised male-to-male anal penetration, and it can be said that it was during this period that homophobia as a concept of fear and hate was first used by a state to condemn its enemies.

One man, Peter Damian, was the prime thinker and instigator of the idea that the evils of sodomy were a major weakness to the social order of Medieval society. Damian, later canonised as Saint Damian, was a Benedictine monk and Cardinal to Pope Leo IX, who came to prominence around 1049AD for writing *Liber Gomorrhianus*, the Book of Gomorrah, a protracted diatribe on the ills of homosexuality and masturbation. In it, he addressed one of the prime concerns of the Inquisition reformers, that of celibacy within the Church. Through his writing, Damian saw himself carrying out a great act of intervention, utterly necessary for the stability and continuation of both the Church and the state. In referring to the biblical story of the ill-fated cities of Sodom and Gomorrah, he gave clear warning to those who ignored the misfortunes of vice and corruption that went on, not only in the towns and cities of Medieval Italy, but also within the Church, that what they were doing would lead to the downfall of civilisation itself. The Church's main function as a pillar of society was to save the world, but it was wantonly contributing to its ruin by allowing sodomites to take up ecclesiastical positions. 'This', he said was 'nothing short of their [the homosexuals'] attempt to sodomise God Himself.'

In *Liber Gomorrhianus* Damian wrote of the 'four types of criminal wickedness': 'Some sin with themselves alone (masturbation); some by the hands of others (mutual masturbation); others between the thighs (intercrural); and finally, others commit the complete act against nature (anal intercourse). The ascending gradation among these is such that the last mentioned are judged to be more serious than the preceding. Indeed, a greater penance is imposed on those who fall with others than those who defile only themselves... The devil's artful fraud devises these degrees of failing into ruin such that the higher the level the unfortunate soul reaches in them, the deeper it sinks in the depths of hell's pit.'

Stark warning indeed. Nowhere in the book, however, does Damian discuss or ask the question as to why people might indulge in such sexual acts, only stating that there would be dire consequences for anyone who did. Just like any homophobia we would recognise today, in Medieval Europe too, it was not, really, about male-to-male sexual behaviour or about masturbation, but rather the idea that such behaviour was a threat to the whole of society and particularly the dominance of the male gender. The thing that threatens is not wrong; rather it is wrong because it is seen as a threat.

If Damian was the first to pose the idea that homosexuality was a dangerous menace that could break the very fabric of society, he was not the last. It has been a recurrent theme in homophobic attitudes ever since. We might, therefore, ask those who hold these views what is it about the heteronormative status quo that makes it so vulnerable and feel so endangered by sexual diversity, and why anything other than narrow sexual conformity is so fundamentally dangerous? Why is the male body the focal point for such concern?

In Medieval times mortality was high, as malnutrition, harsh living conditions and epidemics swept through densely-populated cities with scything regularity. With up to one-in-three children not surviving beyond their fifth birthdays and adults living, on average, only until their mid-forties, it was considered a Christian imperative that fornication should only be for childbearing purposes. This is not the reason for Damian's stance on sodomy and masturbation, however. Had it been, it might be easier to forgive him, as any knowledge of the spread of disease via rats and unsanitary water were centuries off from being understood. No, Damian's start point was that it was against nature and God, and it was vital, therefore, that this behaviour be stopped.

By the thirteenth century, secular laws were being laid down across Europe as states sought to control their populations and the revenue and economies they drove.

Lawmakers took the framework of Justinian Roman law, or the Codex Justinianus – after the reforms of Emperor Justinian, 527AD-565AD – as their guide, in which homosexuality was explicitly condemned, and throughout Medieval times, Peter Damian's *Liber Gomorrhianus* was proliferated by the Church. Sodomy and those who practised it were the enemies of decent, God-fearing people, and of God Himself. This despicable practise which they could not explain, which they saw as an attack and deliberate feminising of masculinity, was at the root of all that was wrong in society. The rhetoric would have been easy to believe when everyone knew that the next epidemic, the next harsh winter or summer of drought, could spell the end for them. Fear of a God who meted out His divine displeasure on Sodom and Gomorrah was often given as good enough reason for implementing the new punitive laws.

On the face of it, by condoning the persecution of one minority to save the majority any dominant group in a society might seem to have found a practical answer to solving a great problem in times of peril when there is no other, easier way to resolve it; and especially so when it is a matter of saving the State and Church. Blaming a minority group deflects the onus of the problem from the actual cause to a perceived threat. Mistrust can then encourage that very group to rise-up and fulfil the prophetic negatives the dominant group say they possess. This is the danger of cultures with one dominant group, where weaker groups are made to suffer and pay over and over again, which ultimately, and ironically, leads to the destruction and overthrow of the society's dominant group. This method of dealing with the root of fear, any irrational fear that cannot easily be explained, by shifting the blame to a minority already on the edge of society and who cannot defend themselves, is horrifyingly simple in the way it works and can be seen throughout history and in societies today.

It is easy to dismiss any sexual practice as an indulgence that can, and perhaps should, be curbed, especially in times of repression, when to flout the law could have such catastrophic consequences, both personally and to the family of the accused. But the primal urge to satisfy ourselves through sex is a powerful, innate driver. Unlike most other animals, we do not have sex purely to procreate – though some religions still advocate that this is the ideal state of being. It is worth reiterating that there are no sexual activities that are exclusive to homosexuals. Sex is a way of bonding, of forming relationships, and inevitably of orgasm (though not always). It is such a powerful instinct that despite the punishments for those convicted of sodomy over the centuries since Medieval times, men particularly have persisted. As an example, in thirteenth century France, a man caught and condemned for sodomy was castrated, if caught again he would face dismemberment and for a third offence, be burnt to death, still men carried on taking the risk. (I'm not sure how it would be possible to get to a third offence without the mechanics to penetrate, or legs to stand on, and in any case either of these punishments could easily lead to death through infection and blood loss. Being the passive, sodomised, was just as lethal, unless you could prove that you were attacked and raped.)

One reason the risk of being caught outweighed the punishment, might have been that it was very difficult to prove. Essentially, to break such prohibited taboos, we must acknowledge just how strong the drive for sexual pleasure is in many individuals – as strong and sometimes stronger than any moral principles or laws of the day. It must be pointed out here that I am talking about consensual sex, and rape or abuse of any kind against anyone of any age cannot be condoned either morally or through law.

In the twenty-first century, individuals' human rights are much more to the forefront, and yet homosexuals have continued to suffer, and even today, homophobia blights our modern, and supposedly liberally open and diverse, society. In the UK, homophobic hate crime has risen over the past few years, but this is in part due to the increase in the number of incidences being reported. Between 2011-2012 the number of cases reported to the police was 4,252 (10% of the total number of hate crimes), in 2016-2017 it was 9,157 (11% of the total number). Figures published by the Home Office show a rise of 46% in reported hate crimes over this five-year period, and though the level of hate crime against the LGBT community does not appear to have risen significantly, how can anti-gay crime and rhetoric be explained when there are now laws against discrimination of homosexuals and homosexuality? Does it come back to the perception of disempowerment of the male gender, and specifically, the shrine of the male body?

Firstly, let us clear up the differences between biology, gender, sexuality and personality. These are four distinct parts of what makes us who we are, but often these traits and natural sciences get muddled up, especially by homophobes. Biology is not the same as gender, and gender is not the same as sexuality; and personality is something altogether different. What exactly are these four 'ologies' and 'alities'?

Biology is the science of life. It is the study of what makes up our physical structure, the chemical composition, the functions, development, and the evolution of the body. Males are born with X and Y chromosomes and females are born with two X chromosomes. Half of male sperm carries the X chromosomes and the other half carries the Y chromosomes. Genes present on the Y chromosome signal development towards maleness and cells within the pregnant female act to deactivate one or other of the chromosomes. In this process, an X chromosome and a Y chromosome determine the sex of the baby as male, while two X chromosomes produce a female. Humans, as well as some other organisms, can have a chromosomal arrangement that is contrary to the typical male/female composition; for example, XY females or XX males, which occurs in about one in 20,000 new-born males. Diagnosis and treatment can be medically unnecessary, but individuals may opt for surgery to make their genitalia appear more male or female. Also, there may be abnormal numbers of sex chromosomes, such as in Turner's syndrome, in which a single X chromosome is present, and Klinefelter's syndrome, in which two X chromosomes and a Y chromosome are present. Other less common chromosomal arrangements include: triple X syndrome, 48, XXXX, and 49, XXXXX.

Gender is a range of characteristics pertaining to, and differentiating between, sex-based social structures. These can differ according to the society in which you belong. They are often entrenched and can be difficult to break. For instance, in Western culture, boys might be thought of as the ones who play with guns, train sets, cars and building bricks, and who rough and tumble. Girls, on the contrary, might be assumed to want to play with dolls, dress up as princesses, wear pink (a gender specific invention that didn't fully take off until after WW2), and they might also choose to play at pretend tea-parties. But girls and boys often choose toys that are non-gender specific or that would typically be played with by the opposite sex. In the adult world similar preconceived ideas might apply when considering men who do labouring work, or women who take on caring roles, such as nursing. These 'rules' are often broken nowadays, but this has only been a relatively recent shift in the way our society views the roles of men and women. It was during the First World War, when women were needed to work in the munitions factories, drive the buses and work on the farms, that the idea of women's liberation from the servitude of conventional female roles was first challenged, and thus the idea that roles could be non-gender specific became more accepted and popularised over the latter part of the twentieth century.

Rather than gender being about male or female specific roles – pink or blue, his and hers – it is considered today that there is much to gain when the focus is shifted to what the individual finds interesting, playful or exciting. In the past, the use of the word 'gender' often referred to someone's sex; today, the acknowledged academic meaning is its context in the social roles men and women take on. This is by no means a modern way of thinking and in fact dates back to at least 1945 and was later popularised by the feminist movement in the 1970s and onwards. The theory behind the women's liberation movement's striving for a genderless society was that human nature is essentially epicene, i.e. it has no characteristics of either sex and social distinctions based on sex are arbitrarily constructed.

Today society has gone further, and individuals who do not identify as male or female might choose to define themselves as non-binary, genderqueer, agender (genderless), transgender or androgyne, among many other labels. Gender is seen as fluid, it is not fixed, and a person might juggle their psychological gender with their social or work-related gender and their gender role within the family.

In other cultures, there are specific third genders that are distinct for being neither male or female, such as the *hijras* of South Asia and the Two-Spirits of the indigenous North-American tribes.

Sexuality is the way we express ourselves as sexual beings. It is our sexual preference, or our sexual orientation, as it is often called. It is the sex we have, or want to have, and what gives us our sexual label; heterosexual, homosexual, bisexual, transsexual, lesbian etc. But sexuality is variable, and often these labels are too restrictive. It can change too, to degrees, throughout a person's lifetime. It is neither fixed nor prescriptive, and is demonstrated in the 'Sexual Spectrum', first established by Alfred Kinsey in the late 1940s, as a system which places individuals somewhere between strictly heterosexual at one end of the scale and strictly homosexual at the other. Most of us fall somewhere in between, and this can change over time.

What about the theory that our sexuality is defined by the influences of nature versus nurture? Sigmund Freud firmly believed that sexual drive was a natural instinct and therefore nature was the determiner to our sexuality. His theory said that humans are driven from birth by the desire to acquire and enhance bodily pleasures, thus whatever our sexual desire might be, it is set within the womb. However, there is another group that believe at least some aspect of sexual desire can be learned. This goes back to the seventeenth century English philosopher John Locke and his theory that the human mind was a blank sheet and that everything we do and learn is based on our environment.

Personality is what makes us individual. It is the combination of characteristics and qualities that makes us distinct from anyone else. This will include our biological male or female traits, our gender roles, our sexuality and any number of other internal or external influences that we experience through our lives.

For openly out homosexuals, it is often their sexuality that is judged before their personality, when other people assess whether they are decent human beings or not, and the fact that they are homosexual often colours the response to a negative one. This is the essence of homophobia; a complete misunderstanding of the difference between what is someone's gender, their sexuality and the biology of the person standing in front of you. And where misunderstanding sets in, so fear grows. Homophobia locks men, in particular, into stereotypical gender roles many of them find hard to live up to.

In her article for PBS Frontline online newsletter 'Inside the Mind of People Who Hate Gays', Karen Franklin says that homophobia and anti-gay violence are often quoted as things that bond young males in gangs, prove heterosexuality and expunge unwanted hidden homosexual desires. Targeting gay men in unprovoked violent attacks is not seen by the perpetrators as hatred towards individual homosexuals per se, but rather an extreme expression of society's expectations of them, i.e. conduct that is within what constitutes as acceptable male behaviour. Motive is not a prerequisite.

The potential of any man, regardless of his sexual orientation, to be labelled as 'gay' and therefore ostracised from his family, school, work or neighbourhood, for being or presenting anything other than the heteronormative, is so damning, even dangerous, that men are pressurised into characterising themselves to a very narrow set of male gender stereotypes. This in turn reinforces societal belief that there is only one rule for how men should be and behave. According to Franklin, the idealised masculine norm of men whose traits are dominance, competitiveness, occupational achievement and heterosexuality is virtually impossible for most men to achieve, yet they still aspire to this cultural standard, which goes back to the Medieval times and was romantically popularised in the empire-building days of the nineteenth century. This ideal is guarded so much that any feminine traits are seen as attacks on the male form – the body itself. Words such as 'disgust', 'vile', 'repulsive' – 'I'd rather lick my dog's butt than kiss a man' – are used by homophobic men to distance themselves as far as possible from any correlation to the perceived 'feminine' traits and characteristics of homosexuals.

For those not fitting the narrow brief of what it is to be manly, being weak or insufficiently masculine is cause enough for the attackers of homosexuals, who see the violence they inflict as justifiable punishment meted out on behalf of society for the shameless 'flaunting' of gay sexuality, and for gays refusing to show any humiliation in their deviance, as a God-given right. The reinforcing of sex gender norms, peer pressure, macho thrill-seeking, lack of education and the underlying threat of male disempowerment all help to explain how individuals end up queer-bashing or using vitriolic homophobic language. The potency that the masculine heteronormative icon holds, over young men especially, through its facade of power and rightful place in the world, when their own circumstances gives them no real power at all, is the pitiful falsehood that is so damaging. Males who aspire to this gender type, yet have no means of realising it due to a myriad of factors in their lives, not exclusively economic or social, may feel their only way to make a mark in the world, to stand out in their community, is to carry out attacks on vulnerable groups, particularly, homosexuals – easy targets which they see as the antithesis of who they are and who they want to be.

Although there are more diverse representations of men these days – different masculinities in the arts, entertainment and sports worlds (though less visible in football) and even in politics – nonetheless there is a revered proliferation of traditional male stereotypical characteristics in the dominant masculine force in our society. The 'power' of the heteronormative perpetuates and effects the way in which men engage with gender equality. Getting to a place where gender equality is not a topic of discussion any more is difficult to imagine because of the deep-rooted fundamental traits of the fixed male psyche that inherently defend against it.

Owen Jones, columnist, author, commentator and political activist, agrees that there have been huge changes, but says there is still a long way to go. 'I wouldn't hold hands in the street, and mental issues are much higher among the LGBT community. Gay is a term of abuse in the playground,' he tells Will Young, on the Homo Sapiens podcast. 'What is going on in society is nothing less than gender policing. There is an expectation of what it is to be a man and how men behave – getting into fights, leering at women, being sporty. If you don't abide by these rules you get people saying, "Stop being such a gay".'

Schools work hard to stop it, but homophobic bullying is pandemic in the playground and the damage caused can be lifelong, leading to drug and alcohol abuse, which is much higher among LGBT people than the rest of the population. It is a well-established fact that the biggest killer of young men is suicide. This is why homophobic abuse can be so dangerous, because it is difficult for men to open up and talk to someone about their problems, especially when their contemporaries are telling them that it's unmanly to talk about your feelings; that it's gay or womanly to do so. The majority of homophobic abuse, according to Jones, is ironically, directed at straight males, and that almost all men will have been subjected to this type of malicious verbal name-calling and been told in no uncertain terms what sort of a man they should be.

'You grow up hearing people use what you are as the ultimate derogatory insult,' Jones says. 'Society tells you you should be heterosexual. It's even subtler than that. There's that awful patronising thing when people say, "Oh, I never would have guessed that you're gay", and you're left feeling almost flattered that your leprosy isn't publicly obvious. Or, when there's that look on a friend's face when someone says to them, "Oh, I thought you were gay too", and they feel completely insulted that they were thought of as being 'one of them', even though, of course, they would say that they back LGBT rights and have plenty of gay friends and have nothing against gay people.'

'All the rights and freedoms we have won have been due to people who were demonised as poofs and perverts and deviants. Alan Turing, whose brilliance at mathematics helped defeat the Nazis, was sterilised and driven to suicide, prosecuted for who he was, and not pardoned until 2013, nearly 60 years after his death. All those that went before us – heroes – are giants and we stand on their shoulders. Yet still some people say, "Look, you got your rights, you got all your laws, what are you bothered about? What's your problem?" As if the laws they gave us were a gift – a gift to be equal – like some act of beneficence.'

How then can we stop homophobia; where each and every anti-gay word a gay teenager hears reinforces their feelings of unworthiness, that they are vile, disgusting and have no place in the world and have nothing to contribute?

It is a simple matter of education; teaching our children that there is a difference between biology, gender, sexuality and personality is a start. Stopping those subtle homophobic words we might hear our work colleagues and friends use, even when they think it's just banter, can enlighten where ignorance lies.

Linda Riley, DIVA magazine publisher and creator of numerous diversity initiatives, who has dedicated herself both professionally and personally to promoting the values of equality, diversity and inclusion, writes:

With so much progressive legislation down the years, it seems all too clear that societal attitudes have some way to go before they catch up with the law of the land. Homophobia and transphobia is alive and well throughout the UK 50 years after sexual activity between gay men was decriminalised.

My daughters, twins of ten, are constantly asked why they have two mums, or where their dad is. Sure, kids will be curious, and in the black and white world of young childhood, questions are inevitable. But when curiosity turns to insistent questioning and then to bullying, we need to ask whether schools, local authorities and other stakeholders are doing enough to normalise what is an increasingly commonplace domestic situation. We do not need a revolution, but we do need to make some simple changes. These changes include ensuring that official forms are gender neutral, rather than asking for the signature of a 'father' and 'mother'. Frontline staff need to be trained not to make assumptions based on outmoded ideas of a nuclear family (I can't tell you how many times I've been asked about my husband or my daughters' father), and schools need to ensure that all pupils understand that, in 21st century Britain, families come in all shapes and sizes.

In the USA, in one of the most compelling surveys I have read in recent times from GLAAD USA 'Southern Stories', it was noted that although many work colleagues would invite their gay workmates to their wedding, they were not so ready to extend the invitation to the children of same sex couples. In this 'always on' digital age, where children are seemingly glued to their smartphones, we also need to hold social media organisations to account. For too long they have tolerated disgusting homophobic abuse, including the vilification of same sex families. Children with two mums or two dads can't avoid coming across this abuse, with a hugely detrimental effect on their wellbeing and self-esteem. These tech giants, quite rightly, do not permit the abuse of – for example – mixed race families, and I call on them to apply the same standards to the LGBT community.

We have come a very long way in a very short time, but these are just the first steps and we must continue to fight, to campaign and to call out injustice where we find it. No child deserves to have his or her family denigrated simply because of their parents' gender, and none of us should rest until such unacceptable prejudice is consigned to the history books.

Many people who hold homophobic views are stuck on the preconception that homosexuals are predatory, that they have an insatiable sex drive and want to have anal sex with every man they come in to contact with, that they want to 'turn' all men gay. Heterosexual men need to be aware that they are not under threat from sexual deviants; that each and every one of us, gay, straight or whatever, should not be defined by our sex lives. There is so much more about being a confident human-being and member of society than just that.

3.
Homosexuality in Literature

The words 'gay' and 'literature' came together in relatively modern times to describe a particular genre of book. It was a means to categorize what has become an increasingly lucrative area of writing, and refers to works of fiction that deal with themes of same-sex love between men, or women (although more recently, 'lesbian literature' has become recognised as a genre category in its own right). The term 'gay literature' may be a modern one, but it is by no means a modern genus of writing. Love poems and letters between male lovers have been written through the ages, exposing innermost thoughts and desires in often explicit and flowery language. The earliest examples were written by the Ancient Greeks.

Ancient Greece

The ancient civilization of Greece provides some of the earliest scriptures of homosexual themed stories dating back more than two thousand years. *Symposium*, a text written by the Greek philosopher Plato in about 385BC, is one of the best known. The symposium in the story's title was an exclusively male, usually aristocratic, dinner party, which was tightly choreographed and overseen by a master of ceremonies, and where men of a similar social standing could discuss and enjoy themselves in a convivial atmosphere. Bedecked in garlands, the participants would recline on couches, either singularly or in pairs, with cushions and low tables from which to eat. The symposium enabled these educated men a forum in which to debate topics and issues of traditional values and morals.

The host of the party in Plato's *Symposium* challenges his guests to give appraisals of Eros, the God of love and desire. The first, Phaedrus, begins by saying that love is the oldest of the gods and therefore the one who does most to promote virtue in people. The second, a man named Pausanias, a legal expert, talks about the distinction between what are considered the nobler and baser forms of love. The baser, or improper, lover he describes as one who searches for sexual gratification and whose objects of desire are women and boys. The nobler lover however, directs his affections towards young men, establishing lifelong relationships. This love is based on honour, where each partner venerates the other's intelligence and wisdom. He goes on to analyse the different attitudes to same-sex love throughout the city-states of Greece; those that have clearly established what is and what is not admissible behaviour, and those that are less clear about the distinctions. Eryximachus, a doctor, suggests that good love promotes moderation and is not restricted to humans, but can be found in music, medicine and much more. Aristophanes talks about a myth where earth was filled with twice the number of people and posed such a threat to Zeus that he cut us all in half. Ever since, we have wandered the earth looking for our other halves to join and become whole again. Socrates relates what he was once told; that love is not a God at all, but rather a spirit that mediates between people and the objects of their desire. At the end of the symposium, Dionysus, the Greek God of wine, whose male lovers included the satyr Ampelos and Adonis, the God of beauty and desire, judges the speeches. Putting the philosophy aside, what *Symposium* shows us is the dynamics of sexuality and sexual attraction in Athens at the time.

Many ancient and classical myths include stories of romantic affection and/or sex between men, and many religious texts tell of Gods transforming from one sex to another. The Greek Gods especially, had no qualms in taking male as well as female lovers. Zeus, the god of the sky and ruler of all the Olympian gods, took the youthful Ganymede, now an icon of gay culture, as his cup-bearer on Mount Olympus, and Heracles, who was attributed with many different male companions throughout his ordeals, had the young Hylas, famed in legend for being abducted by nymphs, among his entourage.

In Homer's epic *Iliad*, the heroic figures of Achilles and Patroclus were not portrayed as homosexual lovers, but in a later version, *The Myrmidons*, a play by Aeschylus, Achilles speaks of 'our frequent kisses' and 'my pure reverence for your thighs' – a reference, perhaps, to intercrural sex. The third century BC statesman and orator, Aeschines, in appraising Homer, says that he 'hides their love and avoids giving a name to their friendship'. It is reasonable to think that Homer would have known that his readers were well educated and literate, and that they would have perfectly understood the 'exceeding greatness of their affection' as meaning something other than just good friends.

Rome

Roman writers and poets also wrote of encounters of same-sex love and the power of penetration. *Satyricon* is one of only two known examples of a Roman novel, and is regarded as evidence of how lower Roman classes lived. It is a mixture of prose and verse that are both serious and comical while at the same time erotic and decadent.

Gaius Petronius, believed to be the author of *Satyricon*, was the *elegantiae arbiter* or 'judge of elegance' at the court of Nero, and a member of the senatorial class who devoted much of their lives in the pursuit of pleasure. The surviving portions of the *Satyricon* text detail the misadventures of the narrator, Encolpius, and his lover, a handsome and promiscuous sixteen-year-old servant boy named Giton, in what at times, according to Raymond-Jean Frontain, Professor of English at the University of Central Arkansas, says 'resembles a sexual carnival'. Encolpius, whose name apparently translates to 'crotch', is endowed with an exceptional phallus, but who offends the god Priapus resulting in a sequence of painful, but generally comedic misadventures. (Priapus was a pastoral fertility god, the protector of livestock, fruit plants and male genitalia, and noted for his oversized and permanent erection. He was a popular figure often used in Roman erotic art and literature, and also the subject of an obscene collection of humorous verses called the *Priapeia*).

Throughout the tale of *Satyricon*, Encolpius has a trying time keeping his lover, Giton, faithful, as he is constantly enticed away by an equally impressively endowed friend and rival by the name of Asclytus. In Roman times, sexuality was interchangeable, and one of the characters, named as his master's heir for the sexual favours he provided well past the age when it was seemly for him to do so, boasts of how he also serviced the mistress of the household, Encolpius' wife. She is outraged, not by the fact that her husband keeps a stable of beautiful male slaves, but that he publicly kisses his favourite in her presence.

The moral of the *Satyricon* story appears to be that denying sexual appetite is a misdemeanour, punishable, in this case, by farce and mockery. In 1969, a controversial film version of *Satyricon* was made by Federico Fellini. It is both grotesque and powerfully homoerotic, but is considered to have lost much of Petronius' humour.

An English translation of *Satyricon,* first published in Paris in 1902, was purported to be by Sebastian Melmoth, a well-known pseudonym of Oscar Wilde. It was clearly not written by Wilde, but by attempting to promote the underground ancient text by linking it to the refined and satirical sharpness of the Victorian Age's most famous homosexual, the anonymous publisher was the first to define and promote homosexual literature as artistic. Professor Frontain says that *Satyricon* is the prototype for many other contemporary gay novels, such as John Rechy's *City of Night* (1963), Daniel Curzon's *The*

Misadventures of Tim McPick (1975), and Luis Zapata's *Adonis Garcia* (1979).

Another notable poet from Roman times was Gaius Valerius Catullus (84BC-54BC), who, through his poetry, made it known to the world that he had fallen in love with another man's wife. He was a fashionable young man, famed for his subversive lyrics, and was Rome's leading poet of the day. His life, as he told it through verse, was beset with love, loss, and politics. While Rome quaked under the rule of Julius Caesar, Catullus wrote some of the most sexually explicit and audaciously erotic poetry of all time about various politicians and his ex-lovers.

There are 117 surviving Catullus poems, and a significant number show his interest in a boy called Juventius, of whom he admired his 'honeyed eyes' and 'delicate lips', and 'longed to give him thousands of kisses'. On the other hand, some of his poetry could be equally brutal:

> *The scenario is ridiculous and too funny.*
> *Just now I caught my girlfriend's little boy*
> *Wanking; If Dione approves, I took him*
> *With my hard-straining cock.*

It's hard not to see this as anything other than assault, but for the Roman male it was considered an assertion of his power to be the penetrator. The passive partner in the scene described above, whether he was willing or not, would have been viewed as effeminate and therefore below the status of the masculine Catullus. To call any man of social standing 'a penetrated man' was a huge insult, with which Catullus famously labelled Julius Caesar himself with in another of his poems.

Catullus' raunchy poems, obsessed with genitalia, full of semen and sex and vicious poetic attacks on leading figures of the day, brought him fame and notoriety. Even today he is infamous for writing what amounts to the crudest opening line ever written in Latin, in the poem

Carmen 16: *'Paedicabo ego vos et irrumabo.'* It was considered so rude that an uncensored modern English translation wasn't published until the twentieth century. It is one of several poems in which Catullus abuses two men, Marcus Furius Bibaculus (who had an affair with Catullus' young male lover Juventius) and Marcus Aurelius Cotta Maximus Messalinus:

I will sodomize you and face-fuck you, bottom Aurelius and catamite Furius, you who think because my poems are sensitive, that I have no shame. For it's proper for a devoted poet to be moral himself, but in no way is it necessary for his poems. In point of fact, these have wit and charm, if they are sensitive and a little shameless, and can arouse an itch, and I don't mean in boys, but in those hairy old men who can't get it up. Because you've read my countless kisses, you think less of me as a man I will sodomize you and face-fuck you.

Often the first two lines and the repeated last line were left out of English translations or left with the original Latin lines in place. The reason that Catullus should have used such acerbic language of sexual penetration seems to have been due to some challenge made to Catullus' masculinity. Catullus also wrote about his lover, Clodia, the wife of his friend, and of her betrayal when she turned her affections towards another man. The result was Poem 64: A mythical tale of an unhappy marriage and a lover's desertion, told through the picture on a bedspread.

Following a brush with Julius Caesar, and a cunning escape, Catullus' end came in an untimely death at the age of thirty.

The Middle Ages

By the turn of the first millennium, attitudes towards same-sex love between men in Medieval Europe had changed. Historians researching manuscripts written by seventh century Visigoths or twelfth century monks are, by default, recording a picture of life across five hundred years of different cultures and societies. What is consistent and easy to establish is the unswerving attitude of the Christian Church towards homosexuality and those who practised it. Discussion about sodomy is almost entirely from the ecclesiastical experience, written down by celibate monks; the privileged few who could read and write. Lay people could not. The power of the church was all-encompassing, above every man, even royalty. It wasn't until 1534 and the Act of Supremacy, brought into law by Henry VIII, that the power of the church was curtailed. This didn't alter how things were for sodomites however, it only meant that the power of law was taken from the ecclesiastical courts to reside with state legislative courts.

Historical biographies of famous personalities such as Richard I, William Rufus, St Anselm and others have brought together snippets of detail evidenced from documents and testimony, and from later third-party accounts, giving an indication that homosexual activity was apparent in Medieval society and must have been tolerated to some degree in certain social confines, though this would certainly have been dependent on the class and status of the men involved.

Paul Halsall of Fordham University explains in *The Experience of Homosexuality in the Middle Ages* that monastic writings about man-to-man love and friendship in twelfth-century Europe are 'some of the earliest evidence we have of the views of homoerotically inclined men'. Contrary to the Churches' official stance on sodomy, some Medieval monks, such as Baudri of Bourgueil, channelled their homoerotic desires through love poems and letters written in the language of spiritual friendship but which are so unrestrained in their description of their feelings of love, it is hard to see them as anything other than passionate, and often erotic, love letters. Ardent with emotion, Egbert, Archbishop of York, wrote to Saint Boniface in about 720AD about his feelings:

I avow the bond of your love; when I tasted it in my inmost being a fragrance as of honeyed sweetness entered into my veins... believe me, the tempest-tossed sailor does not long for his haven, the thirsty fields for their rain, the anxious mother waiting at the bend of the shore for her son, as much as I long to delight in seeing you.

A certain amount of caution needs to be applied to such writings as evidence of gay love rather than that of an overstated passionate friendship written in a style that would be in keeping with the chivalrous language of the day. Even so, it is hard to dismiss the idea that there seems to be something more than just heartfelt kinship towards a fellow man in the words Egbert uses.

Another extraordinarily erotic letter was written by a respected monk and scholar in the court of Charlemagne named Alcuin (circa 735–804), to a beloved bishop, and it reflects incredible intimacy:

I think of your love and friendship with such sweet memories, reverend bishop, that I long for that lovely time when I may be able to clutch the neck of your sweetness with the fingers of my desires. Alas, if only it were granted to me, as it was to Habakkuk, to be transported to you, how would I sink into your embraces... how would I cover, with tightly pressed lips, not only your eyes, ears, and mouth but also your every finger and your toes, not once but many a time.

It is not clear what part physical sex played in these relationships, and though we cannot say for sure that any of the writers was sexually attracted to men generally, their emotional being at the time certainly seems to have been fixated on the men they were writing to.

Other contemporaries of the lovelorn monks were a very different society of young fighting men – the aristocratic and chivalrous elite of the heraldic knights, especially those of northern France. The education of these all-male groups of privileged young men, with little prospect of early marriage, would have been a hot-bed for encouraging clandestine homosexual activity. Richard I, the Lionheart of the Crusades, the embodiment of twelfth century knightly principles, was one of those knights who is documented as having had homosexual affairs. That evidence, however, rests on a contemporary document concerning Richard's relationship with King Philip II of France. In 1187, the chronicler reports, the two men were so close that 'at night the bed did not separate them'. Whether the statement reflected their personal situation of closeness rather than a political one, as suggested by some historians, is debatable, but in an age when public relations had to rely on word of mouth more than anything else, Richard's decision to make it public that he had shared his bed, even metaphorically, with Philip could have represented the analogy of the ultimate demonstration of trust. The brotherhood of love in which the knights invested all their emotions by virtually binding themselves together in these demonstrative and powerful relationships, often during long crusades and military campaigns, is well known.

In the poem *Amys and Amylion*, about treason, forbidden love, loyalty and suffering and subsequent miracles, the story tells of the unconditional special friendship that unites the two knights throughout their lives and beyond. The story seems to have fascinated people in Medieval times, striking a chord with the sensibilities and gallantry of the age. Versions of it can be found throughout European literature.

The depiction of love between Amys and Amylion is perhaps most vividly portrayed towards the end of the poem, when Amys takes in his sick friend who has been in exile for a time. The exclusivity of the bond they share is shown when Amys slays his own children and then anoints the ailing Amylion in their blood. This gruesome scene veers to one of eroticism as Amys bathes Amylion's naked body and then dresses him. This he carries out, not with the attentiveness of a physician caring for his patient but as someone who loves this man more than his own children. In the end, the children are miraculously revived, suggesting that the relationship between the two is sanctified by God. If not, the children would have been lost forever. Upon their own deaths, Amys and Amylion are laid to rest in one grave, together for eternal bliss.

Perhaps one of the greatest legends of Medieval England is that of King Arthur and the Knights of the Round Table. In it the characters are set adventures abundant with trysts, *ménages à trois*, unrequited love and the chivalrous bonds of perfect male-to-male friendship. Arthur, Guinevere and Lancelot form the central triangle of love, while the relationship between Lancelot and Galehot, the Lord of the Distant Isles, appears to complement or mirror the secret affair between Lancelot and Queen Guinevere. Unlike the love between Lancelot and the Queen, it is the bond of union between the two knights that is destined to last for evermore. This unbreakable male-to-male bond occurs often throughout Medieval literature and is perhaps characteristic of the times, when death in childbirth and short life expectancy meant that such a unity with a woman could only ever be temporary. In the ménage à trois of the Arthurian legend, the male-to-male relationship always supersedes that of any role the female played in the tryst, no matter what her social status.

On the battlefield, the towering figure of Galehot, whose strength of forces could so easily have overthrown Arthur's, lays down his arms in awe of Lancelot when he sees him, and after his surrender, Lancelot gallantly accepts Galehot as his companion. Even in death they are inseparable, when Lancelot, at his behest, is buried next to Galehot in his tomb; the headstone is inscribed, 'Galehaut and Lancelot, the best knight who ever bore arms in Britain. Except only Galahad his son.' Thus, the knight Sir Galahad becomes associated with the couple, as if he was their child.

The relationship between Lancelot and Galehot is seen by many to represent one of the greatest homoerotic pairings of literature, and why not?

That night Lancelot slept heavily, and ever he made moan in his sleep, and Galehot, that scarce slept, heard him well and thought all the night through on how he might keep him.' And in the morning Galehot speaks to Lancelot: 'wit ye well that you can have the company of a more powerful man than I, but ye will never have that of a man that loveth you so well.

The two knights, so closely entwined and dependent on each other, epitomise the classical chivalric concept that true male friends share one soul. The implication of this is that these relationships are driven by deeply-held emotive forces, that the men are bonded together through loyalty, completeness, love and soul-sharing, and that they may have been physically attracted to one another. That these stories of Medieval chivalrous knights are filled with underlying homoeroticism is irrefutable, or certainly difficult to discount.

The Renaissance

The period known as the Renaissance took place at different times across Europe and is regarded as the cultural bridge between Medieval and modern times. The principal on which the Renaissance flourished was the rediscovery of classical Greek philosophy. In England, the Renaissance is considered to have started at the beginning of the Protestant Reformation under Henry VIII, in the 1530s. But Renaissance style and ideas did not fully integrate into English culture until the Elizabethan era in the second half of the sixteenth century. This period saw a high point in English literary accomplishment through the works of William Shakespeare, John Milton and others, and brought to the populace by the introduction of William Caxton's printing press.

The Italian Renaissance period started in the fifteenth century when humanists such as Poggio Bracciolini travelled through Europe, visiting monastic libraries, seeking out ancient Latin literature and the histories and rhetorical texts of the classical age. At the same time, the Fall of Constantinople in 1453 brought about a surge of emigré Greek scholars, bringing with them precious manuscripts which had fallen into obscurity. Italian cities such as Florence and Venice became magnets for artists and scholars of all kinds, and subsequently saw a prevalence of same-sex culture and activity. So much so that the Florentines even went so far as to establish heterosexual brothels with the aim of luring young men away from sodomy.

There are three literary traditions or genres which are closely associated with the Renaissance period, and these, according to Rictor Norton, are fundamentally homoerotic:

1. The pastoral tradition, with its mournful laments and lovers' woes, like that of the Elizabethan Richard Barnfield's homoerotic poem *The Affectionate Shepherd.*

2. The Ovidian erotic mythological tradition, with its host of androgynous young men, Adonis, Ganymede and Narcissus.

3. The friendship tradition, with its assertion that the love of man and youth is a higher form of affection than that of loving women, and its belief in the narcissistic phenomenon of 'one soul in two bodies' – as discussed in the Arthurian legend of the Medieval times.

'For an enlightened mind, Barnfield's poetry is no more cloying than many another Elizabethan courtiers' pastoral complaint about the unrequited love of his cruel fair' says Norton. 'From a gay point of view, the fact that the beloved is 'a lovely Ladde' rather than a disdainful maiden, a Ganymede rather than an Amaryllis, is a positive joy and a fountain of friendship upon the monotonous field of heterosexual corn.'

The greatest tragedy of Renaissance literature, Norton says, is that few people were able to read Plato or any of the early poets in their original Greek text, so their nearest archetype to the true Eros was an idealised shepherd's swain.

The artist Michelangelo (1475-1564) was a master of painting heroic masculinity. He regularly employed male models, even for his female figures, including the famous statue of *Night* on the Medici Tombs, which shows a figure whose breasts are obviously superimposed onto a male torso. In 1623 Michelangelo's grand-nephew published an edition of the sculptor's poetry, in which all the masculine pronouns were changed to feminine. This then became the standard edition for nearly 250 years, and it wasn't until John Addington Symonds' studies in 1892, at the archive of the Buonarroti family in Florence, that the censorship was brought to light. Further, it is only recently that Michelangelo's homosexuality has become a generally accepted fact. His earliest lovers included the handsome model Gherardo Perini, who came to work for him in around 1520, and, during the 1530s, the younger assistant Febo di Poggio, whom he called 'that little blackmailer' because of his demands for money, clothes and love-gifts from the artist. In 1532 Michelangelo began wooing a Roman nobleman by the name of Tommaso Cavalieri and became 'an armed Knight's (a Cavaliere) captive and slave confessed'. He wrote to Tommaso:

'...be it as it will: I know well that, at this hour, I could as easily forget your name as the food by which I live; nay, it were easier to forget the food, which only nourishes my body miserably, than your name, which nourishes both body and soul, filling the one and the other with such sweetness that neither weariness nor fear of death is felt by me while memory preserves you to my mind. Think, if the eyes could also enjoy their portion, in what condition I should find myself.'

The *ragazzi,* as they were called, worked as apprentices in the studios and offered other 'services' to the masters. Michelangelo's contemporaries, Leonardo da Vinci, Sandro Botticelli, Benvenuto Cellini and Giovanni Antonio Bazzi, were all publicly charged with sodomy.

The Quintessence of Debauchery, a raunchy play attributed to the libertine John Wilmot, Second Earl of Rochester, and published in 1684, has the distinction of being the first literary work to be censored in England on the grounds of its obscenity and pornography, and not unsurprisingly so, with characters called King Bolloxinion of Sodom and General Buggeranthos, to name just two. The play opens with the King issuing a decree that sodomy is to be practised widely throughout the land. General Buggeranthos reports back to the king that his soldiers don't seem to have had any complaints about the new ruling, rather they are pleased at saving their money they would have previously spent on prostitutes. The play is a caricature of the court of Charles II; a sexually explicit and thinly disguised satire written at the time of the 1672 Declaration of Indulgence, (a statute for the religious liberty of Protestant non-conformists and Roman Catholics).

John Wilmot was infamous during his lifetime for his poetry, satires and lampoons. He was renowned as the wit of Restoration England. However, he was also cursed as the devil incarnate and simultaneously adored by Charles II for his angelic presence, cutting humour, beauty and extravagance. Sexually, he was a free spirit, with many mistresses and just as many liaisons with men, including the Duke of Buckingham at one end of society and at the other, linkboys (those that lit the streetlamps at night), and a certain servant boy, of whom he wrote in a poem:

Then give me health, wealth, mirth, and wine,
And, if busy love entrenches,

There's a sweet, soft page of mine
Does the trick worth forty wenches!

The Age of Enlightenment

The Age of Enlightenment, which approximately spans the time-period from the 1650s to the 1780s, and is known in French as *le Siècle des Lumières*, 'the Century of Lights', was an age of new intellectualism and philosophical thought that dominated the sphere of European thinking and cultural ideas during the late seventeenth and eighteenth centuries. Enlightenment centered on reason as the primary source of authority and legitimacy, and advanced the ideals of liberty, progress, tolerance, fraternity, constitutional government and the separation of church and state. In France, the central principles of 'des Lumières' were individual liberty and religious tolerance, which was a popular opposition to the absolute monarchy and dogma of the Roman Catholic Church. In its scientific approach, enlightenment was eloquently captured in a succinct phrase by the German philosopher Immanuel Kant in an essay he wrote in 1784 called *Sapere aude* (dare to know), a phrase that became widespread and encapsulated the enthusiasm of the times.

When it came to love, enlightenment shone new light on the subject. In the words of the eighteenth century French writer Nicholas Chamfort, whose quotes include, 'There are more people who wish to be loved than there are who are willing to love', also wrote on the topic of love, that it was simply, 'The contact of two epidermises'. What Chamfort expressed in these few words was that love was a scientific process and as such could apply to, and be experienced by, anyone. Love was not the sole territory of the young, the rich, the educated, or even those of opposite sexes; love was inclusive and available to all. It was simply a chemical reaction ignited by two people.

Authors of the time who wished to allude to male-to-male love in their writing did so by including neoclassical themes. Greek characters from mythology became the coded message bearers of a homoerotic subtext. Despite the increased visibility and expression of homosexual behaviour in the arts at this time, and the prospering networks of male prostitution and introduction of molly houses in cities like London, sodomy was still a punishable crime. But since it was so difficult to prove that penetration had occurred, and as two witnesses were required to secure a custodial or death sentence, many men were prosecuted and charged with the lesser offence of 'intent to commit sodomy'. For this they could serve six months or more or be pilloried for two days. Stocks were often erected at sites where sodomites gathered, which simply led to these locations being identified and becoming even more popular. A cruising path across Moorfields was well known as 'Sodomites' Walk', and the south side of St James's Park was notorious for picking up soldiers from the nearby barracks.

Early fiction writers such as Matthew Lewis (1775-1818) masked themes of homosexuality at the heart of Gothic tales such as *The Monk*, in which the main character, Ambrosio, the devout thirty-year-old monk of the title, is smitten by the attentions and idolising of the novice Rosario. Later, Rosario is revealed in fact to be a woman, Matilda. To most homosexuals of the time, the veiled plot would have barely hidden the clear subtext on same-sex love and the problems of misunderstood sexuality.

Another author of the Gothic genre was Charles Maturin, who, in his novel *Melmoth the Wanderer*, dared to write full erotic tension into this scene centred also on a novice monk, this time fleeing and naked:

A naked human being, covered in blood and uttering screams of rage and torture flashed by me; four monks pursued him – they had lights. I had shut the door at the end of the gallery – I felt they must return and pass me – I was still on my knees and trembling from head to toe. The victim reached the door, found it shut, and rallied. I turned and saw a group worthy of Murillo. A more perfect human form never existed than that of this unfortunate youth. He stood in an attitude of despair and was streaming with blood.

Maturin writes with a graphically modern tone. Only in the description does he allow himself a sense of propriety in implying that this is something that would have occurred in the Inquisitions, and reference to the Spanish Baroque painter, Murillo, also gives a cultured seriousness to what is otherwise a homoerotically charged scene in which the protagonist is 'on his knees' worshipping the violently pornographised body of the young novice.

What we need to remember is that the language of male-to-male sexual activity is not an exclusively twentieth century phenomenon popularised by porn movies. Eighteenth century authors, and those before, would have been very familiar with, and no doubt took part in, the delights of such carnal acts, but it was still too risky to write about anal penetration and fellatio in plain terms.

Trial documents from the time, however, do give explicit accounts, as told to the courts by those involved, of the goings on between homosexual men. An illustration of this is quoted by Rictor Norton in *A History of Gay Sex*, in the case of two men who were prosecuted in 1772 for buggering one another in the toilet of the Red Lion pub in Moorfields, London:

Robert Crook, a 19-year-old man who was sharing a drink with Charles Gibson, said: "I went into the yard to make water, he came into the yard while I was making water, took hold of my yard, and began to work it with his hand. He said, 'It was a very good one, and he liked it very well'. He then asked me to go down to the vault [i.e. the bog-house] with him, which I did. There he said 'Did not you know Dick that lived in this house? He had a fine tool, almost as big as my wrist, you are just such a lad as he was, let's see if yours is as big as his.' Then he worked my yard till he made it spend in his hand. Then he pushed me back upon the vault, and worked me in the same manner on the seat of the vault till I did it in his hand; after that he kissed me very heartily; then he unbuttoned his own breeches, put my hand to his private parts, and kept tickling me about ten minutes; he kissed it and rubbed it, then he said 'Now it will do'; he then turned round, and put his naked breech into my lap, and put his hand behind him, laid hold of my yard, and pushed it into his backside, twice or three times, I am not sure which.

From his evidence, it appears that Robert Crook was just as willing a participant in the shenanigans as Charles Gibson. He claimed he was drunk and that he had been forced into having sex with Gibson, but it transpired in court that this was not the first time the two men had been to the vault together and they had been seen kissing in the pub before. After a long trial, both men were acquitted.

During the reign of George III (1760-1820), the earliest known novel containing two characters engaged in an openly homosexual love affair was published. *A Year in Arcadia: Kyllenion* (1805) by Augustus, Duke of Saxe-Gotha-Altenburg, grandfather to Prince Albert, consort of Queen Victoria, is set in ancient Greece, immediately giving it a sense of decorum and propriety. The novel by the German aristocrat features several couples, one of which is a homosexual male couple. The plot is structured around a set of idylls, one for each month of the year, and sees each couple falling in love, overcoming obstacles and living happily ever after. In their story, the two homosexual lovers are 'Alexis the splendid and Julanthiskos, the no less delightful'. Alexis is a young aristocrat who lives in a beautiful palace, and Julanthiskos is his 'hail-fellow-met-well' shepherd. They meet at a dance. Julanthiskos is smitten with the Prince, but Alexis toys with the young shepherd's affections. After various failed romances and tribulations, Julanthiskos chances upon his beloved Alexis, wounded and 'spattered with blood' in the forest. They are discovered together by Alexis' slaves, 'slumbered, mouth on mouth on the soft moss of one of the Kyllenian caves.' The landscape of ancient Greece as the utopia of male-to-male love was acceptable, but even so, some of Augustus' contemporaries felt that his characters 'stepped over the bounds of manly affection into unseemly eroticism.'

The Victorians

The heady days of louche Georgian vulgarity were confined somewhere beneath the genteel sensibilities of the rising Victorian middle classes of the new industrial age. Homosexual characters, storylines and themes of nineteenth-century literature became strange spectres that haunted the pages of many novels, seen and yet not seen, spoken of though never mentioned. Rarely apparent in mainstream fiction, same-sex desire nevertheless held a persistent presence in the sub-consciousness and sub-culture of Victorian life.

Replacing the shameless and immodest excesses in behaviour of the Regency era, Victorian values of puritanism and control, both personal and societal, steadily became the norm and the means by which the status quo of the Empire was maintained. The reality of many people's lives, however, saw glimpses of the soaring prostitution and pornographic imagery that was becoming more widely available.

The Industrial Revolution, at its height in the nineteenth century, saw huge increases in the populations of cities, inevitably bringing together groups of people who otherwise would never have come into contact with one another. For the adventurous, opportunities to explore their curiosities and desires became easily obtainable through sexual subcultures. Wealthy homosexuals came together in private clubs and houses, and ordinary working men cruised the public toilets and parks, as had been the case for many years, and still is today. What had not been so easy before but suddenly became simpler was that in the city it was possible to disappear quickly and become virtually invisible.

Homosexuality as a hidden yet growing sub-culture was pushed into the shadows by the continuing lack of discussion on the matter. Talk of sexual practices of any kind only took place in a legal, criminal or medical context, and the collective willingness not to speak openly of many subjects that were thought of as unspeakable, such as race, women and sex, became the shared peculiar characteristic of the age – one that persists and is still embedded in the British psyche today. Writing about such things as same-sex desire had to be done in either scientific or academic terms, or, in the case of literature, authors had to heavily disguise their underlying sexual messages, and often used homoerotic codes and signals as a sub-text to the initiated. The playwright George Bernard Shaw later commented: 'It was impossible for men to express anything other than ignorance of the phenomenon or the deepest condemnation and personal distancing from it.'

A leading sexologist of the day, Havelock Ellis, saw his book *Sexual Inversion*, the first medical textbook on the topic of homosexuality, withdrawn from sale in Britain and in 1897 a bookseller was even prosecuted for stocking it.

Co-authored with John Addington-Symonds, the poet and literary critic, *Sexual Inversion* established the idea that male 'inverts' were inclined, in various degrees, towards traditional female pursuits and dress, and women 'inverts' the opposite. Today we might describe these characteristics as transgender or non-binary, but such a concept did not exist as a separate identity then. The book, first published in German in 1896, used the term 'inversion' to describe the inborn reversal of gender traits. The collaboration of Symonds' historical analysis and Ellis' knowledge of modern medical scientific theory produced what was the first objective study on homosexuality which did not label it a disease, immoral, or a crime.

In 1883 Symonds had already published, amongst other works, *A Problem in Greek Ethics*, in which he sought to justify sexual relations between males using historical context. He was prolific throughout his life, writing biographies, poetry and his life's achievement, a work on the Renaissance. His private memoirs, written over a four-year period from 1889 to 1893, are the earliest known self-conscious writings of a homosexual autobiography.

John Addington-Symonds was married and had four daughters but was an early campaigner for male-to-male love, referring to it as *l'amour de l'impossible* – love of the impossible. In 1868, he met and fell in love with Norman Moor, who was about to study at Oxford and who became his pupil. According to his diary, Symonds wrote of Moor on 28th January 1870, 'I stripped him naked and fed sight, touch and mouth on these things'. Their relationship inspired his most productive period of poetry. He also translated classical poetry on homoerotic themes, and wrote poems drawing on ancient Greek imagery and language. While the taboos of Victorian England prevented Symonds from speaking openly about his own sexuality or homosexuality in general, his published works contained some of the first direct references to male-to-male sexual love in English literature. In *The Meeting of David and Jonathan*, in 1878, Jonathan takes David 'In his arms of strength / [and] in that kiss / Soul into soul was knit and bliss to bliss'.

Plagued throughout his life with ill-health, Symonds died of tuberculosis at the age of 52 in 1893. Thirty years earlier in 1863, his suffering health was due in part to the stress caused by the rumours that he was having an affair with one of his students. After a further attack of bronchitis in 1877, resulting in violent haemorrhaging, he was told not to spend another winter in England. He journeyed to Egypt, stopping en route in Davos Platz in Switzerland, which became his home for the rest of his life, except for the winter months which he spent in Venice. In his memoirs, he extolled the idea that freedom and strength can be achieved through self-discovery, and said that the more he accepted his homosexuality, the healthier and more invigorated he became. He claimed he felt a powerful sense of liberation at each successive stage of his 'coming out'.

On his death in 1893, Symonds' autobiography was given into the care of his friend and executor Horatio Forbes Brown, with implicit instructions 'to save it from destruction after my death, and yet to reserve its publication for a period when it will not be injurious to my family'. After Brown's subsequent death in 1926, the manuscript was given to the London Library, again with instructions that it could not be published for a further fifty years. The green cloth box containing the manuscript was sealed until 1949, when Symonds' daughter, Dame Katharine Furse, was finally allowed to read it. In 1954 the London Library granted easier access to scholars but did not allow direct quotation, and it wasn't until 1976, after the fifty-year ban expired, that the restriction was finally lifted. In 1984 the manuscript was published, but only about four-fifths of the original full text. Many poems on youths such as Alfred Brooke, early descriptive writings, transcripts of letters sent to him, letters sent by him to his wife, testimonials on several of his academic friends, and much of the material about Christian Buol and Christian Palmy, his 'two friends and fellow travellers' he had taken up with and visited the wine regions of Lombardy, were omitted. What was published though, illustrates the major phases of Symonds' growing self-realisation and self-acceptance of his homosexuality.

Equally important, but quite different, was an underground book called *The Sins of the Cities of the Plain* or *The Recollections of a Mary-Ann, with Short Essays on Sodomy and Tribadism,* by Jack Saul. It is one of the first exclusively homosexual works of pornographic literature published in English. It is suggested that it might have been written by James Campbell Reddie in collusion with the painter Simeon Solomon.

Reddie was a collector, bibliographer and author of erotica, who wrote under the pen-name of James Campbell for the publishers William Dugdale and later for William Lazenby. Reddie was homosexual and never married or had children. In an edition of the pornographic periodical *The Pearl* (also published by Lazenby), Reddie's landlord, Adamo Pedroletti, described the tale of their seduction of a fifteen-year-old boy and Pedroletti's seduction of the boy's mother. One of the earliest publications featuring Reddie's translation work was for William Dugdale's risqué Scottish newspaper *The Exquisite*. Published between 1842 and 1844, *The Exquisite* contained 'a great number of tales from the French, with a few from the Italian, translated for the most part, if not entirely, by James Campbell Reddie.'

The artist Simeon Solomon quite possibly could have been an acquaintance of Reddie's. However, he had left London for Paris in 1874 after his conviction for attempted sodomy in a public toilet off Oxford Street a year earlier, and after his return to England struggled with alcoholism and spent time in the workhouse. Reddie himself left London to return to his Scottish homeland and subsequently died in 1878, three years before *The Sins of the Cities of the Plain* was published by Lazenby. All this makes the pair's connection to the book somewhat tenuous.

Another candidate for the book's authorship might be attributable to William Simpson Potter, who was also a friend of the publisher, William Lazenby, and lived at Cornwall Mansions near Baker Street Station, where the character, Mr Chambon, who befriends Jack Saul, the narrator of the book, also lived. Potter, like Reddie, was a bibliographer and collector of erotic materials, and an eminent authority on the life and works of Cervantes, the seventeenth-century Spanish writer. He also compiled other anonymous pieces of erotica, *A Letter from the East* (1877), and *Letters from India during HRH the Prince of Wales' Visit in 1875/6* (1876).

The Sins of the Cities of the Plain was supposedly the dramatized memoirs of Jack Saul, a young rent boy or 'Mary-Ann'. In the book, Jack, whose real name was John Saul and who originated from Dublin, gets picked up on a London street by a Mr. Chambon. Chambon, charmed by Jack's looks and the tales he spins, invites him to tell his life story for payment.

It is unclear if *Sins of the Cities* is a genuine biography of John Saul's life or a work of fiction based on his notoriety and other stories of the time. But much of what is written about in the book could only have come from a rent boy like John Saul. Dublin Jack, as he was also known, was pre-eminent in two major homosexual scandals and was considered just as notorious in Dublin as he was in London. He became infamous for the sensational testimony he gave at the Cleveland Street scandal trial – the male brothel raided by police in Fitzrovia, London, in 1889. The story of the homosexual brothel was so sensational it was published in newspapers around the world. Prior to this, John was involved in a similar homosexual ring scandal at Dublin Castle in 1884.

In the book, published before these two scandals, Saul is described as possessing 'a fresh looking, beardless face, with almost feminine features, auburn hair and sparkling blue eyes... and endowed by a very extraordinary development of the male appendage'. The 1881 first edition had a run of just 250 copies; a second, published in 1902, sold at the extortionate price of four guineas.

Whoever wrote *The Sins of the Cities of the Plain* could not have known that the legacy of Jack Saul and his exploits would endure in the imaginations of gay men a century later and be the inspiration for books and even adapted for the stage in the play, *The Sins of Jack Saul*. Whoever he was, he would have undoubtedly been very surprised.

Despite the exclusion from the public domain of representations of explicit homosexual desires and practices in popular fiction, it seems that such material was available through small and underground publishers and could be bought if you knew where to look. What is striking about this period is that the same names of aristocratic and artistic men keep appearing in so many of the scandals and accounts of the time. They seem to be connected, purposely or otherwise, through an intricate network, a sticky web that joined one to another. Many of these men frequented the same clubs and establishments and knew full well the risks they faced if they were caught in compromising situations with rent boys and male lovers. They carried on regardless, against the backlash and disapproval of the establishment (of which many of these same men were fully paid-up members), and did so with a stiff upper lip and a good deal of British aplomb.

The Victorians lived in a juxtaposed world of extreme poverty and wealth, in which a tiny minority of well-educated men ruled an empire that stretched across a quarter of the earth's land surface. Their lives were governed by strict rules of etiquette and a patriarchal system that hid an underbelly of psychological discourse, including homosexuality, which boiled just below the surface. For many men it was a dangerous ferment; a time in which homosexuals could explore their sexuality yet at the same time find themselves metaphorically, 'walking the plank'.

The Twentieth Century

The twentieth century brought with it inconceivable advances in technology which allowed for ever faster communications. What had been the stuff of dreams just fifty years before was now commonplace: the telegraph, sending messages across the oceans; the laying of hundreds of miles of rail track, cutting journey times between cities from days to hours; printing presses that churned out daily newspapers and had them delivered to people's doorsteps the same day; telephones, cars, motion pictures – all these new technologies enabled more and more people to 'join in the conversation'.

Social issues such as poverty and equal rights for women were taken up and brought to the attention of the masses through demonstration and what we would call 'media coverage' in the popular newspapers and magazines, and Pathé News film footage was shown in the burgeoning new cinemas that sprung up in every town and city.

After the high-profile cases in 1894 and '95 of the Cleveland Street scandal and the Oscar Wilde trial, public awareness and its willingness to talk about homosexuality very gradually became more commonplace. Though the reality for homosexuals was still the fear of the law and repercussions from a not always entirely open-minded society.

Early twentieth century gay themed novels, many of which were authored by writers using pseudonyms, reflect the introspective nature of denial and hidden homosexuality. *Death In Venice* (1912), by the German novelist Thomas Mann, highlights this quandary, as the protagonist struggles with his sexuality in exactly the same way the author himself did. Interestingly, the film, released in 1971, starred Dirk Bogarde, also a repressed homosexual. The story is of an aging writer who visits Venice, and, suffering with writers' block, finds himself besotted with a teenaged boy. Though Mann always denied his novels had autobiographical content, the release of his diaries after his death revealed just how all-consuming his life had been with unrequited love and passion. Ironically, this new knowledge of Mann's hidden character resulted in a renewed interest in his work.

Another famous novelist, E. M. Forster, author of such classics as *A Room With a View, Howard's End* and *A Passage to India*, had a distinguished reputation for his work, while concealing from the public his own homosexuality. In 1913, he wrote *Maurice*, a story of male-to-male love about Maurice Hall, a young upper-middle class man and his personal struggles with his sexuality. Hall realises early on, even in boyhood, that marriage was never going to be the path he would follow. Let down by his lover, Clive, a boy he meets at university, who reveals that he does intend to marry and live a normal life, Maurice makes an appointment to see a hypnotist to try to cure himself of the scourge of his homosexuality. The hypnotist claims to have a fifty percent success rate, but after one visit it becomes clear to Maurice that the hypnotism has failed.

Eventually Maurice finds and falls in love with Scudder, an under-gamekeeper, but Scudder threatens to blackmail him. The continued failure of his hypnotherapy sessions leaves Maurice with only one option, to leave England for France or Italy, where same-sex desire is more tolerated. When asked by Maurice if he thinks it will ever be safe for men to love other men in England, Lasker, the hypnotist, replies, 'I doubt it. England has always been disinclined to accept human nature.'

In *Maurice*, Forster tackled many of the issues surrounding homosexuality in Edwardian England; curing therapies, class division and blackmail. A hundred years later, these same issues still manifest in some areas of society, though marked improvements in both legal and societal terms have been made.

Although a close-knit circle of Forster's friends had read the manuscript, *Maurice* was not published until 1971, after his death. He resisted submitting it because of the furore he knew it would cause and even wrote a questioning note on the manuscript to this effect, 'Publishable, but worth it?'

Maurice was made even more controversial because of the novel's happy ending. "A happy ending was imperative," wrote Forster, "I was determined that in fiction anyway, two men should fall in love and remain in it for the ever and ever that fiction allows." William J. Mann said of the novel, "Alec Scudder was a refreshingly unapologetic young gay man who was not an effete Oscar Wilde aristocrat but rather a working class, masculine, ordinary guy ... an example of the working class teaching the privileged class about honesty and authenticity — a bit of a stereotype now, but back then quite extraordinary."

The twentieth century was marked by two dreadful world wars which threw many social stereotypes and the norms of acceptable behaviour into question. Men thrown together in cramped and dangerous conditions on the Western Front in the 1914-18 Great War found solace in the old virtues of male-to-male bonds, so beloved by the ancient Greeks and the Romantics of their great-grandfathers' generation. The blackouts in London and other cities during the Blitz of the Second World War provided clandestine opportunities for homosexuals to meet under the cover of darkness and anonymity.

One writer who best described this time of unparalleled extremes during the interregnum years of the two world wars was Christopher Isherwood. In *The Berlin Stories*, he captured completely the hedonistic atmosphere of Weimar Berlin of the 1930s. Isherwood, who fully embraced his homosexuality, was drawn there by its reputation for sexual freedom and thus made it his home. For the opportunities the city provided for homosexuals, Isherwood wrote of John Henry Mackay's *Der Puppenjunge – The Boy-Doll* – 'It gives a picture of the Berlin sexual underworld early in this century which I know, from my own experience, to be authentic.' In 1931 he met Jean Ross, a young nightclub singer who was the inspiration for his character of Sally Bowles in *Goodbye*

To Berlin, which was later made into the musical *Cabaret,* with Liza Minnelli playing the part of Sally.

Though writers still had to remain vigilant if they were not to fall foul of the law, it was becoming possible, in theory at least, to be and live life as a homosexual man, so long as what you were writing about was not overt and/or explicit on the subject. In general, the public were beginning to grasp the idea that writers, as well as artists, could be that way inclined, and great authors suddenly fell into the same category as great artists. This of course played to the inversionist theory that the appreciation of art and a natural bent towards the artistic was predominantly a feminine trait. Working the docks, being policemen, miners and many other 'manly' professions could not possibly be the career of choice for the inverted homosexual. The public was safe – there was no need for panic. For when did anyone come into close contact with an upper-class, educated author or artist?

4.
Art & Homoeroticism

What is homoeroticism? Is it merely the art of acceptable soft-porn, or has it something deeper to offer? And who puts it on their walls? The official definition of homoerotic is: 'concerning or arousing sexual desire centered on a person of the same sex'. The concept of homoeroticism, as an emotion, is something intrinsically different from that of homosexuality. As the definition from the Oxford Dictionary above states, homoeroticism does indeed arouse feelings of desire characterised with homosexuality. However, homoerotic feelings are fleeting and temporary, as opposed to the permanent reference to sexual identity in the classification of *being* homosexual.

Homoeroticism as an art form is a much older concept than that of homosexuality. Homoerotic art has sustained a place in aesthetics ever since man began to draw on cave walls, and certainly since its proliferation in ancient classical times, and resurgence in the Middle Ages. We can see it in beautifully-decorated Ancient Grecian vases, on carefully crafted Roman silver wine goblets, such as the Warren Cup, in the Italian Renaissance and in mainstream art ever since.

Many examples of male-to-male homoeroticism in visual art leave little to the imagination. Its abundance and explicitness for instance, in the Ancient Greek and Roman periods might have something to say about the times in which it was made; that it was a visible expression of an open society which included homosexuals within it. This is not always the case, and Nazi Germany in the 1930s is an illustration of how one set of rules can apply to something such as the proliferation of athletic naked male statues, promoting the image of the ideal male aesthetic, while at the same time the state condemned homosexuals to the concentration camps. This extreme highlights the differences between homoeroticism and homosexuality.

One of the most iconic homoerotic images we are familiar with is that of the youthful St Sebastian tied to a tree and shot through with arrows. The perfect and near-naked body of the youth stands limp yet winsome, captured at the precise moment of destruction, on the orders of the Roman Emperor Diocletian, for trying to convert Romans to Christianity. However, this is not an accurate telling of the story of the not-so-young Sebastian's martyrdom, though it has been depicted this way ever since Mediaeval times. The truth is that Sebastian was a middle-aged man who survived the arrows shot into his body by the Pretorian Guard in an execution staged more like a gruesome session of target practice, only then to suffer a worse fate later when he was stoned to death and his body thrown unceremoniously into the Roman sewers. But it is not this final, ignominious death we see recalled in art, but the anguished moment his flesh is impaled by the soldiers' arrows.

The earliest known representation of St Sebastian is depicted in a mosaic in the Basilica of Sant'Apollinare Nuovo in Ravenna, Italy, which dates between 527AD-565AD. Pointedly, there are no arrows. The first paintings of St Sebastian, as we would recognize him, are those by the sixteenth century Italian Renaissance artist Guido Reni. Reni painted a series of six images in which St Sebastian is depicted tied to a tree-stump, a lost look written on his face, beseeching his God, while the arrows stick out at hideous angles from his untainted flesh. Pain, torment and a saintly grace are the emotive feelings portrayed. So the question arises: why was this martyred Sebastian depicted in what can only be described as a vision of homoerotism, when on the face of it the true story was anything but?

The answer is not simple and clear-cut. At the time, Bologna was annexed under Papal rule and this period saw the construction of many churches and religious establishments, and artists such as Reni were in high demand. St Sebastian, martyred for his stand against the paganism of old Rome and for converting to Christianity, was a popular saint and one the Romans gave prayer to, to keep them safe from the plague. He had, after all, survived the arrows, so his blessing was seen to stave off the evils of disease which were thought to pierce the body from without. But why portray him as a lithe youth, tied to a tree, appealing to God for his mercy? There are many explanations, and only Reni himself could fully explain his motives. It is doubtful that he would be able to divulge his innermost thoughts on any sexual connotations in his paintings, for he apparently 'turned to stone' in the company of women. Physical sex for Reni was nigh on impossible. He lived with his mother until her death, after which no other woman was allowed into his house. There is, however, no evidence or suggestion that he was homosexual. Rather, it seems that he saw youths, both men and women, as virginal and untouchable. Thus, he paints Sebastian impaled by the arrows, the phallic symbols of outside forces, yet he is still pure of virtue, like the Virgin Mary. On this level the painting has a universal appeal, and as the German novelist Thomas Mann said of Reni's masterpieces, 'Grace in suffering, that is the heroism of St Sebastian'.

For a deeper homoerotic meaning, we might look to the Japanese writer, film-maker and keen sadomasochist Yukio Mishima, for whom Sebastian's martyrdom symbolises the erotic pleasure of pain. Another S & M fetish is that of being tied or tying someone up; making a sex partner passive and entirely vulnerable to your desires. Being out in the open too, for all to see, speaks to us about vulnerability, exposure and voyeurism. All these underlying nods towards sexual pleasure and desire feed into the homoerotic theme. Added to that potency is our enduring fascination with the actual moment of St Sebastian's torture and impending doom, which we witness, and which touches us all in his helplessness. His face never shows the agonies his perfect body is having to suffer; he bears it with absolute dignity – a message, perhaps, that we can all identify with, homosexuals especially.

But what about less obvious examples of homoeroticism? Take for instance a painting such as John Minton's *Horseguards in their Dressing Rooms at Whitehall*, which recently featured in Tate Britain's exhibition 'Queer British Art 1861-1967'. On first inspection the viewer might see Minton's painting as an innocent study of a soldier sitting on his bed during some down time, preparing his kit and brushing his bearskin. However, it was well-known in the 1950s (the time the painting was commissioned to commemorate the Queen's coronation) that some of these handsome young guardsmen had a reputation for being willing participants in what historian Matt Houlbrook, calls 'an institutionalised erotic trade'. Accounts of men cruising for sex in the vicinity of the Guards' barracks go back hundreds of years. Even the War Office was well aware of those who were 'afflicted with homosexual tendencies [being] strongly attracted towards soldiers… particularly of the physical requirements and standards of deportment required by the Guards.'

Thus, a gay man viewing *Horseguards* might interpret the otherwise seemingly domestic scene as one filled with overt erotic meaning, and take away from it an altogether different emotional context from that of the heterosexual viewer.

In the young guard, sitting on the side of his bed within arm's reach of the empty bed next to his, we might imagine the night-time scenario where he lies there listening to his dorm mate breathing. Is he remembering something as he perches on the edge of the bed in his bare feet, his white braces carelessly undone and flung across the bed behind him, his beautiful red guard's tunic hanging on the wall in prominent position above his head? On the bed, his brightly-polished black boots are displayed conspicuously towards the front of the picture, and over the bedcovers a number of unspecified and phallic-looking objects are strewn. Even his arm, thrust inside the bearskin, seems to send a distinct message. All these images might spark references a homosexual man would recognise, yet viewers are permitted only to imagine what he and his fellow barrack mates might get up to when they're not on parade or guarding Buckingham Palace. Nothing in the picture is overt or obvious, everything is left to interpretation and ambiguity; but shiny black boots and the splatter of white across the bed covers are clear signposts for those in the know.

This is the case in much artwork, homoerotic or not. Metaphoric meanings and pointers are purposefully put there by the artist to trigger certain responses and emotions in our brains, as we cast our eye over the canvas, working our way around it, deciphering and decoding the story; and we do this entire analytical operation in just a few seconds every time we look at a piece of art. Art, and particularly homoerotic art, appeals strongly to our subconscious mind, and our brains assemble an incredible ability to interpret what is before our eyes, as we delve into the artwork and make sense of it. A landscape such as John Constable's *The Hay Wain* is, by virtue, non-homoerotic. It could be assumed that the scene is simply there to be enjoyed. Though perhaps as it was painted in 1821 at the height of the industrial revolution, it might have been Constable's intention to jolt a memory of a time when the world was slower, more idyllic. The fundamental difference between art that is homoerotic and art that is not is that homoerotic art is meant to arouse as well as tell a story which can be translated to the viewer's own agenda and life experiences.

How does this happen? What precisely is going on inside our brains when we look at art?

In a study, researchers at University College London monitored the brains of volunteers while they were shown different paintings, one every ten seconds, and asked to rate each one according to how much they liked it or not.

The test was carried out on dozens of people, picked at random, but who had little prior knowledge of art and would therefore not be unduly influenced. Their instant appreciation of the images they were shown was clearly apparent in their MRI brain scans, which detected increased blood flow to areas in the orbitofrontal cortex where cells were vigorously responding.

Increased dopamine, which is transmitted through the brain as a reward motivator, and the brain's frontal cortex, are both known to be instrumental in the feelings of desire and affection, and in evoking the pleasurable affects often associated with romantic love and drug taking. In the painting study, the volunteers' blood flow to these regions increased by as much as ten per cent. As expected, viewing the paintings also triggered responses in the volunteer's brains that are associated with visual understanding and object recognition, but also activity in the regions of the brain associated with emotion, inner thoughts and learning. These instantaneous, cognitive reactions going on in our heads as we look at art appear not unlike the deep emotions we experience when we gaze at someone we love or feel a strong attraction towards. Beautiful paintings by artists such as John Constable, Ingres, the French neoclassical painter, and Guido Reni, produced the most powerful pleasurable responses in the volunteers, while less visually attractive paintings by artists such as Hieronymus Bosch, Honoré Damier and the Flemish artist Quentin Massys led to the smallest increases in blood flow activity.

'What we found,' Professor Semir Zeki of University College London explained in an interview with *The Telegraph*, 'is when you look at art, whether it is a landscape, a still life, an abstract or a portrait, there is strong activity in that part of the brain related to pleasure. The reaction was immediate and what we found was that the increase in blood flow was in proportion to how much the painting was liked.'

Humankind clearly appreciates beauty in art and we have done so since the dawn of time. Is there a deeper reason why we feel the effects of art as intensely as we do?

In the growing field of neuro-aesthetics, which studies the relationship between aesthetic pleasure and neurological functioning, the role that so-called mirror neurons play in art appreciation has been studied, and the findings are revealing. Mirror neurons are cells in the brain which respond in equal measure when either performing or observing the same action. Their job is to act as an important component in our innate survival mechanism. When we see something in nature – penguins huddled together in the cold, a cheetah hunting down a small deer or more potently, another human being experiencing pain – mirror neurons enable us to see ourselves in that cold, dangerous or frightening place and we anticipate how that experience would feel to us. Prime examples of this instinct are when our stomachs tense at the sight of blood or when we flinch when we see others hurt. This ability to empathise and feel emotion without actually having to be involved in the scenario also applies when viewing art. Even though the images that move us might vary among individuals, this ability to be aesthetically moved, sometimes to tears, appears to be a universal one.

According to research carried out by New York University, the ratings participants in their study gave to paintings of various subject matter they were shown showed very low agreement levels, revealing that the artworks that people found moving, for whatever reason, varied from one individual to another. As we know, individual taste in art is almost boundless. The study's participants were asked to rate a selection of paintings from 1 (lowest) to 4 (highest) in response to the question: 'How strongly does this painting move you?' It was explained that the rating they chose could cover all their emotional connectivity to the painting, from beautiful to strange or even ugly. Interestingly, MRI readings from the participant's brain activity showed that their sensory brain regions responded to the paintings no matter what their individual rating for each of those paintings was. However, the most moving paintings produced activity in regions of the brain which respond when we think about things that are personally relevant, such that might be connected to our own personality traits and daydreams, or when we think about our future.

The *Smithsonian Institute Magazine* cites the example of another study carried out by Professor David Freedburg of the Columbia University, in which ten subjects were asked to examine the wrist detail in Michelangelo's *Expulsion from Paradise*. Using a technique called transcranial magnetic stimulation (TMS), the researchers monitored the participant's brain patterns.

Expulsion from Paradise is part of Michelangelo's great Sistine Chapel masterpiece, and the detail used in the experiment was Adam's wrist as he bends it backwards in defence of a sword strike by an angel expelling him and Eve from the garden of Eden. 'Just the sight of the raised wrist causes an activation of the muscle,' says David Freedberg. This mirroring connectivity explains why, for instance, when viewing Degas' ballerinas, people sometimes say that they experience a sensation of movement and dancing. This, and the other studies, explain just how deeply we relate to art when we see paintings of others in dire straits, divine encounters or peaceful moments, and why we feel those emotions with them.

This same mirroring effect, of course, is going on when we view homocrotic art. The difference here is that the viewer needs to be able to read the 'hidden' messages. On one level, viewing a work such as Minton's *Horseguards* might simply produce a feeling of appreciation for the story the artist is trying to convey, that of contemplation and quietness, preparing for the big occasion (the Coronation) and what that moment of responsibility must feel like, or on a deeper, homoerotic level, the mirroring neurons react to the individual component images of strewn white braces, bare feet, and the barrack room setting, which can trigger strong sexual responses. In other paintings, the sight of a perfectly-formed penis might trigger 'feelings' in our own genitals, just as Adam's bent wrist triggered muscle contractions in the study's participants. Thus, art depicting muscled torsos, languishing youths and classical heroes elicits deeper emotions than simply those aroused by the beauty of the male form before us.

Homoerotic appreciation of the male body has long been identified in works by masters such as Leonardo da Vinci and Michelangelo, and more explicit sexual imagery can be seen in the Mannerist style of European art which emerged in the latter years of the Italian High Renaissance around 1520, and in the style of Tenebrism, also called dramatic illumination, where stark contrasts between light and dark are used with great theatrical effect, and where the darkness itself becomes a dominating feature of the image. Artists such as Agnolo Bronzino, Carlo Saraceni and Caravaggio were often severely criticized by the Catholic Church for the overtly 'homoerotic' content in their telling of classic religious stories. But how did they get away with it?

In Caravaggio's *Bacchino Malato*, for example, the boy portrayed is dressed as the Roman deity Bacchus (the face of whom is that of Caravaggio himself) and rests his head on his naked shoulder, peering out towards the viewer with what could be described as a provocative, alluring pout. In a lot of his work, Caravaggio's unseemly and some would say, inappropriate use of nudity, appears to goad the audience. Take for instance the pose of Cupid in *Victorious Cupid* painted in 1602, where an angelic boy sits with his legs splayed, exposing his genitals and the cleavage of his buttocks for all to see, with nothing but a carefree, enticing grin across his face. In this, and many of his paintings, it is as if Caravaggio is daring the viewer to acknowledge what is ostensibly obvious in his depiction of bared shoulders, tempting smiles, the sensuousness of parted lips or the delights of exposed genitalia. Despite the variations in religious themes, Caravaggio painted what could be seen as a series of sexual come-ons for public spectacle. A deeper look at his work however, finds that his message is perplexing, often juxtaposed; and that he intended for his paintings to be enigmatic rather than instantly readable, as well as to be enjoyed for their technical artistry. Today we are so used to seeing naked images of perfection in all manner of poses and contextual positions that it is difficult for us to appreciate the impact such lifelike work would have had on those who were fortunate enough to view it at the time.

Throughout Caravaggio's life, scandal and notoriety followed him. He was condemned as the 'antichrist of painting' for his use of his extreme naturalistic style. Notably, the *Madonna of Loretto*, which now hangs in the Basilica of Sant'Agostino in Rome, was widely criticized at its unveiling for the shocking portrayal of the Mother of God leaning nonchalantly against a wall in her bare feet while holding the baby Jesus in her arms as if she was a down-on-her-luck mother from one of the *borgate* districts of the city. His work however, was popular, and commissions and the burgeoning religious market in Rome, as the Catholic Church sought to attract Protestant converters back to the faith, meant that he was in demand. After his death though, he was largely forgotten, and draperies were added to some of his paintings to cover up the rather more conspicuous male genitalia and buttocks. It wasn't until the twentieth century that his genius and his mastery of light and dark began to be fully appreciated.

The skill of the Renaissance artists to paint nudes with ambiguous layers of meaning into their masterpieces, which are still on display in many churches, museums and art galleries around the world today, is testament to the fact that although the Church was often vocal in its disapproval, artists still produced works that could both stun by their beauty and at the same time cause outrage, often resulting in turmoil in the artists' personal lives.

By the nineteenth century, artists such as Simeon Solomon, Thomas Eakins and Henry Scott-Tuke used the classical figures of Hyacinth, Ganymede and Narcissus in paintings that were unequivocally homoerotic in their interpretation. The new 'classification' of homosexuality in the late 1800s made it more difficult for artists to paint freely without the label of 'homosexual' being attached to them. In 1873, Solomon himself had to flee London after being arrested in a public urinal at Stratford Mews Place off Oxford Street and was charged with attempted sodomy. His career was cut short, and a year later in Paris, he was arrested again for the same offence and sentenced to three months in prison.

In modern history, there was a brief period in the twentieth century when the proliferation of male nude art exceeded that of the female nude, and none more so than in Germany where the revolutionary theme of the 'Lebensreform' – literally 'life reform' – became a cult of the body.

The Leslie-Lohman Museum of Gay and Lesbian Art in New York curated an exhibition of one of the German artists, Sascha Schneider, who benefitted from this fraught and contradictory period that grew up and developed under the whimsical title of the Health and Hygiene Movement. An extension of the Arts and Craft Movement, Health and Hygiene was a direct response to the continual industrialization of the European nations and the fear that modern life was weakening the strength and drive of its youth. The movement promoted a return to the classical principles of nurturing the mind and body, of the youthful pursuit of outdoor exercise, and preferably naked as the Greeks would have done it. In Germany, this became a forward-looking and at the same time backward-looking philosophy, where the romanticized vision of youth, strength and beauty allowed for artists to paint, sculpt, and photograph the naked male body in what looked like strikingly obvious homoerotic poses, while at the same time promoting an idealized vision of the future.

Sascha Schneider came to understand the limits of a world that accepted homoeroticism but would not accept homosexuals. He contributed to *Der Eigene*, the world's first gay periodical, founded by Adolf Brand in 1896, but in the end, he was forced to resign his post at the Weimar University and fled to Italy.

Mid-twentieth century artists such as Andy Warhol, Jasper Johns and others developed their own visual codes by which to express homoeroticism. It wasn't until the Stonewall Riots in New York in 1969, and the subsequent growth of the Gay Liberation Movement, that there was a marked turning point in the popularisation of gay culture and homoeroticism. Modern-day work by fine artists such as Paul Cadmus, one of the first openly gay artists, Matthew Stradling, Cody Furguson and many others, have all made a strong contribution to the field of homoerotic art.

Nineteenth century homoerotic photography, such as that by Wilhelm von Gloeden and Vincenzo Galdi, (a pioneer of Italian erotic photography and renowned for breaking the taboo against showing the erect penis), changed direction in the 1960s, moving away from the stylised documentary setting and veiling models in Ancient Greek costumes in scenes that would otherwise be considered pornographic, into areas of fine-art surrealism by the likes of James Bidgood and Arthur Tress. Gallery censorship and legal restrictions were also challenged in the late 1970s and 80s by Robert Mapplethorpe, who further broke down the barriers between what constituted art rather than porn with his shockingly exposing S & M and fetish photo studies.

I posed the question at the beginning of this chapter, 'What is homoeroticism, and who puts it on their wall?' For centuries art was made for, and commissioned by, men to view and enjoy, and those who could afford it were the aristocracy, the wealthy, and the Church. We can assume, therefore, that Renaissance masterpieces that included male nudity and references to male-on-male, or solo masculine sex, had to be what those wealthy patrons wanted hanging on their walls, in their country houses, palaces and religious institutions. This is a simplistic analysis of course, and there were undoubtedly other layers of subliminal messages at play within the context of where a 'homoerotic' painting hung. Notwithstanding the undertones of homosexuality in appreciating homoeroticism, it appears that people on the whole enjoy viewing the naked male form; we like to see flesh and muscle, see it pitted against unthinkable foes, and in those pseudo-classical and biblical religious scenes, we imagine ourselves and how we might feel, react, win or fail.

There is another characteristic, that of friendship and brotherhood, strong connotations of which are encapsulated in homoeroticism. Like the sisterhood that binds women, men should be bold in recognising homoerotic emotion as something separate from homosexuality. Sigmund Freud put it this way: 'Rather than being a matter only for a minority of men who identify as homosexual, homoeroticism is a part of the very formation of all men as human subjects and social actors.'

Much of the sensual art we experience speaks to us on a bisexual, androgynous level. Often it is difficult to immediately tell the sex of the figure portrayed, but in them it is possible to see ourselves and the more skin unencumbered by clothes, the more potent the feeling of oneness with the characters and their situation or predicament.

Art, as proven by research, is good for us. It is calming, gives us a sense of pleasure and sometimes even erotic feelings, but more importantly perhaps, it demands of us to question what exactly the messages are that we are asked to decipher. We should, therefore, spend more time in front of works of art. We should embrace and enjoy art for all the good it brings us – especially homoerotic art.

5.
Sodomy across the Empire

On the prevalence of homosexuality in the military, where one might expect a natural inclination for homosexual men to draw closely together in ready-made homosocial groups, a lot of academic discussion can be found on ancient armies who treated man-to-man desire as part of the accepted beneficial order of bonding fighting men together, but there is little evidence of such things in the armed forces of modern history. Evidential records prior to 1700AD are sparse, other than a few sodomy cases bought to court by the English Admiralty, and in those cases none of the prosecutions apparently involved any naval officers. This lack of substantiated documentation is due in part to the fact that it wasn't until after the English Civil War (1642-1651) and the restoration of the monarchy in 1660 that King Charles II thought it prudent to keep a band of Royalist soldiers on permanent standby. His new regiments became Britain's first standing army. Similarly, the Royal Marines were formed at about the same time as the Duke of York and Albany's Maritime Regiment of Foot, which soon after became known as the Admiral's Regiment. Until that time, recruiting men to fight for king and country was done on an ad hoc basis, either by pay or by press-gangs, as with the Royal Navy.

Evidence of homosexuality within these close, male-only institutions only become apparent after the first Mutiny Act was passed by William III, who took the crown in 1689, and as a response to the mutiny of a large portion of his army who remained loyal to James II. A direct consequence of the Act was that military courts were given authority by Parliament to exercise jurisdiction in matters of discipline within their ranks and to hold courts-martial. However, the reason few documents survive is that in the opinion of most army officers at the time the civil legal process had little in common with the prosecution of military discipline. Instead, they preferred to use the informality of the regimental hearing to that of the general courts-martial and until 1805 they kept no written records of such proceedings. Witnesses and members of the informal courts took no form of oath. A general court-martial, on the other hand, was conducted with much greater formality. It was convened by an army commander and consisted of at least thirteen officers. Both the members of the court and the witnesses were sworn in, and a full transcript of the case and evidence was made. It is through these general courts-martial that the evidence of prosecutions for sodomy gradually start to appear.

Throughout the late seventeenth and early eighteenth-centuries, trial transcripts and the last confessions of condemned men in the form of printed pamphlets were extremely popular and a source of entertainment for London's coffee-shop patrons. The final confessions of sodomites, written by unknown authors at the side of the clergymen who administered the last rights, and sold as moral parables to the public in the form of short novellas of the trial, including the characters from inside the court, were particularly popular. The readers, playing devil's advocate through the realism of the stories, were asked to identify either with the condemned man or the accuser, in what was ostensibly voyeuristic eroticism.

The transcript of the trial of Captain Edward Rigby in 1698, who was charged with inciting nineteen-year-old William Minton to commit sodomy at his lodgings a few days after accosting him at a Guy Fawkes firework display in St James' Park, is an explicit example. The narrative explains what happened:

Rigby had said to Minton, "That the French King did it, and the Czar *of* Muscovy made Alexander, a carpenter, a Prince for that purpose," and affirmed, "He had seen the Czar *of* Muscovy through a hole at Sea, lie with Prince Alexander." Then Rigby kissed Minton several times, putting his tongue in his mouth, and taking Minton in his Arms, wished he might lie with him all night, and that his lust was provoked to that degree, he had — [i.e. ejaculated] in his breeches, but notwithstanding he could F[uck] him; Minton thereupon said, "sure you cannot do it here," "yes," answered Rigby, "I can," and took Minton to a corner of the room, and put his hands into Minton's breeches, desiring him to pull them down, who answered "he would not, but he (Rigby) might do what he pleased." Rigby pulled down Minton's breeches, turned away his shirt, put his finger to Minton's fundament and applied his body close to Minton, who, feeling something warm touch his skin, put his hand behind him and took hold of Rigby's privy member and said "I have now discovered your base inclinations. I will expose you to the world to put a stop to these crimes." Thereupon Minton went towards the door, Rigby stopped him, and drew his sword, upon which Minton gave a stamp with his foot, and cried out "Westminster", then the Constable and his Assistant came into the room and seized Rigby.

In court, Rigby declared that he had been set up and that he was drunk. Luckily for him his punishment was more lenient than it might have otherwise been. He was sentenced to two hours on each of three days at the pillories in three different locations, incurring the utmost humiliation, a fine of '100l' to the King, and one year in prison. After serving his prison sentence, Rigby exiled himself to France. In 1711 he commanded the French warship *Toulouse*, which was engaged by two English ships and badly damaged. The *Toulouse* was towed into Port Mahon in the Mediterranean. Here, Captain Rigby managed to out-manoeuvre the British, found his way onboard a Genoese ship lying at anchor and escaped back to France again. For a man who was the first recorded victim of entrapment, he had the tenacity and talent for getting away. He was highly regarded by the French for his skills as a sea captain and well paid for it, though it was said his pleasures were very expensive.

Another seafaring community, which was most active between the 1660s and 1730s, was the pirates. Their trials were also of the utmost interest to the public. Though they were portrayed as manifestly criminal in nature, whose felonious activities were against property, as opposed to the sodomite whose crime was the violation of the body, the pirate's carnal desires were always questionable, and were as much about danger and unpleasantness as his pilfering career was. Pirates were seen as someone with an unnatural craving to live in an all-male, closely confined social order, much like his holy antithesis, the monk; and on the periphery of a normal, law-abiding society, bound only by a loose code of rules applicable to no one but the pirates themselves. A certain Captain Hacke, for instance, spoke of his crew being made up of 'all run-aways, some having merited the gallows, others fire and faggot for sodomy.' Evidence that pirates practised sodomy is all but non-existent, as there is no documentation of life on board a pirate ship. There is plenty of evidence that sodomy was part of life aboard ships of the Royal Navy and that sailors such as Captain Rigby had to bridle their sexual desires whilst they were on land, which they would have otherwise gratified at sea. It can, however, be safe to assume that pirates would have been less than scrupulous in relieving themselves of their sexual desires both at sea and, no doubt, on land as well. There was a distinct difference, however, in the way trials concerning pirates were reported to those of other sodomite cases involving Royal Navy seamen – the sodomites were never made into rapscallion heroes.

In the army, circumstantial reports endure of sodomy occurring at isolated army garrisons or within the poorest and lowest ranks. For example, soldiers in the town of Candia, modern-day Heraklion in Crete, who were besieged there from 1648-1669, were, according to reports, 'horribly devoted to sodomy'. There are also trial reports of instances that took place between soldiers and civilians, such as that of Thomas Lane, a foot-soldier, who in 1707 was indicted for assaulting Richard Hemming and Samuel Baker on London Bridge. Lane, according to the transcript, 'pulled out his nakedness and offered to put it into his [Hemming's] hands'. Lane said in his defence that he had been at St Thomas' Hospital, and 'coming over the bridge, stopped to make water', and that Hemmings' hand slipped 'upon his nakedness, and such like frivolous stuff.' Despite him making light of what happened, pleading his good character and his many years in the service of King William and the present Queen Anne, the jury found him guilty.

It was at this time, during the reign of Queen Anne, that concern about the increase in homosexuality began to grow. One of the main promoters for the spread of the vice, it was thought, was the importation of Italian opera into England.

The eighteenth century novel Fanny Hill, or Memoirs of a Woman of Pleasure, published in 1748, expresses the popularly-held belief that sailors were less than fussy when it came to sex. In this quote, Fanny's alarm is raised during the act of sex with a sailor: 'he was not going by the right door, and knocking desperately at the wrong one, I told him of it. 'Pooh!' says he, 'my dear, any port in a storm.''

There was a widely held suspicion of the period that the Royal Navy was a bastion of homosexuality, but for the men who lived in that secluded world, the topic was either totally absent or taboo, not least because penalties for committing sodomy on board a Royal Navy ship were severe and more so than they were on land. The threat of death was the ultimate deterrent, and some have argued that finding a private place onboard a cramped man o'war would have been very difficult, making it almost impossible not to be detected. When it did occur, it was often covered up or treated as a lesser charge of 'uncleanness', which covered a catalogue of offences including 'improperly conducted excretory activity', i.e. going to the toilet in non-designated areas of the ship, 'a general lack of hygiene', or 'homoerotic behaviour'.

Judicial record keeping improved from the late eighteenth century onwards and transcripts of Royal Navy sodomy trials and accounts from the Napoleonic wars contain information not previously found in similar documents from earlier cases. Research suggests that during the Seven Years War (1756-1763), there were eleven courts-martial for sodomy, of which four defendants were acquitted and seven were given lesser charges of indecency or 'uncleanness'. Considering the scale of the naval population engaged in the war at the time, between seventy and eighty thousand men, this number of cases seems extremely low and does suggest that many incidents, if brought before the commanding officers, were simply dealt with on board.

The furtiveness of seamen who found pleasure with each other is testified in the case of Lorenzo Greenard and Thomas Fuller, who were discovered playing with each other's genitals one night under a launch on the *Vengeance* in 1802. They were both sentenced to death. Also, that year, John Holland and John Reilly were so drunk on board the *Trident* that they made no attempt to hide what they were up to. Their behaviour so upset their messmates that the master-at-arms was summoned. When he arrived on the scene he caught them in a flagrant, uncompromising position and had to literally prise them apart. He reported to the court-martial that having examined the penis of one of the men, he found it to be 'fit for action'. Both these men already had bad reputations and Reilly had it on record that he had kissed another sailor before while drunk. They, however, did not receive the death penalty, but their sentences were still harsh; Reilly received 600 lashes and Holland 300. Had they been more discreet in their behaviour they might have got away with it. It was only that their conduct had been so intolerable to their shipmates that they were reported. Lashings for these sorts of offences were twice those for mutiny or desertion and sentencing by the courts-martial seems to have been arbitrary. It is impossible to say why one sentence was meted out in favour of another.

There is evidence of degrees of tolerance among sailors towards those they knew to be homosexual but who acted discreetly. Sergeant George Pewtrer, a marine with 14 years' service, and Michael Millard, a marine drummer, were both accused of indecent acts on board the *Defiance* in 1808. Their hammocks were known to be adjacent to one another. One marine reported that he had seen them cuddling, another that he had stumbled upon them locked in an embrace and kissing underneath a gun. No one, it seems, was unduly concerned by their behaviour and one witness even went so far as to say that he 'never formed any opinion upon it.' The pair were acquitted, probably not least due to the testament of their character witnesses.

There are two schools of thought about homosexuality in the Royal Navy; one held that it was so inconsequential to the running of the fleet that it was in many cases brushed under the carpet, while the other view was that officers and seamen so feared the consequences of being caught and the harsh penalty they would face that they simply did not indulge. Whatever the actual situation, there was an inherent public perception that the Royal Navy was a haven for sodomites.

Another odd contradiction is that the press-gangs who trawled the pubs and quaysides of English ports for victims had no hesitation in who they collared when it came to finding men for the King or Queen's ships – someone's sexual predilections were no guarantee of them not being clubbed and dragged off. As in the case of William Bailey, who, despite bringing numerous witnesses to court to testify in his defence, saying that he was 'frequently in women's company', was sentenced to stand at the pillory for sodomy. He managed to escape that fate, only to be pressed into service with His Majesty's Navy by a passing press-gang which had no scruples in setting about Bailey's captors and bringing the convicted sodomite onto a Royal Navy ship. With a price of up to ten shillings for each man pressed, it's perhaps not surprising that the press-gang took the law into their own hands, brawling with the 'butchers' to get at Bailey.

With the expansion of the Empire and battalions of men being stationed on far-flung garrisons away from home for months at a time, warnings of widespread homosexual activity came out of the colonies. Fear of a moral contamination in the native environment made it a matter of urgency to insert anti-sodomy provisions into a new Indian Penal Code. In 1825 a mandate was handed to Thomas Babington-Macauley, renowned historian and politician, to chair the Law Commission of India into drafting the code.

The British explorer Sir Richard Burton, who was famed for his travels and explorations of Asia, Africa and the Americas and his command of twenty-nine languages, amongst his many other talents, which were as varied as geographer and soldier, spy, poet and fencer, claimed that there was what he called a 'Sotadic zone' that circumnavigated the globe between forty-three degrees north of the equator and thirty degrees south in which 'unnatural affection' thrived. The zone took in the northern shores of the Mediterranean in a belt approximately 780-800 miles wide, including Southern France, the Iberian Peninsula, Italy and Greece, and the coastal regions of Africa, from Morocco to Egypt. Eastwards it encompassed Asia Minor, Mesopotamia, Afghanistan, Sind (modern-day Pakistan) and the Punjab and Kashmiri regions of India. In Indo-China the belt broadened further, taking in China, Japan and Turkistan; then the South Sea Islands and the New World, where, 'at the time of its discovery, Sotadic love was, with some exceptions, an established institution.' In this belt-region under the sun, Burton claimed that 'the vice is popular and endemic... whilst the races to the north and south of the limits, here defined, practise it only sporadically amid the opprobrium of their fellows, who, as a rule, are physically incapable of performing the operation and look upon it with the liveliest disgust.'

At the age of twenty-four, whilst stationed just outside Karachi, then a small town of 'two thousand souls', but which supported no less than three brothels specialising in boys and eunuchs and being the only British officer who could speak Sindi, Burton was directed to make enquires and to report back. He undertook the task and wrote about it in his *Terminal Essay from Pederasty: Volume Ten of the Arabian Nights*, which gives a glut of detail, probably indicating his own first-hand experiences.

British officials at the time feared that their soldiers and colonial administrators – particularly those unaccompanied by their wives – would turn to sodomy in these decadent, hot surroundings. Lord Elgin, Viceroy of India between 1894-1899, gave warning that the British garrisons could become 'replicas of Sodom and Gomorrah' as soldiers succumbed to the 'special Oriental vices'. For many Victorian men, soldiers and government officials alike, the restrictions on sexual freedoms back home were irresistibly lifted once abroad, and especially in India. The availability of concubines, eunuchs and lotus-eyed prostitutes were overpoweringly seductive to the extent that the incidences of venereal disease at the turn of the twentieth century among the those in the army and stationed at home in Britain was 40 soldiers per 1,000; in India it was 110 per 1,000.

At his residence in the north Indian district of Shimla, Lord Kitchener, the First World War general, now most commonly recognised from the famous army recruitment poster 'Your Country Needs You', was Commander-in-Chief of India from 1902-1909, and continued a habit he had indulged in greatly in his days in Egypt by surrounding himself with an eager bunch of unmarried officers nicknamed 'Kitchener's happy band of boys.' As one journalist put it, Kitchener personified the 'Officer's failing... a taste for buggery.' Lord Kitchener wasn't the only one indulging his sexual preferences in the Shimla foothills. From its earliest days as the summer retreat for the Raj, Shimla became a place for British administrators, government officials, and convalescing and holidaying soldiers, to enjoy some restorative fornication in an atmosphere of 'gaiety, frivolity and sexual indulgence.' It was a far cry from the morality of tight-lipped Victorian England.

The expansion of the British Empire into every tropical corner of the world provided no end of possibilities for sexual experimentation. As historian Roy Porter put it: 'For many English travellers, exotic parts and peoples were realisations of fantasies, sources of sexual or mystical discovery, havens for scoundrels and screwballs, ways of jumping the rails of Western Classical-Christian Civilization.'

6.
The First World War - Homosexuality Under Fire

The ancient army known as the Sacred Band of Thebes, was a unique fighting force; certainly nothing like it has been recorded in military history since. In modern times such a battalion of men, made up of warriors and their male lovers, would have been unthinkable, and largely because of the myth that homosexuals were incapable of bravery under enemy fire. This untruth also stretched to include women, since fighting and courage on the battlefield were not seen as feminine attributes. Despite both homosexual men and women displaying immense courage and fortitude in the face of terrible danger in all sorts of scenarios, often at personal risk, still it was assumed for many years, and especially so for homosexuals, that they would turn and run when faced with life-threatening situations rather than stand and help their comrades.

For women, flexible gender roles were seen as a practical answer to the problem of a shortage of labour in heavy industry and the munitions factories. With the shortage of men, the women's labour force was a positive and worthy contribution to the war effort. But for men between the ages of eighteen and 41 (51 by 1918), and physically fit (the basic rule of thumb was that if any man turned up at the recruitment office appearing healthy, able and of age, no further questions were asked), opposition to their perceived gender role as soldiers or sailors, was unthinkable and unacceptable. Conscientious objection, though unpatriotic, could be forgiven in women, as it was seen as a natural feminine instinct to uphold peace above all else. A mother's innate wish not to see her son die in warfare was entirely normal, but for men who declared themselves conscientious objectors, not only were they cast as cowards and instantly made pariahs, but their very masculinity was also brought into question. Through necessity, the male population was defined as warriors, and even those who were too old, too young or infirm to fight were expected to support the war by any means through their jobs. Women, even when given their newly-acquired flexible gender roles, were still seen as the mothers of the nation, holding the family together and the guardians of morality. Woe betide the woman whose sobriety or fidelity was brought into question. The separation allowance paid to a soldier's wife or mother could be withdrawn at any time by the government for misconduct.

Before the war, in 1908, there was a case of scandalous proportions of homosexual conduct which wrought havoc to the German Government. The Eulenburg Affair, as it became known, was the culmination of a series of courts-martial and trials that centred around a homosexual affair between Prince Phillip of Eulenburg-Hertefeld and General Kuno, Graf von Moltke. Accusations and counter-accusations were made, and the phrase 'Liebenberg Round Table' came to be synonymous with the homosexual circle that surrounded the Kaiser. The affair received widespread publicity and was the biggest domestic scandal in German politics of the time, leading to the first major public debate on homosexuality in Germany, comparable to that of the trial of Oscar Wilde in Britain ten years earlier. The case was propaganda gold to the British and homosexuality was accordingly associated with Germanness and remained so throughout the First World War.

Given this climate of social and authoritarian control, it is little wonder that homosexual men signed up in their droves, kept their heads down and went off to fight alongside their brothers and friends; and why wouldn't they, given that they felt the same patriotic sense of duty to defend their homeland and way of life as any other Tom, Dick or Harry?

Evidence of homosexual activity between serving men during the First World War, and for that matter the Second World War, is sparse. Being caught would have resulted in a court martial and a sentence of at least two years' imprisonment. Of the four million men serving in the British forces in WW1, records show that just over 304,000 were courts-martialled for offences ranging from insubordination to sleeping while on look-out duty, and even murder. Of those, just 22 officers and 270 enlisted men were court-martialled for homosexual offences. Considering the questionable recruitment process and more pertinently, the constant stress they were under, this number is very small. Many more must have hidden their homosexuality or that their fellow comrades turned a blind eye; for privacy, in the conditions in which they lived and fought, would have been difficult. However, some psychologists and historians cite evidence that suggests there was much more homoerotic emotional feelings between men than there was sexual activity, which might indicate that homosexuality was as repressed in the trenches as it was in civilian life.

French laws prohibiting sodomy were repealed in 1791 during the revolution, and so theoretically, under the law, homosexuality was legal in France. There are sketchy accounts of French families who lived near the front line taking pity on love-struck British soldiers and offering them a place to carry on their secret rendezvous. However, in general, the French attitude towards homosexuality was essentially no more liberal or tolerant than it was in Britain. They too associated it with effete Germans.

In 1916, a far-right Independent Member of Parliament, Noel Pemberton Billing, announced that homosexuality was infiltrating every aspect of British society and that German agents were working on the streets as part of an espionage ring out to entrap the unsuspecting youths and men of Britain. He wrote an article in *Vigilante* magazine in which he claimed that Prince William of Wied, Prince of Albania, had in his possession a 'Black Book' in which

47,000 British men and women of 'moral and sexual weakness' were named, and which the Germans planned to use to 'exterminate the manhood of Britain by luring men into homosexual acts'. He also claimed that, 'incestuous bars were established in Portsmouth and Chatham, and in these meeting places, the stamina of British sailors was undermined. More dangerous still, German agents, under the guise of indecent liaison, could obtain information as to the disposition of the Fleet.' Following a disagreement over Parliamentary procedure and refusing to be seated, claiming that Germans were 'running about the country', Billing was ejected from the House of Commons and suspended as MP in July 1918.

On both sides, the governments tried to enforce normal sexual behaviours. Men at the front and their womenfolk back home were both encouraged to abstain for the duration of hostilities. The traditional social limitations that would have otherwise disallowed straying were, in many cases, ineffectual. Being away from home, families torn apart and the overwhelming strains brought about by war, meant that though the war could be brutal and devastating, some found it also provided a way to experience sexual liberation for the very first time. The heroic image of abstinent soldiers dedicating their every thought and waking moment to victory, with nothing else at all on their minds, was rather undermined by the rapid spread of venereal disease, which exactly reflected the sense of sexual adventure the men, many of them still virgins and away from home for the first time, so eagerly craved and desired. To alleviate the spread of VD at the Front, and to free up beds for those injured in actual combat, both the German and French militaries set up 'safe' brothels just behind the front lines, where prostitutes were medically checked. British military authorities did allow their soldiers to visit the French brothels as a necessary evil, but they came under increasing pressure from civilian groups such as the Association for Moral &

Social Hygiene to discontinue such an open tolerance for the soldiers' promiscuity.

The down side of self-restraint was pent-up torment and angst, and there is a lot of documented evidence from serving homosexuals who could not be open about their sexuality. An anonymous soldier told of his experiences and why he did not act upon those feelings and desires. 'There was no sexual contact with anybody in the services. The simple reason [for me was] I got promoted to sergeant from corporal. As you're getting promotions, you couldn't take no chances. I had several chances mind you, with two or three different private soldiers I knew. You can gauge 'em, but the point is, when you come to look at it, you say to yourself – well, is it mind over matter? You say to yourself, 'No, I mustn't'. You're jeopardising your chances, because if something happened, you're going to get court martialled.'

Wilfred Owen, the famous war poet, wrote to his cousin in 1918: 'There are two French girls in my billet, daughters of the Mayor, who (I suppose because of my French) single me out for their joyful gratitude for La Deliverance. Naturally I talk to them a good deal; so much so that the jealousy of other officers resulted in a Subaltern's Court Martial being held on me! The dramatic irony was too killing, considering certain other things, not possible to tell in a letter.'

Back in Britain the authorities came down hard on women, young and old, who propagated what they called 'khaki fever' by openly flirting with any man they came across in uniform, and as losses mounted at the front, so the emphasis back home bore down even more heavily on men, not only in their response to join up and fight, but also to father sons for an ever-dwindling male population. Thus, the morality of anyone entering into a homosexual relationship, however brief, had never been more questionable, for not only was it illegal, it was unpatriotic.

Magnus Hirschfeld, in his studies for the British Society for the Study of Sex Psychology, found a rise in what he euphemistically called 'pseudo-homosexuality', which he claimed was the result of heterosexual men engaging in same-sex activity. There was an outcry from the military authorities, who saw this as the beginning of a complete breakdown in masculine warrior behaviour. Controversially, Hirschfeld maintained that homosexuals were actually better equipped to deal with the emotional rigours of combative war, as they were well used to suppressing any emotions to do with love or bonding to other males.

For some homosexual men, living and fighting on the front line gave them the subconscious permission to demonstrate outward displays of emotion and affection that in any other situation at home would have been seen as abnormal or deviant. Love and compassion between soldiers who shared a six-foot dugout was a positive factor in the well-being of the men. Some homosexuals thrived in this unnatural environment, showing that strong emotional ties between men encouraged morale, and that heroes and bravery were not the sole preserve of macho stereotypes. When the British stiff upper lip was subjected to the horrors of war at close quarters day-in day-out, all pretence of what was or was not acceptable masculinity were soon forgotten. For many struggling with their sexual identity, the front line provided that ideal situation in which it was possible to be both a warrior and a nurturer.

One well-documented story tells of a young German soldier who was carried off the battlefield by four of his close comrades on a stretcher back to the field hospital, after suffering terrible injuries in a bomb blast. With little aid or comfort from drugs, he lay on his sick bed in terrible pain, his leg completely mangled. When he did find the strength to write a letter, it was not to a sweetheart or wife, but to his boyfriend back home. 'I crave a decent mouthful of fresh water, of which there isn't any here,' he wrote in his final letter. 'There is absolutely nothing to read; please, do send newspapers. But above all, write very soon.'

His boyfriend, known simply as S, and hundreds of miles away, was unable to do a thing. The suffering of the dying soldier and his lover, helpless at home, was exactly the same ghastly predicament as that experienced by many thousands of other men and women all over Europe. In a cruel twist of fate, the letters S wrote back to the Russian front to comfort his boyfriend never reached him. The young soldier died alone, not knowing if his boyfriend ever knew his fate. In April 1916, their story was told via a letter S sent in to the Scientific Humanitarian Committee, the German publication for WhK.

After the war, his was among many voices insisting that the German government were obligated to them, the 'inverts', as they were commonly known, regardless of the biology of their sexuality. Science as a reasoning argument in the homosexual's fight for equality was now being replaced with a direct set of demands that they deserved to have their rights respected as much as any other citizen.

It was during the First World War that the first seismic movements in understanding homosexual sexuality and the benefits to society of their equality were first recognised. Ideas of citizenship, respect and equality for women, workers and homosexuals, especially so in Germany, were beginning to gather momentum. It wasn't until the groundswell of popularity which brought about the rise to power of the Nazis that a stop was put to all that.

7.
London Between the Wars

Social changes that had begun with the First World War continued through the years of the Depression that marked the twenties and accelerated again in the period leading up to and during the Second World War. In those interregnum years, women assumed a new collective sense of purpose and emancipation. Factories offered better conditions, higher wages and more interesting work, and freedom was gained away from the subservient duties of domestic service. Maids and under-footmen left the confines of working for the upper and middle classes in their droves. Female factory workers challenged gender norms in many situations, demonstrating that they were more than capable of carrying out skilled labour tasks in jobs that had once been closed to them. In public they were able to conduct themselves differently as well, wear less constricting clothing, and contribute to society in ways undreamt of before the Great War. In other respects, such as equality and pay, women were still paid less than men, and they lacked the independent economic and political power to make sweeping changes; women were given more opportunities, but they were never equal to men.

By the 1920s, the social changes which had been brought about by and for women meant that there was also a greater awareness and acceptance of other minorities, including homosexuals, at least in urbanised areas. At the same time there was greater mobilisation in this period, which meant that there were now opportunities for gay men to find themselves and each other that simply hadn't been there before.

In a newspaper article from 1916 it was reported that 'painted and perfumed travesties of men' were seen openly leering at passers-by in London's Piccadilly. 'Certain bars and restaurants are meeting places for these creatures', the newspaper went on, adding that it was 'lamentable to know that their victims or accomplices are largely drawn from the ranks of the British Army.'

What the newspaper observed was a lively and highly visible 'scene' that bloomed like a rare flower, or perhaps an unsavoury weed, from the shadowy underworld of the West End and Central London during the First World War and throughout the inter-war period. In 1924 the *Sunday Express* noted, 'our new decadents… at Covent Garden [opera house], at the Alhambra [theatre in Leicester Square], and wherever Sergie Diaghilev [the Russian art critic and ballet impresario] had his seasons… Rouge and powder are known to this co-fraternity of nastiness.' The Dilly Boys, as the painted young 'queans' and rent boys who plied for trade in and around Piccadilly Circus and The Strand were known, were the modern versions of Dickens' pick-pocket gangs in the novel *Oliver Twist* – Fagins' wretches grown up and corrupted into a lucrative and destructive sex trade. The screaming, effeminate caricatures these young 'felons' portrayed exemplified the meaning of what it was to be homosexual to the onlooking, and side-stepping, general public. They were the punks of their day. Long before youths and teenagers formed tribes like the teddy boys, rockers and mods of the fifties and sixties, this group of over-the-top, loud and anti-social fairies, who dipped in and out of normal daily and nightly life like a flock of flamingos, portrayed a persona that was, in reality, a ridiculous misrepresentation of the homosexual, but one which made the public take the view that all men who wanted to have sex with other men must be like this. According to historian Matt Houlbrook in his book *Queer London: Perils and Pleasures in the Sexual Metropolis 1918-57*, London in the first half of the twentieth century was much queerer, where coiffured and rouged-up poofs wearing lipstick were an everyday sight in the West End. Houlbrook talks about three distinct gay stereotypes which seem to have increased their 'visibility' in the pre-Second World War decades. There was the showy 'quean', the 'normal' working class man, and the respectable gentleman homosexual – and each was caught in a malaise of yearning and disgust. The West End poof or 'quean', though tolerated to a degree in working-class neighbourhoods, remained, as he does today, a constant target for abuse from the very working-class men and labourers he desired. He was despised by the gentlemen gays for his crass affectations and gross parodying, and for the spectacle that always surrounded him, like some horrifying pantomime.

The working man, so craved by both the other groups, enjoyed the sexual freedoms the anonymity of the city provided him, but his manly self-image meant he could only ever denigrate the 'queans' in front of his mates and extort money from his upper and middle-class gentleman friends. But it was the respectable gentleman homosexual who had it most tough. Enthralled by the dangers and excitement of illicit liaisons in public toilets and in the alleyways and notorious streets around the gaily patronised public houses, of which his stiff-upper-lip respectability would have otherwise denounced, the gentleman gay lusted after those virile working lads or the bits of trade who frequented these places, both of whom, he knew, would never accept his middle-class dream of a passionate man-to-man love affair and domesticity in the suburbs. He lived an invariably dark and shadowy 'other life', unknown to his family, work colleagues or the rest of the world. Encounters between these two groups were permitted, so long as the masculinity and dominance of the working men were never brought into doubt. For some tough young working-class bachelors, a lack of money and private digs of their own, together with societal condemnation towards premarital sex, enabled a culture in which relieving an older gay gentleman of a few shillings for a blow-job or more was an acceptable demonstration of his masculine prowess and ability to make money.

Venues in areas such as Edgware Road, particularly in the 1920s, thronged with homosexual gentlemen, as well as domestic hotel staff and army lads from the barracks in Regent's Park and Knightsbridge. In the East End and South London, the 'queans' were a familiar presence in many pubs, and the area around Waterloo was well known for tough working-class men who could be approached with a reasonable chance of success.

For ordinary working-class people, the perception of homosexuals was of men who were louche, limp-wristed and essentially feminine, and public moral attitudes found the vision of painted young men mincing about the centre of London increasingly scandalous. In December 1932, *The News of the World* euphemistically reported, to save the sensibilities of its readers, on a police raid of a men-only dance in Holland Park, London, where thirty police officers burst in on a 'ball' taking place in a private house. 'About ten per cent were women, and women of a particular class, not prostitutes, but another sort of woman. The remaining 90 per cent were men, men of a class well known to the public in London, men who speak to each other endearingly and dress effeminately'. 'One man,' the newspaper added, was spotted wearing 'only his pyjama trousers'. The organiser of the ball, Lady Austin (otherwise known as Austin S., a twenty-four-year-old barman from Barons Court), was arrested along with 59 others. Austin did not go quietly, but instead, stalling in front of a particularly good-looking policeman, he told the inspector apprehending him that the young police officer was 'too dishy to be a real policeman,' and that he 'could love him and rub his Jimmy for him for hours.' At the inspector's caution, Austin retorted, 'There is nothing wrong in that. You may think so, but it is what we call real love – man for man. You call us nancies and bum boys but before long our cult will be allowed in this country.'

There are anecdotal accounts of men picking up other men in the circle at the Empire and at the Prince of Wales in Leicester Square, preferring the relative safety of cruising the theatre galleries rather than the numerous cottages, bars and clubs that proliferated throughout the city. Each of these locations was the pick-up area for a distinct type of man. It was well known, for instance, that if you wanted a bit of rough you'd look round the cottages in Covent Garden. Or, according to school teacher Bernard Williams, 'On the other hand, if you wanted the theatrical trade you'd do some of the cottages round the back of Jermyn Street, or if you did the cottage at Waterloo Station you'd have a good class of trade there, dear.'

In what must be the first-ever guide to the capital's cottages, *For Your Convenience*, published in 1937 by one 'Paul Pry', was a barely-disguised compendium of London's public gents' toilets, put together for the amusement of those seeking relief other than from a full bladder. The subtitle on the frontispiece could not be clearer: 'A learned dialogue instructive to all Londoners and London visitors, overheard in the Théléme Club and taken down verbatim by Paul Pry.' What other reason could there be for such a book other than to guide homosexuals to the capital's best cottages? The book is written in the form of a conversation between two members of a gentleman's club, the Thélème, which itself seems to be a reference to the pseudo-religion *Thelema* organised of the notorious occultist, Aleister Crowley, who saw himself as its prophet, encouraging his followers with the mantra, 'Do what thou wilt.' In *For Your Convenience*, the older gentleman becomes increasingly interested in the younger man's knowledge of where 'relief' might be found in the capital's lavatories and remarks that the facilities on Goodge Street were closed because they had been abused. The younger man explains: 'places of that kind which have no attendants afford excellent rendezvous to people who wish to meet out of doors and yet escape the eye of the 'busy' [policeman]'. In what could be taken, on the surface of it, to be an innocent conversation, the book ends with a clear innuendo remarked by the older gentleman as the pair trot off to the club's toilet together, 'I'm coming that way too. Lead on, my boy.' The end-paper map depicts lavatory attendants reclining in the foreground bearing their brushes like attendants at a Roman orgy with ostrich feather fans, and the located lavatories are indicated as tented pavilions scattered across central London.

Popular music-hall songs of the time also made open reference to homosexuals, the new social acceptance of homosexuality and the increasingly indistinguishable differences between the sexes. One well-liked song, with the title *'Masculine Women, Feminine Men'*, released in 1926, was recorded by Frank Harris and many other artists of the day, and included these chorus lyrics:

Masculine Women, Feminine Men
Which is the rooster, which is the hen?
It's hard to tell 'em apart today
And say…
Sister is busy learning to shave
Brother just loves his permanent wave
It's hard to tell 'em apart today
Hey Hey!

Being gay in the 1920s and 30s, certainly for those working behind the scenes in the theatre, film and popular entertainment industries, received a certain level of tolerance that had not been seen before, and would not be again until the 1970s. Even so, box office stars could not live openly gay lifestyles. Hollywood actor William Haines, who had a string of successful lead roles in major films in the twenties, had his career cut short in 1935 when he refused to give up his partner and lover, Jimmy Shields. Haines was lucky and went on to establish a thriving interior design company, ironically supported by many of his Hollywood friends such as Joan Crawford.

By the mid-nineteen thirties, the political world stage had changed. Frivolity, gaiety and the exploration of individualism ceased. Europe was preparing for war and homosexuality was again seen as divisive, dangerous and weak.

In London, the Public Morality Council, a quasi-official authority which had been formed in 1899 to combat vice and indecency in the capital, was given special dispensation to monitor 25 gay pubs in the West End. The PMC, whose members included representatives of the major religions as well as education and healthcare leaders, reported eleven pubs for 'irregular conduct', resulting in numerous arrests of rent boys and their clients. A prosecution was also brought against the Caravan Club in Covent Garden, which advertised itself as 'London's Greatest Bohemian Rendezvous' and 'the most unconventional spot in town.' It was, according to neighbours who complained about it to the PMC, 'frequented by sexual perverts, lesbians and sodomites... an absolute sink of iniquity, your prompt attention is respectfully craved.' Membership to the club was a shilling or 1/6d on the door, and six weeks after opening it had a membership of over 400 and attracted many more casual visitors. The club opened in July 1934 and shortly after was put under surveillance. In August it was raided and the subsequent court proceedings in October at the local Bow Street Magistrates caused a sensation. Once the nature of the charges became public knowledge it was inevitable that people would be curious. Crowds of up to 500, mostly porters from the nearby Covent Garden Market and local office workers gathered outside the court, and as each defendant arrived they were met with 'What ho, Gerald!' and roars of laughter and cheering from workmen on the roof of the Royal Opera House opposite. The crowd was good-natured, but the police were forced to intervene to keep the road open.

Verdicts were delivered on 26 October. Jack Neave, who ran the club, was sentenced to 20 months' hard labour, and Joseph Reynolds, who financed it, 12 months' hard labour. William Dodd, a shop assistant, got three months' hard labour. The *Daily Express* described Neave as a man of striking appearance: 'He has black hair, which hangs over his shoulders. He wore a frockcoat, large black stock tie, and a soft frilled shirt front. He is a man of tremendous strength.' The rest of the defendants were either found not guilty or received shorter sentences, which with time already served resulted in their immediate release. The defendants were mostly in their early twenties, and their occupations included artist, window dresser, waiter, messenger, dancing partner, painter, schoolmaster, traveller, milliner, clerk and salesman. In his final summing up, the judge described the club as 'A foul den of iniquity which was corrupting the youth of London.'

The Pubic Morality Council continued its work until 1969, concentrating on the wider morass of sexual immorality and pornography, particularly regarding the theatre, the cinema, radio and television.

A further insistence on the Metropolitan Police to exert their powers came from the army's London District Command, which saw such disreputable clubs, cafés and bars as a corrupting threat to its servicemen. Military Police began patrolling undesirable premises, barring young soldiers from entering and calling for the Met to close them down. The police, however, were put in a difficult position. Officers could enter an establishment and grant approval, as well as verify the landlord's suitability prior to licensing, but their capacity to keep the place under surveillance was tightly regulated. Firstly, surveillance could only be carried out on the authorisation of a senior officer and raids on premises could only be conducted with a magistrate's warrant. Even then, the club could re-open under a new name and with new management in just a few days. The Met were therefore reluctant to act with any formality and only did so under pressure of specific complaints from the public and the military authorities. Police operations did take place, famously at the Caravan Club and other establishments such as the Running Horse and Melodies in Shepherd's Market, but only after intervention from the Admiralty and the Royal Air Force in the latter two cases.

External pressures did eventually bring about the reorganisation of police procedures and were further developed as anxieties about the corruption of vulnerable young servicemen intensified with the onset of the Second World War. Under the Defence Regulations and Emergency Powers Act, 1939, police officers were empowered to close down venues that were deemed disorderly, and could do so without any legal process. Surveillance of nightclubs and pubs already known to the police increased, and the effectiveness of the closing orders was such that they did not need to raid every dubious pub or club in town, but rather one closure or conviction was enough to effect 'the cleansing in other premises where such perverts congregate.'

The carefree optimism and frivolousness that marked the period after the First World War had changed by the mid-thirties. Whilst social changes had ostensibly shifted the emphasis of the class system and altered the face of British life, there was an understandable seriousness in the years that led up to the Second World War. Even so, arrests and convictions for gross indecency of homosexual men in the pre-war period, and indeed throughout the war, were few in comparison to the number made in later years.

8.
The Second World War

In 1939, the British Army was made up of an all-volunteer force and was tiny in comparison to that of the German Wehrmacht. Its main purpose was to garrison the Empire, working as localised law-enforcers and peace-keepers. The Royal Navy on the other hand, was the largest fleet in the world and was Britain's main line of defence.

An official number is hard to pin down, but over the course of the Second World War, Britain, her Empire and Dominions raised approximately 8.5 million men for military service, and of those between 3.5 and 5 million were British citizens. Taking the mean figure of 4.25 million, it is likely that at least 106,000 of those serving were homosexuals or bisexuals. This is based on data from Britain's National Survey of Sexual Attitudes and Lifestyles – a probability sample survey using 15,162 people aged 16–74 years undertaken in 2010–2012, in which 2.5% of men identified as gay or bisexual. Interestingly, 6·5% of men reported having had same-sex attraction, and 5·5% that they had experienced same-sex sexual activity. It is recognised that men who have sex with other men do not necessarily identify as homosexual. It is very likely then that in the theatre of war, away from home, often fearful and missing loved ones, and living in cramped conditions, sexual activity between soldiers or sailors would have been more prevalent and accepted than on civvy street in peacetime. The segregation of hundreds of thousands of men into crowded barracks, officers' messes and ships' berths which before the war had been served by a force of under a million men, had to accommodate four times that number from 1939 onwards. Under these circumstances the norms of civilian life were unsurprisingly, and frequently, put aside. Sailors on leave in ports could often be seen dancing together in the packed dance-halls, an offence that would have brought arrest during peacetime; in far-flung destinations, soldiers also regularly performed in exotic and highly popular drag shows, often with explicit homosexual themes, to rapturous applause from the troops they entertained. Intense emotional relationships were easily formed between men who could be physically demonstrative in ways they would have thought unthinkable at home.

The Second World War was a terrible and tumultuous period in modern history. Estimated numbers of those killed range from 50 to 80 million, with civilian casualties accounting for up to two thirds of this number. After the defeat of Nazism and the slow, continuing social liberalisation of Western democracies, together with the advances in technology that allowed for better media communication in film, print and radio; the war-time experiences of ordinary gay men started to be heard for the first time. Society until then had only ever expected homosexuals to be flamboyant sissys, and the ones most people heard about were aristocratic socialites, artists and writers; those who were in positions that allowed them, or more accurately, gave them some choice in the matter of expressing their homosexuality through their art or closely-guarded peer group. In time, ordinary men who lived, fought and survived the desperate times of the Second World War became the first generation to be given the opportunity – albeit decades later – to speak about their experiences, and their wartime homosexual encounters, and even to live openly gay lives.

However, the post-war period was in fact a harsher time for homosexuals. There was a sudden increase in prosecutions caused by a shift in operations on the part of the Metropolitan Police covering the West End and areas around Victoria, South Kensington and Hammersmith. A return to full manpower after the war aided the Met in their decision to put more men on vice duty. The increased visibility of homosexuals on the streets of central London made them easy targets and a way of demonstrating to the public that the police were determined to clean them up. Though many of the dilly boys and prostitutes moved in the same circles as thieves, pimps and drug addicts, their clients were mostly ordinary men from the suburbs. The resulting police actions saw the number of cases brought before West London magistrates increase from just six in 1942 to 168 in 1952. The ensuing panic in the press about greater and more pervasive homosexual activity in London, fuelled by the pronouncements of individual judges, convinced the police of the importance of making arrests.

Shortly before he died in 1999, Dudley Cave, an openly gay man who signed up to fight in 1942, reflected: 'They used us when it suited them, and then victimised us when the country was no longer in danger. I am glad I served, but I am angry that homophobia was allowed to wreck so many lives for over 50 years, after we gave our all for a freedom that gay people were denied'.

How did the military deal with the need for men to fight in the war, against the difficulties and concerns they had in allowing homosexuals into the ranks? Homosexuality, after all, was still an offence both in civil society and the military. The Ministry of Defence did provide guidelines on the matter and what it saw as an acceptable model soldier. Many envisaged gay soldiers serving in the ranks as incompatible with a military lifestyle, and it was not only the Commanding Officers who felt this way. There was a deep mistrust and misunderstanding about homosexuality and years of a general lack of information about homosexuals and the effects of having them fighting alongside heterosexual soldiers led to a weeding out of suspects at the recruitment stage. The unabashed raconteur Quentin Crisp attempted to join the army in 1939. When he appeared for his physical examination, Crisp was asked if he was homosexual. He told them that he was, but the examination was still carried out, in case he was lying. This caused great consternation among the doctors, Crisp recalled. 'They were terribly flustered, rushed about and talked to each other in whispers.' Crisp was summarily refused entry and his Army Medical Exemption papers stated why – that it was on the grounds of his 'sexual perversion'.

Quentin Crisp might pose an extreme example, as the personification of the public's narrow view of homosexuality, but his exemption from joining-up was not the general experience of other homosexuals. As the need for men of fighting age grew ever more desperate, the Armed Forces found they did not have the luxury of being able to exclude any number of men on the possibility that they might be unsuitable due to their same-sex desires. Nevertheless, the military took very seriously the negative presumptions about homosexual soldiers and reports were commissioned to answer questions on their behaviour. Military psychiatrists warned of psychopathic personality disorders that would render homosexuals unfit to fight. One study, by Charles Anderson, on sexual offenders in the British Army emphasised, disparagingly, that homosexuals, 'achieved gratification from those of their comrades who turned towards them as substitutes for women.' He also said that they were known to 'dominate the group, obtain love, respect and acknowledgement of prowess. He must lead, cannot be led and finds it intolerable to be in a position of obeying.' Of the cases Anderson studied, more than a third, he said, 'had Fascist leanings', and he concluded that 'homosexuals form a foreign body in the social macrocosm.' He supported the wartime policy that offenders should be quietly invalided out of service and given advice on medical treatment, unless a court martial was required. Psychiatrists of the day often suggested that men who cracked under the strain of war were 'feminine' and 'latent homosexuals'. There was also concern that such 'socially and emotionally stunted individuals' were 'rewarded' by being excused from combat. One remedy was that they should be immediately sent back to the battlefields and threatened with disciplinary action 'should their symptoms reappear.'

There were of course, no scientific methods to determine whether a recruit was homosexual or not. Crude guidelines suggested that those who displayed feminine bodily characteristics, even to the extent that their pubic hair might be of a womanly quality; or those who dressed in a feminine way and had about them a female manner, or those who showed an uncertain nervousness when standing naked before a medical officer, should be disregarded forthwith for military service. The infamous 'bend over' routine of humiliation that each recruit had to endure in the examination, was to gauge whether their rectum was 'patulous' - expanded. It stands to reason that none of these so-called traits of the homosexual took into account that most homosexual men are not effeminate or passive, and if they indulge in anal intercourse at all, many men only do so as the 'top' active partner.

The Nazis' view on homosexuals was less spurious, if not nihilistic. SS leader Heinrich Himmler pronounced in 1940: 'When a man in the Security Service, the SS, or in the government, has homosexual tendencies, then he abandons the normal order of things for the perverted world of the homosexual. Such a man drags ten others after him, otherwise he can't survive. We can't permit such a danger to the country; the homosexual must be entirely eliminated.' The idea that a homosexual man can 'drag ten others after him' is absurd, but it does play to the irrational fear that homosexuals are predatory and that once persuaded to take part in same-sex activity, there is no going back. Whether it is enjoyable or not, one is forever tarnished. The irrational concept of the influence of homosexuality on other men also reinforced the dread of 'contagion', putting homosexuals into the category of 'disease' spreaders – a favourite propaganda tool of the Nazis.

Quentin Crisp, meanwhile, went on to enjoy his war years, especially when the young American GIs began landing in Britain in 1942. He describes this time with excitement in his autobiography, *The Naked Civil Servant*: 'Labelled 'with love from Uncle Sam', and packaged in uniforms so tight that in them their owners could fight for nothing but their honour, these 'bundles for Britain' leaned against the lamp-posts of Shaftesbury Avenue or lolled on the steps of thin-lipped statues of dead English statesmen.' Cruising the streets of London during the blackout, and enjoying brief encounters with the GIs, Crisp commented, 'Never in the history of sex was so much offered to so many by so few.'

In 1941, Dudley Cave joined up to the Royal Army Ordnance Corps. He was twenty-years old. His experience was different from Crisp's, in that he had no questions or warnings about homosexuality in the army put to him by the recruitment officers who interviewed him, and there was nothing explicit about it on his enlistment forms. 'People were put in the army regardless of whether they were gay or not,' he told the activist Peter Tatchell in an interview. 'There was none of the later homophobic uproar about gays undermining military discipline and effectiveness. With Britain seriously threatened by the Nazis, the forces weren't fussy. Homosexual soldiers were more or less accepted.'

Cave's experience of serving in the army as an openly gay man during the war was different from what might be expected. He recalled overhearing two soldiers gossiping about him, one referring to him as a nancy-boy, while the other protested that he couldn't possibly be because he was 'terribly brave in action'. Cave realised then the dilemma homosexuals posed to straight soldiers. In their minds he could not be brave and homosexual at the same time; the two ideas were incompatible with each other. Despite the tittle-tattle, the worst prejudice he faced in the army was being shouted at for 'holding a broom like a woman.'

Cave freely admitted that he had a reputation and was renowned for providing his fellow soldiers with sexual favours, and even supposedly straight men made use of his talents. When one keen sergeant took a dislike to Cave and tried to charge him with being out of the barracks after lights out, the Commanding Officer, who knew exactly what went on in the mangrove swamps at night, swiftly dismissed the charges. He had the wisdom to understand that the furtive goings-on in the dark were 'a useful relief from the stress of war'. On a day-to-day basis, neither the commanding officers nor Cave's fellow soldiers showed any concern about fighting alongside homosexuals. 'All the gays and straights worked together as a team. We had to, because our lives might have depended on it,' Cave said.

The unofficial version was that concerns or objections to homosexuals serving in the army were often ignored, and anecdotal stories by the men themselves suggest that even soldiers who were caught in the act often got off relatively lightly, with nothing more than a reprimand. Some did face punishment however. The unlucky ones were handed a few weeks' hard labour to 'knock the queerness out of them', whilst others were quickly transferred to break up potential relationships.

Though it remained a criminal offence, for some heterosexual servicemen, same-sex sexual activity was considered preferable to going with prostitutes and catching VD. Signs were up everywhere warning: 'Remember; they are waiting – syphilis and gonorrhoea.' And, 'She may look clean, but – pick-ups, good-time girls, prostitutes, spread syphilis and gonorrhoea.' Or as one poster spelled it out, 'She may be a bag of trouble…'

Some homosexuals, like Cave, could be open about their sexuality and were protected by their comrades as 'mascots' and even considered good for boosting morale. When Alec Purdie received his call-up papers, his gay friends told him not to go; that he didn't have to join up. '"Tell 'em you're queer!" they said, but I was determined to do my duty,' Alec recalled. Fate landed him in one of the many army entertainment troupes and he spent half the war in a dress and high-heels with 'lashes and slap', in remote camps in India entertaining the troops. Putting on shows in the field hospitals was particularly difficult though, he said. 'These lovely boys, who had had terrible things done to them and were trying to clap and laugh at me. It was too awful.'

Talking candidly, long after the war, straight infantryman, Ted Denith said: 'Before the war they were chorus boys in the West End, we had one in our battalion. He would pucker his lips putting his lipstick on and say, "I must look pretty for the Germans."' Denith thought the young soldier just as brave as the next man, if not more so, 'because he had to be extra brave in front of the straight lot. The fact that they have always had this thing of being sissy, lacking in backbone, is absolute rubbish. They were very brave indeed.'

Sex between the men seems to have been kept within rank. 'We had a couple of officers and they were terribly concerned about being found out. Of course, we all knew,' said Denith. 'But they never let on. The soldiers didn't mind a damn if people knew they were gay.'

One DSO made advances to him, but Denith declined. 'He was a lovely fella. It didn't change anything between us. When you're in a serious situation, you couldn't care less what someone's sexuality is; when you're up against it and you know you might be dead tomorrow, sexuality doesn't come in to it.'

Were they having sex at every opportunity? 'Absolutely not', according to Denith. 'If they were they kept it to themselves. They were just as sensitive about sex as any of the rest of us were. As heterosexuals we didn't parade our copulating.'

Was having a homosexual in the bunk next to you or in the shower with you a problem? 'Anybody alongside you in a battle situation is a bonus. It's really of no consequence. Montgomery was as gay as you like. It's nonsense to suggest that being gay reduces your ability to lead. As for showering, the first thing the gays would say when they got in was "oh, what a lovely bum!" Nobody took any notice, it was just a joke.'

Other soldiers who were taken prisoners of war found the unrealities of the battlefield heightened to even greater extremes. In an unpublished memoir, *The One Who Didn't Get Away*, by a heterosexual gunner by the name of J H Witte, lurid details are revealed not only about his own sex life but also of the homosexual sex among PoWs at the camp where he was held in Italy. Witte describes the love affairs between 'boy friends' and their 'girl friends', who were the female impersonators that entertained in the shows put on in the camp's theatre, and a corporal in the Military Police who was 'violently' in love with one of the 'actresses'. The pair went missing during one roll call and the Italian guards who found them snuggled up under a blanket put them into solitary confinement together for a week. Being incarcerated in such close quarters was either enough to break their relationship or strengthen it still further. Witte maintains that homosexual liaisons existed between all ranks of prisoners and took many forms, from parcel sharing to holding hands and from heavy petting to full-on sexual relationships.

Ralph Hall, a working-class lad from London's East End, was drafted into the RAF in 1940. He wrote hundreds of impassioned letters to his boyfriend, Monty Glover, a well-heeled architect and keen photographer, and was himself a decorated First World War soldier. In his letters, though they would have been heavily restricted under censorship rules, Ralph managed to convey much of what life was like away from home with comforting reassurance. He wrote about manning a gun battery during the night raids on an airbase he was stationed at and of day-to-day trivia, such as sharing with his comrades a cake Monty had sent him, and how they all ribbed him for calling out Monty's name in his sleep after a drunken night of beer drinking. Ralph was in every respect just like the other men, writing letters to their sweethearts, sketching out their daily lives and dreaming of the time they would be together again when peace came.

Another enthralling story to come out of the Second World War is that of Fighter Pilot Ian Gleed, or 'Widge', as he was known to his chums, due to his diminutive size and penchant for using the word 'wizard' at every opportunity. He survived the Battle of France and the Battle of Britain and on Christmas Eve 1940 he became Squadron Leader and commanding officer of 87 Squadron. In 1941 he was promoted to Wing Commander and took charge of the Ibsley Wing, making fighter sweeps across the Channel.

In 1942, while Hitler and the Nazis were at the height of their power in Europe, the threat of an imminent invasion however had subsided, and Britain's new battlefront was in North Africa. It was in this year that Gleed's autobiographical book *Arise to Conquer* was published. Gleed described in detail in his memoir the daily lives of RAF pilots and their terrifying sorties and dog-fights over the Channel and France. What he also alluded to was the frisson of homoerotic behaviour that went on in the mess and billets between some of the young pilots.

A doctor's son, Gleed was born in Finchley, London in 1916. Educated at Tenterden Prep and Epsom College, he had private flying lessons and flew solo for the first time at the age of 19 at the London Aeroplane Club in Hatfield in 1935. He was also a keen sailor, and it was through this pastime that he met famous literary friends, such as Somerset Maugham and the journalist Hector Bolitho, an intelligence officer in the Royal Air Force Volunteer Reserve, who, astonished at the young man's tenacity and sense of adventure, encouraged him to write down his experiences. Over the next few years Gleed wrote his memoir.

The book opens with what can only be described as a rather spiffing country house weekend party with friends. 'That morning the batman woke me with his usual smile.

"Seven-thirty and a nice morning, sir." It was September 3rd 1939, I was twenty-three. I turned on the wireless and listened to some music from Paris. After a few moments I heard Billy next door starting his French lessons on the gramophone, and at the end of the corridor Micky was singing in the bath. [Later that same day] "Play me squash Micky; we can have a swift game before dinner." I liked playing with Micky because we were about dead equal and always made each other run all over the place. I beat Micky by one game. We ran to our rooms dripping with sweat. I yelled to the batman to grab me a bath, turned the wireless on – more news; what I heard of it was exactly the same as the four o'clock version – stripped in front of the fire, shoved a dressing gown on and sprinted along the corridor to the bath.'

This scene of posh young men filling their time idly, with its homoerotic undertones, either intentional or not, belies the daily heroics of Gleed and his fellow pilots. In the book, he writes about his first raids, the nervous breakdown he suffered not long after, and the air-battles over France; of becoming an ace fighter pilot and being awarded the Distinguished Flying Cross (DFC) for his valour. It is a remarkably honest account considering the restrictions imposed on him and the publishers by the War Office. Censorship at the time would have meant that every word was subject to the highest scrutiny. Even so, the gallant adventures of the dashing young ace were an opportune piece of propaganda not to be missed.

What his writer friends made of the manuscript is not known, but one detail that did concern his publisher was Gleed's self-confessed state of bachelorhood. The accounts of stripping naked and jumping in and out of bed with his fellow pilots, however innocent that might have seemed, was not the conventional portrayal of wholesome romantic male heroism. Thus, it was felt that a girl back home written in to the story would make his character more suitably rounded and appealing, especially to female readers. Thus, a girlfriend by the name of Pam was invented, much to the surprise of his family and friends, but none of them realised that Gleed was, in fact, homosexual.

In an interview with the BBC in 1998 for the *Timewatch* programme *'Sex and War'*, Christopher Gotch spoke about his relationship with Gleed. As a new recruit, from the outset he found that Gleed was fixated on him, and he became the centre of his attention. To the 18-year-old Gotch, the gap between him and Wing Commander Gleed, who had two or three ribbons and even at that point was a famous air ace, 'was quite something'.

'One day I was sitting in the mess, reading, when I felt these eyes boring into me. I looked up and saw the Wing Commander staring at me. I looked back at my paper, and in that moment Gleed got up and left.' After a few minutes of playing out the charade in his head, then deciding to forget it, 'I went up to my room, and there he was, sat by the window looking through my photo album. "Can I help?" I asked him. Without saying a word, he stood up, walked over to me and gave me a great big kiss, which took me somewhat by surprise, but being a product of a public school, it wasn't exactly strange. He asked me to come to his room that night, and so we started having sex together. He was the first bloke who ever buggered me. He had charm, he had personality and he had a car, and he used to take me up to London and introduce me to people. I remember one day we flew down to his boat on the Scilly Isles, which in war-time was really something.'

Making eye contact and lingering, knowing looks that remain for just a split second too long, were often the means through which soldiers and sailors would identify one another as potential fair game. As one sailor put it, 'Pretty soon you'd get to know one or two people and then you'd start branching out. All of a sudden, you would have a vast network of 'friends' just through the eye contact thing.'

Even though Gotch's parents were very liberal in their attitudes – nudity at bath-times was a norm and the bookshelves had on them copies of Havelock Ellis and Marie Stopes – his father was virulent towards homosexuals, saying that the letter 'B' for bugger should be branded on their foreheads for all to see. In nice families, homosexuality, if it occurred between adolescent boys, was something they soon grew out of; it was only perverts that continued it into their adult life.

The RAF was home-from-home for many well-educated public-school boys who were quite used to sharing dorms and beds together. As there was nowhere to stay on the airfield where they were based, Gleed and Gotch were billeted together in a hotel in Exeter, along with other pilots in the squadron. Had their relationship ever been discovered, the pair would have been court martialled. Luckily this never happened, but there was one incident, Gotch recalled, when it was a close shave and he had to hide in Gleed's wardrobe.

To the outside world, not privy to the way of life of these young men, it was unthinkable to imagine that Britain's fighter pilots might have indulged in same-sex sexual activity. Even at the publishers, no one thought to edit out or question the nuggets of homoerotic information Gleed had, wittingly or not, divulged through his writing. For instance, there was the occasion when he says he shared a bed with another pilot in France. Of course, bunking together would have been perfectly reasonable, but, as Gleed recalls: 'We had found several old friends at Merville, who were in the other squadrons there. Eventually I wandered down the road with young Banks, with whom I had offered to share my room. He was a young boy who was looking very tired. He had come out three days before, having ferried a new Hurricane over to us. After asking the lady of the house to wake us at four-thirty, we retired to our room with a couple of candles, stripped and leapt into bed naked. When the candles were blown out I lay in bed and thought. Oh, hell, I suddenly remembered, I hadn't told anyone where we were sleeping. My thoughts wandered. In two minutes, I was asleep. [In the morning] There seemed to be nowhere to wash, so we just didn't bother. We thanked Madame very much, and after a difficult few moments gave her fifty francs for our lodgings.'

Displays of affection between pilots were seen as nothing more than bonhomie, and sex, if it went on behind closed doors, was treated with oblivious disregard. Some say Gleed comes across as a tragic figure. This may be in part because the reader knows the nature of his tragic outcome, but it might also be due to the gung-ho, spiffing narration of his story, told in the vernacular of his class, making it feel like a sad attempt at covering up.

Working on a second book, Gleed wrote poignantly, 'It's strange how confident I feel that I shall survive this war.' The end, however, came one April afternoon in 1943 while on patrol over the Cap Bon peninsular of North-Eastern Tunisia. His Spitfire was shot down over the sand dunes near the sea on the western coastline. He was twenty-six. He was buried at Tazoghrane and later reburied in the Military Cemetery at Enfidaville, in Tunisia in April 1944. After Gleed's death, 'Pam' received dozens of letters of condolence from the public.

His mascot, *Figaro*, the little mischievous cartoon cat from Disney's *Pinocchio*, which he had painted onto the side door of his cockpit, was the only fragment of the aircraft recovered from the crash site. It was donated to the RAF Museum in 1971. It is currently not on display.

As the war ended, the public's one desire was to get back to a state of normality as quickly as possible. Rationing however, did not end for another nine years, until July 1954, and whole areas of cities remained bomb-sites well into the 1960s and 70s. Women were expected to return to the same domesticated lifestyles they had predominantly led prior to working in the Land Army or the munitions factories; army recruits from across the Empire were also expected to want to return to their homelands, and homosexuals found they were again subjected to the old draconian laws that would have them imprisoned, or worse, chemically castrated. But for many, the experience of war gave rise to the lowering of social and gender barriers. Men living together in close quarters, sharing every emotion and their most intimate moments, were now aware of homosexuals for the first time and their preconceived ideas that such men were cowardly, that they were psychologically damaged perverts, they found not to be true. Homosexual men also discovered themselves for the first time. They began to realise that they were worthy citizens, able to contribute to society as much as any other man and yet still have same-sex desires. The two were not incompatible. It took another twenty years, however, before the law changed in 1967 and the Sexual Offences Act partially decriminalised homosexual acts between consenting male adults over the age of 21. In the meantime, for men returning to civvy street, it must have felt like the clocks had gone backwards.

9.
Are We Here to Protect Our Mothers?

In 1948, Alfred Kinsey, the American zoologist, published *Sexual Behaviour in the Human Male*. Its sequel, *Sexual Behaviour in the Human Female*, was published five years later. Both these books came to be known collectively as The Kinsey Reports. Kinsey worked at Indiana University and was the founder of the Kinsey Institute for Research in Sex, Gender and Reproduction (more commonly known as the Kinsey Institute). The books caused immediate shockwaves when they were published and were highly controversial, not least because such taboo subjects were being discussed openly. Based on studies carried out by Kinsey into sexual behaviour, the Kinsey Reports challenged conventional beliefs about sexuality.

Kinsey's research is the primary source often quoted for the estimate that 10% of the population is homosexual. His conclusions, however, were based on findings that were not absolute, and even Kinsey himself shied away from restrictive labels such as homosexual, heterosexual or even bisexual, saying that contrary to being static, sexuality was more prone to change and divergence and even to intensify over a lifetime. Instead of the common labels available to describe sexuality, Kinsey invented a seven-point scale:

0 = Exclusively heterosexual

1 = Predominantly heterosexual,
only incidentally homosexual

2 = Predominantly heterosexual,
but more than incidentally homosexual

3 = Equally heterosexual and homosexual

4 = Predominantly homosexual,
but more than incidentally heterosexual

5 = Predominantly homosexual,
only incidentally heterosexual
6 = Exclusively homosexual
and X) No socio-sexual contacts or reactions.

Data from the reports states that nearly 46% of the male subjects 'reacted' sexually to persons of both sexes throughout the course of their adult lives, and that 37% of males had at least some homosexual experience that led them to orgasm. The study also reported that 10% of male subjects were 'more or less, exclusively homosexual' and that 8% were exclusively homosexual for a period of at least three years between the ages of 16 and 55. 4% had been exclusively homosexual after the onset of adolescence and up to the time of the interview. The data for the *Kinsey Reports* was gathered via in-depth, face-to-face interviews with 5300 white males and 5940 white females.

In the *Final Report and Background Papers of the American National Institute of Mental Health's Task Force on Homosexuality*, Paul Gebhard, a Kinsey research associate and later director of the Institute, reanalysed Kinsey's data to eliminate the sample bias. He refined the figures to show that between one-quarter and one-third of white male adults with a college education had had an 'overt homosexual experience since puberty', and mostly during their adolescent years. Weighting the figures by marital status, Gebhard estimated that 4% of the white college-educated males surveyed by Kinsey and close to just 1% of white females, were predominantly or exclusively homosexual.

Today, the Kinsey Institute is careful in its attitude towards the Kinsey Reports, and is quick to point out that the data should be viewed within its historical context. For instance, the samples used are best extrapolated 'for younger adults, particularly the college-educated; they are poorest for minorities and those from lower socioeconomic and educational levels; and the original male sample included institutionalized men.' Gebhard described Kinsey's sampling method as 'quota sampling accompanied by opportunistic collection'.

Later surveys, such as one carried out in 1974 with a volunteer cohort of 2036 people who filled out a questionnaire, showed data that indicated 7% of males and 3% of females had homosexual experiences during more than three years of their lives. In comparing this data to Kinsey's, Morton M Hunt, the author of *Sexual Behaviour in the 1970s*, adjusted Kinsey's 37% figure for males having had some same-sex contact to orgasm to 25%, and the 4% exclusively homosexual figure for males to 2-3%.

In the UK, the Office for National Statistics produced figures for *Sexual Identity* in 2016 in which it reported that 2% of the UK population (just over 1 million aged 16+) identified as lesbian, gay or bisexual. More males (2.3%) than females (1.6%) identified themselves as LGB, and of the population group aged 16 to 24, 4.1% identify themselves as LGB – the largest percentage within any age group that year.

All these surveys provide interesting data and carry on the work first started by Magnus Hirschfeld in Germany in 1903, but do they give a definitive answer to the question, How many people are homosexual? The simple reply is no. There are two main difficulties statisticians need to overcome when trying to ascertain how many people are gay; firstly, what exactly should they be measuring? Is it behaviour, desire or identity? As discussed previously, sexuality, personality and gender are separate and distinctive, but which may be interpreted as being all one thing or an amalgamation of atypical characteristics. Through knowledge gained conducting surveys over time; the question content, wording, and categorisation for sexual orientation have all been extensively tested. Evidence from a report by Peter J Aspinall, of University of Kent, for the Equality & Human Rights Commission indicates that posing the question, 'which of these best describes yourself?' is better for instance than asking,

'which of these do you consider yourself to be?'
Researchers might also take the report's advice when it
comes to labelling a question as 'sexual orientation',
'sexual identity', or even simply 'sexuality', which have
all caused concern or confusion among some respondents.
Keeping the response categories to a minimum including
an 'other' category and dispensing with ones such as
'prefer not to say' or 'unsure', also gives better quality
data, as respondents will tend to opt for the most
meaningful response to their personal situation. 'How you
think of yourself' helps the respondent in recognising that
a process of 'best fit' is also involved in the survey and not
one where a singular category is assumed to be an exact
description of a person's sexual orientation.

Putting aside the intricacies of survey questions and
categorisation, what is certain is that homosexuals have
been a part of every society's culture throughout history,
and though invariably a small group, they are a minority
who afford some power and influence within their wider
societies. Where would the world be, for instance, without
its gay artists, writers, musicians, actors, thinkers and
leaders? And the bus drivers, bakers and candlestick
makers? Until the time when all people feel at ease and
able to talk openly about their sexuality without fear of
recrimination and homophobia from friends, family,
colleagues and neighbours, there will always be a bias in
any survey taken that asks about sexual orientation. People
will lie or leave such a question blank for countless
reasons. They might consider it an affront to be asked
about their sexuality, especially so for older generations
who might view it as something that is intensely private
and the business of no one else but themselves. Covering
up their true identity from those dearest to them might also
lead to questions on sexuality being passed over. Gay
mums and dads in heterosexual marriages are a prime
example. In communities that still stigmatise sexual
diversity as at best a tolerated characteristic, but more
commonly, as a negative rather than a positive trait, it

should come as no surprise then that truly definitive data is still not available.

Still, according to the Department of Trade and Industry, there are 1.5 to 2 million gay men, lesbians and bisexuals in the UK's 30-million strong workforce. Over recent years there has also been an encouraging growth in both big and small companies promoting their LGBT-friendly brands to entice the huge gay economy into buying their products and services. Research into the economic clout of the pink pound shows that the gay community is worth tens of billions, and having gay people represented in advertising certainly has the desired effect when it comes to decisions made at the point of purchase. A lifetime of prejudice can be swayed in favour of those companies and organisations that give a positive message to their would-be LGBT customers.

Perhaps what we would do well to look at, rather than dry statistics, is the reason homosexuals are such an important and vital part of humanity. Simply put – why are we here?

On the face of it, and from a purely evolutionary point of view, homosexuals should not exist. Let's take a moment to think about that. To sustain a species and increase the gene pool, the concept of same-sex sexual activity does not make sense – it is irrational. If a biologist were to invent a new species, they might be forgiven for not including diversity in sexuality for the very reason that it is a self-fulfilling road to extinction. Yet since time began there have always been a significant minority of homosexuals found in all cultures and throughout history. But why? If homosexuality was a blip in the chemistry of evolutionary genetics, surely natural selection over millennia would have erased such a peculiarity from the gene pool long ago?

Italian geneticists at the University of Padua, Italy, have submitted an explanation as to how and why such genes have survived, given also the fact that many gay men do not have children. Their findings also undermine the contentious theory of a single 'gay gene'. What they discovered in their research was that women who were related to gay men, especially the mothers and aunts on their mother's side, tended to have more children, and that this boost in fertility more than compensated for the lack of children fathered by their gay sons and nephews, thus keeping 'gay' DNA in circulation.

'We have finally solved this paradox,' says Andrea Camperio-Ciani of the University of Padua. 'The same factor that influences sexual orientation in males promotes higher fecundity in females.'

Camperio-Ciani's research team questioned 98 gay men and 100 straight men about their closest relatives. The sample size of the two groups combined totalled 4600 people. They found that female relatives of gay men had more children on average than the female relatives of straight men, and that this effect was only seen on their mother's side of the family. The mothers of gay men produced an average of 2.7 babies compared with 2.3 babies born to mothers of straight men. And maternal aunts of gay men had 2.0 babies compared with 1.5 born to the maternal aunts of straight men.

Camperio-Ciani does not believe in the one single gene theory to account for the effects his study shows. It might be more to do with humans having a preferential bias of sexual attraction towards men, he surmises, thus disposing men towards homosexuality and women to be more heterosexual, causing them to have more babies. The tendency of a trait such as this to be passed through the female line also backs previous research suggesting that some of the factors involved in homosexuality are embedded in the male X chromosome, the only sex chromosome passed down by women. 'It's a combination of something on the X chromosome with other genetic factors on non-sex chromosomes,' he says. A tentative note is required here, for even if the maternal factors identified by Camperio-Ciani's team are linked with male homosexuality, the research team's calculations suggest that they account for as little as approximately 14% of incidences.

Could environmental factors play a more significant role in gene development? 'Genes must develop in an environment, so if the environment changes, genes go in a new direction,' Camperio-Ciani explains. The findings do indeed support earlier research which found that when mothers have several sons, the younger ones are progressively more likely to be gay. This might be due to changes in the mother's immune system with each successive son she carries. Camperio-Ciani calculates that the contribution of this 'big-brother effect' on male homosexuality is 7% at most. Added together, the maternal and immune theories, account for about 21% of male homosexuality, which leaves 79% of its causation still a mystery. In conclusion, Camperio-Ciani says 'Our findings are only one piece in a much larger puzzle on the nature of human sexuality.'

Identical twins pose yet another conundrum. Studies have found that if one identical twin is gay, there is about a 20% chance that his sibling will also be. This implies a greater predisposition than pure chance, but it is lower than one might expect for two people with the same genetic code. Other academics and researchers believe that to fully understand the evolution of homosexuality we need to look at how homosexuals fit into the complexities of society and its wider culture.

Dr William Byne, editor-in-chief of LGBT Health, thinks that sexuality may well be inborn, and that it could be far more complicated than some scientists suppose, noting that the inherent attributes of homosexuality could be paralleled with that of say, divorce, but, as Dr Byne states: 'social science researchers have not searched for "divorce genes". Instead they have focused on heritable personality and temperamental traits that might influence the likelihood of divorce.'

Byne says that although many studies have hypothesised biological factors as the basis of sexual orientation, there is no substantial evidence at present to back this theory. In the same way however, there is no compelling evidence to support any singular social or psychological explanation either. He proposes an alternative theory, in which personality traits interact with familial and social environments as the individual's sexuality emerges. 'Because such traits may be heritable or developmentally influenced by hormones, the model predicts an apparent non-zero heritability for homosexuality without requiring that either genes or hormones directly influence sexual orientation per se.'

The American author and cardiologist Dr James O'Keefe favours yet another theory regarding the evolutionary basis of homosexuality. He says that the reason homosexuality has been a constant and necessary part of civilisation is that it is about the survival of the family unit. From Homo sapiens through to modern mankind, we have been wired to be highly social creatures who enjoy the contact of close family bonds, and these strong emotional ties to our families and tribes are an intrinsic part of our makeup. These same traits can be seen in other animals where social interactivity occurs and where homosexual activity has also been recorded. It is evident that strong social connections determine how well we do in life, and those without these traits and the opportunities of bonding networks often suffer because of the lack of them.

Homosexuality, says O'Keefe, provides the community with those specialised talents and unusual qualities of personality; creative, artistic, altruistic and caring. Homosexuals are often quick-witted, funny and sensitive, and all these behaviours set them apart from other hunter/warrior types of male. From an evolutionary perspective, it is these distinctive characteristics that are critically beneficial to the family and consequently society as a whole. In this scenario, diversity is nature's secret weapon to counteract imbalanced chaos. If all men were warriors we'd be constantly fighting. Likewise, if all men were homosexual, we would have vanished from the earth long ago.

But how can it be that one person's sexual orientation can be so entirely different from another's? O'Keefe says it comes down to epigenetic tagging. For each male son born into the family, the chances of the next boy being born gay go up 33% (as in the 'big brother effect'). Is this then a form of natural birth control, where the fourth or fifth son born will be naturally engineered to be homosexual, thus keeping the population at a sustainable level? In ancient tribes, this could well have had the effect of determining whether the group survived or not.

Another study discovered that severe prenatal stress leads to a heightened level of hormones that can 'switch on' the epigenetic tag, predisposing the male foetus to be homosexual. Indeed, this study showed that 37% of gay males reported that their mothers had suffered severe stress during pregnancy, as opposed to only 3% of heterosexual males. Could it be then that the mother is 'protecting' herself? That she is unwittingly, yet naturally, fulfilling her needs for her newest son to be that caring, altruistic, creative person required to keep her and the rest of the family safe? It is a very interesting concept and does appear to help answer the question of why homosexuality exists and not against the order of nature as some think, but that it is nature's delicate prescriptive remedy for dealing with environments and times that would otherwise harm the family unit and therefore society as a whole.

The scientific study of homosexuality is by no means finished. It is clear, however, that nature intends for gay people to be born, and that it is a very special thing.

Find Dr James O'Keefe's video by Googling 'Homosexuality – It's About Survival Not Sex'

10.
A Short History of Gay Porn

There are countless examples of images from ancient times of pornographic art painted onto murals and vases and crafted into sculptures. With each century and each new advancement in technology, art has utilised new innovations to its own ends, and never more so than in the proliferation of homoeroticism and pornography. From hand-tinted Georgian postcards, depicting every sexual act imaginable, to the neo-classically staged sepia photographs of Wilhelm von Gloeden, homosexuals through the ages have, through each new artistic invention and technique, been fed a steady diet of man-on-man love and sex, both in the name of art and for pure gratification.

Wilhelm von Gloeden was known for his Athenian studies of Sicilian boys whom he photographed in and around his home in Taormina, Sicily, between 1890 and 1910. His artistry in using the relatively new medium of photography started out as a hobby, but by 1893 his work was being exhibited internationally. The public had not seen anything like it before. Real-life models, such as two boys caressing an ionic column, were posed and photographed in intimate studies, mimicking the popular Pre-Raphaelite style. Like any artist, Gloeden's success was due to his meticulous preparation, using light and innovations in filters and the use of special body make-up made from milk, olive oil, and glycerine to enhance the contours and hide any blemishes on his models.

Gloeden did not produce pornographic images. Though his more explicit nude studies were filled with homoeroticism, they were only ever traded to his friends. It is these portraits, however, that Gloeden is most widely known for today. What these 'private' photographs show is that there was most certainly a market for salacious homoerotic imagery, even if it was dressed up as art, and there are other more explicit examples of pornographic pictures from the late Victorian period, taken by anonymous photographers to satisfy the demand.

The first pornographic moving picture was an American film called *Free Ride* made in 1915, in which a moustachioed salesman picks up a couple of seemingly drunk girls in his car along a deserted road. After a while he stops the car to take a wee, which is shown to the audience in full view. Intrigued to see what he's up to, the two girls get out of the car, and, before you know it, they're all having sex on the ground. The salesman remains fully clothed, but there are graphic shots showing exactly what is going on.

There is also a fragment of a French film called *Le Coucher de la Mariée* (Bedtime for the Bride), made in 1896, it is reputedly the first time sex was performed on film. Only a minute and a half of the original remains, so it is difficult to tell whether anything actually happens or not. What the viewer sees is a portly gent on his wedding night, trying to entice his new bride out of her dress and into bed. She coyly removes her clothing behind a screen, tossing it languidly over the top, while her fidgety husband sits at the dressing table, waiting impatiently on the other side. Hardly pulse-racing stuff, but if, as we are led to believe, the couple do have sex, it must have been both shocking and at the same time exhilarating to watch for an audience that would have presumably been entirely made up of men who were just as frustrated as the husband portrayed in the film.

The French were pioneers in the use of cinematography in the making of pornographic films. Another film, *Le Ménage Moderne du Madame Butterfly*, made in 1920 and loosely plotted around the story of Puccini's famous opera, is the oldest known film in which hardcore homosexual sex is shown. Cannily, by depicting heterosexual, bisexual and homosexual acts in the film, it might have been made to appeal to as wide an audience as possible. The male-on-male sex, however, is shown as deviant and the heterosexuality of the characters is firmly established, suggesting that the sex that happens between the men is essentially bisexual, as it occurs whilst also engaging Cio-Cio San (Madam Butterfly) in sex. Disturbingly, the homosexual (or is he bisexual?) character, is a badly-treated servant who is subjected to an aggressive act of anal and oral sex from Pinkerton for simply not opening the door for him to the boudoir quickly enough. The forceful assertiveness of the sex is controlled in the end by a certain amount of humour on both sides. As the film closes, Pinkerton flashes his buttocks enticingly towards the camera and the audience beyond.

The Surprise of a Knight is widely acknowledged to be the first full-length gay pornographic film. Produced in the United States in 1929, it portrays stereotypical characterisations of homosexuals as being essentially inverts and passive. The plot opens with a woman preparing herself for a gentleman caller. The viewer is in on the conspiracy however, for the woman in question is clearly a man dressed in women's clothing. The gentleman caller arrives, and the woman begins to seduce him. After a few fumbled gropes, which the woman half-heartedly recoils from, the couple start kissing. The woman then proceeds to do oral sex on him, then flips over on the settee to reveal her bottom. Anal intercourse takes place, but actual penetration is not shown. After their copulation, the man walks off camera, and the woman reveals her secret to the audience by lifting her skirt. The final frames show the two dancing together; the passive quean with her costume disrobed and the gent fully dressed and obviously happy with the experience he's just had. The audience are left to make up their own minds as to whether the gentleman knew all along that the woman was a man in drag, and that therefore he was copulating with a man, or if it was a complete surprise to him, yet he still rather enjoyed it. A storyline of sorts was a prerequisite in early experimental pornographic films, which concluded with a moral dilemma for the audience to go away and think about. Whatever the scenario, the men who appeared in these early films were portrayed as either completely stupid, as in the case of the gentleman caller; inverted bisexual passives, in the case of the servant, or aggressive heterosexuals, as in the character of Pinkerton in *Le Ménage Moderne du Madame Butterfly*.

In a later 1930s film, *A Stiff Game*, the passive role of the one giving oral sex is performed by a black man on a white man. Some say that this dates the film much later, possibly to the 1950s. In all these early porn films the viewers are made to feel that they should distance themselves from the passive roles and identify instead with the poor, hapless, duped idiots who (just like the men sitting in their seats watching) are simply out for an innocent good time and unwittingly get caught up in something they would never normally do. As the final intertitle of *Free Ride* states, 'Men are men in the open spaces', implying that man's innate inclination to fornicate knows no bounds; it matters not where they are or with whom they find themselves doing it. In these films lust is always rewarded to the socially-dominant male and, usually resisted against at first, but inevitably enjoyed by the weaker partner in the end, when they succumb.

In a way, the message has some good intentions: 'It is okay to have sex with other men, so long as you don't intend for it to happen; sometimes these things do happen, but it doesn't mean you're abnormal.' Of course, the flip side of this is that the homosexuals *are* abnormal, sissy, passive inverts, and homosexuality as a choice can never be a desirable normality.

When viewing gay pornography from the beginning of the twentieth century through to the no-holds-barred, modern-day hard-core porn films, the role of masculinity and what it means to be a man has inextricably changed. The Roman idea that to be the passive partner in a male-to-male sexual relationship was the lesser, more demeaning role, has meant that this stereotype has prevailed for more than a thousand years, and is deeply set into our subconscious. However, and as graphically shown in the early stag and gay porn films of the twenties and thirties, the dominant male role does not come out untainted or with any integrity, as the Roman male would have done. Rather he is ridiculed for his inability to make wise choices around sex. He can only hope that the scenario he finds himself in might end in some tomfoolery or a bit of locker-room larking about to cover up any embarrassment. He is led by his penis rather than his brain. This is the characterisation which tars all men, homosexual, heterosexual or anything in between; that there is only ever one motive for the male of the species, and that is orgasm, and that testosterone-fuelled men will always seek to be in control.

Homosexuality is shown to be even more puzzling in a 1950s all-gay film called *Three Comrades*. There is no dramatic context, the plot has been ditched, just three men in an active homosexual threesome. 'As you will notice, these fellows are all hung heavy from continually getting Blowed Off!' says the intertitle, in slightly odd English. Then, after the 'Grand Finale', another intertitle declares, 'Aw shit, I'm disgusted, so let us quit!' If the film was intended for a gay audience, why, one wonders, is there the need for the expression of disgust? Perhaps the film was meant to be included as part of another concoction of exotica for a straight audience to observe the 'great freaks of passion perform'. Or perhaps the intertitles just lost something in translation.

It isn't until the 1950s and 60s that men starring in gay porn films begin to be portrayed as equals engaging in consensual sex. What the audience now wanted to see was a choice of 'role' to identify with, therefore neither participant could be duped or made to look stupid. The power of the penetrator was beginning to decline.

Most commentators look to the 1971 film *Boys in the Sand*, directed by Wakefield Poole and starring Casey Donovan, as the first modern gay porn film and the one that started a golden era. It was the first to include credits, for example, enabling it to cross over into mainstream cinemas. Its importance, and relevance, are also highlighted by the fact that it preceded *Deep Throat*, the first heterosexual mainstream porn film, by a year and it was promoted with an advertising campaign unprecedented for the porn industry. Poole's inspiration to make the film came after having seen a gay flick called *Highway Hustler*, about which he said, 'This is the worst, ugliest movie I've ever seen. Somebody ought to be able to do something better than this.' Later he said, about *Boys in the Sand*, 'I wanted to make a film that gay people could look at and say, 'I don't mind being gay - it's beautiful to see those people do what they're doing.'

The film is in three 'acts'; Bayside, Poolside and Inside, in which Donovan meets three different men. In the Poolside scenario, we see how far equality had come, as both actors flip-flop, taking it in turn to have oral and anal sex with each other. The film became renowned for its Kama Sutra inventory of gay sexual positions, and the freedom in its expression of an idealised gay lifestyle at the sun-drenched Cherry Grove beach resort on Fire Island in New York. It also, inadvertently, fed the growing surge for gay liberation.

In the 90s, after an understandable lull during the 1980s as AIDS took hold, the gay porn star Joey Stefano became the first exclusive 'power-bottom', equalizing and closing the gap between the dominant and passive roles. Before that, porn stars who bottomed were seen as over-affected, fey and dispensable muscle-Marys. Stefano changed that perception. He was the first passive partner to be in control of his body and what he wanted from his on-screen partner. Starring along-side Jeff Stryker – another gay porn icon of the day – in *On the Rocks* (1980), Stefano demands of a good-looking young Matt Gunther, as they work out in the gym, 'Why you so interested in my body?' Later, when the two of them have been joined by Stryker, Stefano demands Gunther penetrates him, but in no way is Stefano simply being the receptacle for the other man's orgasm – he's getting exactly the enjoyment he desires, and after he ejaculates, it is he who 'presents' Gunther for Stryker to then have intercourse with. Gunther, while fully amenable, is not Stryker's equal, as Stefano clearly is.

Joey Stefano had a wild but short career, starring in 58 gay porn films and posing in Madonna's *Sex* book in 1992. He also appeared in two of her music videos and was linked to David Geffen, the Dreamworks mogul. Tragically, he died of a drugs overdose in 1994 aged 26. His family never realised he was a gay porn star, only that he made a living modelling.

Today, the making of gay pornography is not confined to studios, camera technicians, directors and actors, but is as much the territory of anyone with a digital camera or smartphone. The porn industry, meanwhile, strives to keep up to date and relevant with this burgeoning amateur scene by reflecting gritty realism in its own studio-based high-definition films. While three to five minutes filming in a public toilet on a shaky mobile phone, or a sex-session set-up and filmed in someone's bedroom, is a two-way turn-on both for the viewer and the film-maker, who writhes and ejaculates to camera knowing that thousands of men are watching and doing just the same. These amateurs are the uninhibited modern porn stars of today and some even make money from it performing on request for virtual currency.

As a footnote – shooting a scene in a studio porn film does not earn the actor huge sums of money. They will earn incrementally more for each position or sex act they are willing to engage in, but generally they will earn about £300 per session. This is dependent also on star status, but even those contracted to film production companies do not earn vast fortunes as might be expected. Their careers are often short-lived, prone to emotional and psychological damage, and there are health risks, including one of the most common, priapism, a condition resulting from blood not being able to flow back from the penis after orgasm and characterised by erections that last longer than four hours or are unrelated to sexual interest or stimulation. As a precautionary note one should be careful wearing too tight a cock-ring or popping too many Viagra tablets.

As more advances in sensory technology progresses, so the porn industry will develop to take advantage. Already, anal plugs and other sex toys called 'teledildonics' can be connected to the internet and punters can pay to stimulate amateur porn-stars in their bedrooms thousands of miles away. Virtual reality and other technologies can add further sensory engagement to the porn viewing experience. A product called RealTouch uses a high-tech orifice which includes heaters and servomotors inside, to realistically recreate the sensations of a porn scene while watching at the same time. In 2016, PornHub delivered 91.9 billion online videos. That's equal to about twelve and a half videos watched by every human on the planet. Whatever is thought about the moral issues of pornography, it is undoubtedly here to stay and the rise of amateur porn film-making supports a seemingly unstoppable voraciousness for it.

11.
Change Around the World

America

The second half of the twentieth century saw the birth and rise of Gay Liberation as a worldwide movement. It was first ignited by the Stonewall riots in Greenwich Village, New York, in June 1969. The demonstrations, often violent, between the police and crowds of homosexuals were a result of a police raid on the Stonewall Inn, in the early hours of the morning of 28th June. It led to six more days of protest and clashes with police on Christopher Street and in nearby Christopher Park. If British laws were seen to be draconian, the US criminal statute allowed police to arrest people who were simply wearing less than three gender-appropriate pieces of clothing. Bars and clubs were routinely shut down, as the selling of alcohol to groups of homosexuals was enough to validate the argument that it caused disorderly and unruly behaviour. These regulations were in fact overturned in 1966, but police harassment of the gay bars and nightclubs continued in the same vein.

Stonewall Inn was registered as a private 'bottle bar' which did not require a liquor license as the clientele were supposed to bring their own alcohol with them. There was also a sign-in policy which gave the club an air of exclusivity, but which also enabled the Mafia bosses who ran it to know who was using their establishment. Wealthier customers were often subjected to blackmail.

The Genovese Mafia family bribed New York's Sixth Police Precinct to ignore the activities going on at the club. Without any interference, costs were cut to the bone. For instance, there was no fire exit, no running tap water behind the bar, and the toilets were filthy and often overflowed. Nevertheless, Stonewall Inn soon became an important venue for New York's gay men to meet. It was cheap to get in, allowed dancing and welcomed drag queens. Young runaways used the place as a refuge. Unskilled and jobless, these young men, who lived on the streets, could stay in the warm and the relative security of the club for the admission of $3. They could stay all night, there was no hassling to buy drinks, and it kept them from the dangers of sleeping rough or being arrested for vagrancy. When it was raided, these kids fought for what was, in effect, their family home.

Police raids on other gay establishments often occurred, but owners were usually warned beforehand by bent coppers on the Mafia payroll. On the night of 28th June, the Stonewall Inn did not receive a tip-off that they were about to be raided. Discovering the bootleg alcohol, the police arrested thirteen people, including employees and people violating the gender-appropriate clothing statute. A crowd gathered outside and became increasingly agitated at the brutality of the police handling of both customers and staff. The touch-paper was lit when one lesbian was hit over the head by a police officer as he tried to manhandle her into a police-wagon. She screamed out for the crowd of onlookers to do something. Within minutes bottles and cobblestones began to be thrown and a riot ensued involving hundreds of people. Some of the police officers, together with those they had arrested and some bystanders, were forced to barricade themselves inside the bar, which the mob outside attempted to set alight as they stormed the building. The fire brigade and riot squad were deployed and eventually the crowd was dispersed, but further protests, with growing numbers of people, continued to flare up around the area over the following days with cries of 'Fag Power!' 'We're the Pink Panthers!' and 'Liberate the bar!'. The *New York Post* reported that hundreds of gay people were heard chanting 'Gay Power!' and 'We want freedom!' Gay journalist Dick Leitsch reported, 'Coming on the heels of the raids of the Snake Pit and the Sewer, and the closing of the

Checkerboard, the Tele-Star and other clubs, the Stonewall raid looked to many like part of an effort to close all gay bars and clubs in the Village.' He was struck also by the bravery of the crowd. 'Fifty or more homosexuals who would have been described as 'nelly' rushed the cops and took the boy back into the crowd. They then formed a solid front and refused to let the cops into the crowd to regain their prisoner, letting the cops hit them with their sticks, rather than let them through. It was an interesting side-light on the demonstrations that those usually put down as 'sissies' or 'swishes' showed the most courage and sense during the action. Their bravery and daring saved many people from being hurt.'

Although the Stonewall uprising did not, by itself, start the gay rights movement, it was a galvanizing force for LGBT political activism, leading to numerous gay rights organizations being formed. In 2016, President Obama designated the site of the riots – Stonewall Inn, Christopher Park, and the surrounding streets – a national monument in recognition of the area's contribution to gay and human rights.

Germany

In 1950, a year after The German Democratic Republic, GDR (East Germany), was officially constituted, the Berlin Appeal Court decided to reinstate the old pre-war Paragraph 175, the provision of the German criminal code which made homosexual acts between men a crime. It had been notoriously reformed in 1935 by the Nazis in their persecution of homosexuals, and thousands were sent to their deaths in the concentration camps.

A revision in 1957 made it possible not to prosecute what was otherwise illegal activity which, because of the lack of any consequence, was recognised as posing no real danger to society. This was a direct response to the socialist ethos that the individual was simply part of a far more important national socialist system, and the relatively few cases being brought before the courts were of little significance to society. This ruling effectively removed Paragraph 175 from law, and homosexual acts between consenting adults ceased to be punished. In 1968, a new criminal code was adopted, Paragraph 151, which provided sentencing of up to three years' imprisonment for anyone over the age of eighteen engaged in same-sex sexual acts with those under that age. Finally, in 1987 a Supreme Court ruling quashed a conviction on the basis that 'homosexuality, just like heterosexuality, represents a variant of sexual behaviour. Homosexual people do therefore not stand outside socialist society and the civil rights are warranted to them exactly as to all other citizens'.

Just over a year later, in 1989, Paragraph 151 was struck from law, removing all reference to homosexuality from East German criminal law.

The democratic government of West Germany, however, were less sympathetic, and after the war, with the Allies' demands that all Nazi laws should be abolished, the new government was allowed to decide for itself whether or not to leave the expansion of Paragraph 175 which the Nazis had implemented in 1935. On May 10, 1957 the Federal Constitutional Court upheld the decision to retain the 1935 version, claiming that it was 'not influenced by National Socialist politics to such a degree that it would have to be abolished in a free democratic state'.

It is estimated that 100,000 men were implicated in legal proceedings between 1945 and 1969. About half of these were convicted. The rates of conviction had risen by 44 percent, and in the 1960s, the number remained as much as four times higher than it had been in the last years of the Weimar Republic. Legal experts continued to debate the future of Paragraph 175. While it was generally agreed that homosexual activity was immoral, they were divided on whether or not it could be considered unlawful if it was practised between consenting adults in the privacy of their own homes. These experts appeared to have forgotten, or intentionally disregarded, the work of such eminent Germans as Magnus Hirschfeld, Karl-Maria Kertbeny and Karl Ulrichs, with their firm belief that homosexuals were not born that way, but rather fell victim to seduction. Their unproven concerns were that if freed from criminality, homosexual men would intensify 'their propaganda and activity in public', putting male youths at risk. A proposed amendment was drafted, stating: 'Concerning male homosexuality, the legal system must, more than in other areas, erect a bulwark against the spreading of this vice, which otherwise would represent a serious danger for a healthy and natural life of the people.'

It shows an intent to make the already Nazified Paragraph 175 even more rigid in their determination to wipe out homosexuality. Thankfully it was never adopted.

By 1969, past anxieties about declining birth rates no longer held control over government policy-making and homosexual men were no longer seen as a threat to reproduction. With the new Social Democratic Party in power, it was also acknowledged that the role of the state was to protect society from harm and the law should only intervene in cases that involved force or the abuse of minors, i.e. 'sex with a man under the age of twenty-one, homosexual prostitution, and the exploitation of a relationship of dependency, such as employing or supervising a person in a work situation'. These reforms were implemented into Paragraph 175b. Bestiality was also removed. In 1973 further reforms were made, lowering the age of consent to 18 (it was still not the same as that for heterosexuals, which was 14), and only sex with a minor under the age of eighteen remained unlawful. In 1986, the Green Party, and the Bundestag's first openly gay politician, Herbert Rusche, tried to remove Paragraph 175 altogether from the statute. However, this was opposed, and it remained part of German law for eight more years. In 1990, after the fall of the Berlin Wall and reunification, a period of four years was devoted to bringing East and West German legislation into line with each other's. Finally, in 1994, 123 years after its inception into German law in 1871, Paragraph 175 was struck from the legal code.

Australia

Steven Lindsay Ross is a proud member of the Wamba Wamba from Deniliquin, New South Wales. He is also homosexual. Whilst today many indigenous Australians identify as LGBT, there is little or no recording of homosexuality in pre-colonial societies of Australia. Early twentieth-century anthropologists reported evidence of polygamy amongst the Aborigines but none of same-sex sexual activity, though this might well have been down to misinterpretation or squeamishness.

The first laws surrounding homosexuality in Australia were those inherited from the British at the time of colonisation in 1788. Then the punishment for sodomy was death. It was reduced in 1899 to life imprisonment. The first recorded execution in Australia for sodomy was in 1828, and the victim was the Chief Mate of the *Royal Sovereign*, a whaler that had put into Sydney for supplies and for the health of the crew who were suffering with scurvy. The officer, Alexander Brown, a young man under the age of thirty, and three other young apprentice seamen, were arrested and confined in separate cells in the Sydney gaol 'on disgusting charges'. From the court proceedings, the statements of Brown's fellow seamen are revealing, both in their accounts of what they saw and heard, and their willingness to expose Brown and put him at the mercy of the law, whilst undoubtedly knowing what the outcome would mean for him.

This is what James Burns, the ship's steward, said in his witness statement:

In July 1828, the ship being off Japan, I saw the Chief Mate, Mr Brown, lying upon the Apprentice James Phillips, but I saw no motion. On the 20th of July, on a Sunday morning between 5 and 6 o'clock, I was in my bed in a cabin facing Mr Brown's. I saw Mr Brown go into his cabin and soon after the boy, Edward Curtiss, followed. After some talking there was silence. Afterwards, when I heard nothing, I got up from my bed. Looking thru' a crack in Mr Brown's cabin door, I saw Edward Curtiss on his hands and knees on the deck, and his front being towards me, I could not see whether his trousers were unbuttoned. Mr Brown's head and the upper part of his body I could see, and he was in motion backwards and forwards. After looking two or three minutes I went on deck and beckoned to the Third Officer, George Robinson.

Robinson's statement followed:

Between 6 or 7 o'clock, tho' I can't be positive to the precise time, the Steward came and beckoned to me and made motion ensuring silence. I went down and looking thru' the crack of the door of Mr Brown's cabin, the Steward whispered me: "Brown is in Curtiss", but I could not see Brown. The boy Curtiss was on his knees and hands on the deck and quite still. The crack of the door is very small, and I could not see more than the boy's shirt was crumpled up near the shoulders. In about 3 minutes I went on deck. I saw Curtiss in about half an hour more come up on deck and his face was very red. In about a quarter of an hour more I went into my own cabin and then saw Mr Brown come out of his cabin. Sometime after, about the month of August, as I was coming down the main rigging, Mr Brown was going forward, and Captain King was standing abreast up the capstan with Captain Grey and I heard Brown say: "There is three more as guilty as myself", and mentioned the people's names, but of that I cannot be positive. Afterwards I went on the quarterdeck and the boy Lister being there, I heard him say to the effect that Brown had done the deed once or twice with him.

John Coombs, in his statement, said, 'whilst the ship was off Japan I heard the boy Phillips confess that Brown had been connected with him unnaturally and that the Captain asked him how much of Brown had been into him and he said that about 3 or 4 inches, he could not say exactly. The Captain said: "was it water that came from him?" He said: "No. It was thick, flabby, stuff." He said it had happened only once.' The ship's carpenter, John Stewart, reports similarly in his statement, 'I heard the boys Lister and Phillips voluntarily confess that Brown had been indecently connected with them and the boys afterwards confessed the same to the ship's company in my hearing.'

The court records state that of the three boys, it was Curtiss and Lister who were 'feloniously, wickedly and against the order of nature, consenting to and did permit the said Alexander Brown, in manner and form aforesaid, to have a venereal affair... to the great displeasure of Almighty God.' The Chief Justice, summing up, said, 'The law has made your offence capital. It is one at which nature shudders; and it therefore only remains for me to pass upon you that sentence which is affixed to the crime of which you were convicted.' The death sentence was then passed. The charge against Phillips was dropped, as he had not consented.

The *Sydney Monitor* reported the execution of Alexander Brown on 27th December 1828:

Between the hours of nine and ten o'clock on Monday morning, seven unhappy culprits expiated by the forfeit of their lives, the crimes of which they had been convicted during the present Criminal Court sittings. Their names were John Iron, James Holmes, William Owens, John Welch, William Bayne, and Alexander Brown, the Chief Officer of the Royal Sovereign whaler, convicted of a crime which cannot be mentioned, the others were bushrangers, all guilty of capital felonies. From the time of their sentence, there was but one man who appeared to entertain a hope that mercy would be extended towards him. That man was Brown. His former respectable situation in life encouraged him in this expectation, and his hope was rather strengthened than abated when he learned that the life of his youthful companion in crime was spared. Lister, the boy who was convicted with Brown, the Chief Mate, for the unnatural crime, has been respited during pleasure.

The Chief Justice, Francis Forbes proclaimed: 'Prisoner Richard Lister, a lad who was apprentice on board the same ship, should be pardoned on condition of his immediately leaving the Colony.' The fate of Edward Curtiss seems to have slipped from the records, but also being a ship's apprentice and aged between fourteen and seventeen, he was probably pardoned as Lister had been.

Viewing the court proceedings and press coverage of the case highlights the abhorrence of sodomy held in public opinion. But it cannot be that such behaviour was so rare aboard ships that this was the only case of its kind to have come before the courts. As mentioned previously, to report such activity would have been at the discretion of the Captain as to whether he took the matter further when the ship reached port. Brown's shipmates seem to have had little or no qualms about reporting the incident to their superior officers. James Burns spent two or three minutes spying through the crack before he fetched officer George Robinson, giving him ample time to assess the situation and the consequences of reporting it. Reporting Brown could have been for any number of reasons. Was it that Burns simply took a dislike to him? Was he an unpopular crew member? Did he target the apprentice boys?

Of the few cases of sodomy that resulted in execution in Australia between 1828 and 1867, all were for offences of rape against minors, and none of these occurred at sea.

The assumption therefore must be that despite the consensual aspect of the sex, it was probably Brown's coercive behaviour that resulted in his demise.

Throughout this period, the convict transportations from Britain caused a significant imbalance in the colony's population, both within the sexes and between free settlers and prisoners. Convicts were largely kept in isolation away from the opposite sex, and with sentences stretching from seven years to life, homosexual behaviour was common. It has been well documented since, but there was also much concern about rampant sodomy between the prisoners even before the first convict ships landed. Royal Navy Admiral Arthur Phillips, first Governor of New South Wales and founder of the first British penal colony, wrote to his superiors to discuss the limits of his powers over the prisoners. To his mind, there were only two offences that warranted the death penalty – murder and sodomy. 'For either of these crimes I would wish to confine the criminal until an opportunity offered of delivering him to the natives of New Zealand and let them eat him. The dread of this will operate much stronger than the fear of death.'

In 1822 an official enquiry was launched into a sexual scandal that resulted from the movement of thirty female prisoners to the male-only prison farm at Emu Plains. Rumour had it that the women were placed there to prevent continual 'unnatural crimes' being committed by the male prisoners. By the 1830s free settlers were demanding an end to the transportation of convicts, citing their immoral fibre as a major factor affecting the development of the colony. The thinking was that criminality, including homosexuality, was a character trait that was passed down from one generation to another. Convicts were seen as the lowest stock from which to populate a nation. Anti-sodomite rhetoric was utilised with great effect and eventually led to the cessation of the convict transportations in 1857. The emergence of gold mining however, led to a further increase in free migration and settlement, as reported in the *Argus* newspaper: 'No wonder that seamen were running away from their ships, printers from their type, doctors from their drugs. In fact, everything has assumed a revolutionary character.' It was just like the Wild West.

Homophobic attitudes within the indigenous community can be largely attributed to the Christian missionaries who forbade Aboriginal and Torres Strait Islanders living under the church's care and under government orders, from practising traditional culture. It was from this period that the idea of homosexuality being sinful became a common view within the indigenous community - one that still prevails today.

Steven Lindsay Ross, talking about the strong belief of traditionalism amongst the Aboriginal peoples says: 'this is dangerous, because it glues us to the past [and] those who have maintained their culture and those who have lost it.' Indigenous people who struggle to come to terms with their sexuality are often told that homosexuality is not part of their culture.

Gregory Phillips, a Waanyi and Jaru from North West Queensland, is an academic who specialises in indigenous health. 'When I was coming out and trying to reconcile being gay with my Aboriginal culture, I was told by an elder very close to me that being gay didn't exist traditionally. He told me it's bad and all these awful things would happen to me.'

The Aranda, the Aboriginal people who lived in the Flinders Ranges of Central Australia and numbered perhaps two thousand in population at the turn of the twentieth century, had a system of 'boy-bride' mentoring, much like that practised in other African tribes. Fourteen-year-old boys would be taken under the wing of older men who had themselves gone through the initiation of subincision and would mentor their 'boy-bride' in hunting and other life skills. Subincision is the removal of a section of the foreskin from the penis which involves slitting into the *corpus spongiosum*, the column of sponge-like tissue that surrounds the urethra and ends at the glans, or more commonly, by slitting the urethra itself. Over an adult male's lifetime this repeated cutting, the blood from which was used to glue feathers to the body for important ceremonies, and was spread on the backs of other initiates, resulted in the penis opening into an erectable flap, much like a hooded snake, rather than the usual shaft-shape, possibly to give the impression of a vulva on the underside of the penis. The origins of this form of mutilation are unknown but might lie in the mimicking of hermaphroditism, in which the rarity of dual sexual organs might have been seen as something special and therefore to be emulated.

The relationship between the 'boy-brides' and their mentors was close and necessarily so, given that the two had to rely on and trust one another explicitly when they were in dangerous situations out in the wild. Sexual intimacy was part of that bond and it is no surprise then that early anthropologists chose to ignore this side of the intimate relationships within the Aranda when they first reported their findings.

In 1973, the Australian and New Zealand College of Psychiatry Federal Council declared homosexuality not to be an illness. They were the first such body in the world to do so.

Argentina

The Argentine tango is synonymous with the smoky nightclubs of Buenos Aires in its heyday in the 1940s and 50s, with its intricate and often explicit movements and sultry dancers, the man leading the woman. But the origin of this beautifully stylised dance of love-making is very different from what you might think.

In the latter half of the nineteenth century, millions of European migrants crossed the Atlantic in hope of a better life. The ports of entry in the Rio de la Plata in South America – Montevideo in Uruguay and Buenos Aires in

Argentina – welcomed the migrants from Italy and Spain, most of whom were young men looking for adventure, to make their fortune and work. They brought with them the music of their home towns and villages; the sounds of flamenco guitars, violins and the bandoneon. They brought their dances too; the waltz, the polka and the lively, triple-time Polish folk dance, the mazurka. When they arrived, they heard other rhythms; traditional Argentine folk music and dance, and the Cuban habanera, often performed to the music of Bizet's Carmen, and added to this exotic mix were the African Bantu-inspired dance rhythms of the Candombe.

With far more men than there were women, the men congregated in the bars and clubs and a style of dance was born to entice women to the sexiest male dancer. Shunned by the upper and middle classes, the sensual intensity of the tango soon became a favourite of the barmaids and girls working the sleazy nightclubs and bars in areas around the docks. Young men in neighbourhood gangs would practise new steps and moves together for months in order to be the ones who won the attentions of the girls over their rivals.

The tango grew in popularity as well-liked street musicians were brought together and introduced thousands to the spellbinding dance of courtship. The best tango orchestras were booked up far in advance and in the golden age of the 1940s, people would tango all night long. Different neighbourhoods had different variations on some of the moves and fights would often break out at the highly volatile dance competitions, called *milongas*.

The myth that the tango was born and performed in the seedy bordellos hides the true picture – that it was men dancing with men that originated it. The risqué leg thrust between the legs of the partner was a representation of what the young men would like to do to the girls. However, it made for some very intimate manoeuvres between the male dancers and gave the opportunity for gay men to dance closely together without being noticed.

There were even some male dancers who would only 'follow' and would be fought over for their *abrazo* and *enganche* – embrace and hook/hold. The tradition of men dancing with men continues today, with fathers teaching their sons the steps at home. In the early twentieth century the streets of Buenos Aires were dangerous at night and the city nightlife was sordid, so fathers considered it their cultural duty to nurture and pass on the tradition of the tango to their sons. It had become the dance of Argentina.

There is still a conservative view that the tango should only be danced between a man and a woman, but the tradition of male couples dancing together is making a comeback. The Queer Tango movement was founded in Hamburg, Germany, in 2001, and was the setting for the first gay/lesbian *milonga*. La Marshall, home of the first queer *milonga* in Buenos Aires, opened in 2002 and every year since, the Queer Tango Argentina Festival has taken place there, attracting same-sex tango couples from all around the world.

12.
The Scourge of the 1980s – HIV/AIDS

'There is now a danger that has become a threat to us all. It is a deadly disease and there is no known cure. The virus can be passed during sexual intercourse with an infected person. Anyone can get it, man or woman. So far, it's been confined to small groups. But its spreading. So, protect yourself and read this leaflet when it arrives. If you ignore AIDS, it could be the death of you. So don't die of ignorance.'

This was the 'Monolith' TV advert voiced over by actor John Hurt for a major Government public awareness campaign at the height of the AIDS panic in 1987. It was broadcast during peak viewing times and the leaflet mentioned was delivered to every household in the United Kingdom, with the chilling warning, 'Anyone can get it, gay or straight, male or female. Already 30,000 people are infected.'

The idea behind the monolithic tombstone which was posted on billboards across the country and used in the TV ad was to shake the public into taking charge of its sexual behaviour and health. At the time, the World Health Organisation reported over 43,000 cases of AIDS covering 91 countries, and the predictions were that there was likely to be a worldwide epidemic of massive proportions.

The first reported cases of AIDS (Acquired Immune Deficiency Syndrome) were in the United States in June 1981. The origins of the Human Immunodeficiency Virus (HIV), the cause of AIDS, is widely thought to have been through transference from chimpanzees to humans, probably through eating chimp bushmeat, or through contact with infected chimp blood via hunters in Southern Cameroon. In 1999, researchers found a strain of SIV in chimpanzees (the Simian Immunodeficiency Virus found in monkeys and apes which attacks their immune system) which was almost identical to the human variation, HIV. Research revealed that the chimps had themselves hunted and eaten two small species of monkeys, the red-capped mangabeys and the greater spot-nosed monkeys, which had subsequently infected the chimps with two different strains of SIV. These two strains then joined together to form a third virus known as SIVcpz, which was passed on to other chimps, and it was this strain that was also infectious to humans. The researchers concluded that it proved chimpanzees were the source of HIV-1, and that the virus had to have crossed species from chimps to humans. It is thought that this transference took place as early as the 1920s. Research into the genetics of hundreds of tissue samples from people infected with HIV over the last 50 years enabled the creation of a virus family tree which has traced the origin back to a common ancestor from Leopoldville, now called Kinshasa, in the Democratic Republic of Congo (DRC), in about 1920. At that time, the city's population was booming, and with the influx of large numbers of male labourers, prostitution followed. The Congo river connected the growing city to other cities, and rail lines carried thousands of workers to mining towns such as Lubumbashi on the border with Zambia.

Studies of blood samples taken from a man living in Kinshasa in 1959 were shown to carry HIV. This is the earliest verified case. There had been other, earlier cases of death caused by immune deficiency infections in the same area, suggesting that HIV might have been the cause, but these could not be verified as no blood samples remained. Continuing improvements to the rail, road and river transport links during the 1960s, combined also with an increase in sexual activity and the sex trade, made for 'perfect storm' conditions, allowing the disease to spread easily. It is thought that it probably crossed the Atlantic to America via Haitian professionals returning home after work assignments in the DRC.

In the early 1980s cases of otherwise rare diseases such as Kaposi's Sarcoma, a rare cancer, and PCP, an equally rare lung infection, were being reported among the gay communities of New York and California. It was not understood why these rare cancers and infections were concentrated in this group, but the conclusion was that an infectious disease was the cause. By mid-1982 the same spread of atypical cancers and infections was also being reported amongst haemophiliacs and heroin addicts, and by September that year, the acronym AIDS was being applied to a list of diseases and conditions where the patient had 'no known cause for diminished resistance to that disease'. In 1983, researchers at the Pasteur Institute in Paris isolated and identified HIV. In the UK that year, 17 cases of AIDS were reported. By the following year, that number had risen to 108. Though the UK Government's 'Don't Die of Ignorance' campaign was accused of scare-mongering, and it certainly did scare people, history now hails it a success. In other European countries, such as France, Spain and Italy, where the authorities were slower to react, the number of HIV infected cases were double that of the UK. However, in sub-Saharan countries of Africa the figures are stark and alarming. In countries such as Botswana, Swaziland and Zimbabwe estimates suggest that two-thirds of the population are infected. Not everyone in the UK was behind spending millions of pounds on those whom the then Chief Constable of Greater Manchester viewed as 'swirling about in a human cesspit of their own making.' He was not alone in this line of thought and for the first few years nothing was done to alleviate the problem. Had those who were dying not been homosexuals and drug addicts, there would certainly have been a more immediate response. Nevertheless, it was recognised that the danger of continuing to do nothing was far greater and would cost the NHS far more if predictions of UK HIV infection were to reach the estimated 300,000 cases within five years, which experts believed they could. 'Don't Die of

Ignorance' was launched via a Cabinet Committee rather than through Number 10. As Norman Fowler, the Secretary for Social Services at the time, said, 'It wasn't a natural subject for Margaret Thatcher.'

Fowler admits that they knew there were risks in running such an apocalyptic campaign and that the adverts could increase fear rather than educate the public about the risks. Ultimately, they did both, and very effectively. A lot of people stopped having sex altogether and for quite some time, but the campaign did get everybody talking about sex and the implications of unsafe sex and promiscuity. The impact was immediate, and the television adverts seem to have had a long-lasting impression on the popular consciousness, instilling a sense of doom which even today is easily recalled by anyone old enough to remember it.

Diana, Princess of Wales, was not shy about courting controversy, and when it came to her opening the UK's first HIV specialist ward at the Middlesex Hospital in London, she pointedly shook the hands of patients without wearing a surgical mask or latex gloves and sat closely to talk with them. In this moment she did in one stroke, or click of a camera lens, what the authorities had failed to do – ease the panic somewhat and dispel some of the myths that surrounded AIDS. Myths such as – could it be contracted through touch or even the merest drop of saliva? When experts were telling people that there was no danger from 'a peck on the cheek' but then warning against 'swapping saliva', it was difficult to know what to believe and what not to. Did this for instance include drinking from the same cup or shaking someone's hand not knowing where it had been? Diana was instrumental in making a stand against the swell of bigotry and ignorance that surrounded the disease, and yet those myths continued and even today some still exist. Kissing or sharing a toothbrush, for instance, cannot transmit the virus. It cannot be transmitted through skin-to-skin contact or saliva. Here's the technical bit direct from HIV.Gov: 'You can get or transmit HIV only through specific activities. Most commonly, people get or transmit HIV through sexual behaviours and needle or syringe use. Only certain body fluids – blood, semen, pre-seminal fluid (pre-cum), rectal fluids, vaginal fluids, and breast milk from a person who has HIV can transmit it. These fluids must come into contact with a mucous membrane or damaged tissue or be directly injected into the bloodstream (from a needle or syringe) for transmission to occur. Mucous membranes are found inside the rectum, vagina, penis, and mouth. In general, there is little to no risk of getting HIV from oral sex. But transmission of HIV, though extremely rare, is theoretically possible if an HIV-positive man ejaculates in his partner's mouth during oral sex.'

While Diana was being photographed visiting AIDS patients in 1987, Mrs Thatcher, at the Conservative Party Conference in the same year, was making a rallying statement to party back-benchers who had joined an increasingly vociferous public backlash against what many saw as the 'promotion' of homosexuality in society. 'Children who need to be taught to respect traditional moral values are being taught that they have an inalienable right to be gay,' she said.

The result was the introduction of the infamous Section 28, or Clause 28 as it is sometimes known, of the Local Government Act 1988, which affected England, Wales and Scotland. The amendment was enacted on 24th May 1988 and stated that a local authority 'shall not intentionally promote homosexuality or publish material with the intention of promoting homosexuality [or] promote the teaching in any maintained school of the acceptability of homosexuality as a pretended family relationship'.

Rising public negativity was revealed in a British Social Attitudes Survey which reported that 75% of the population said that homosexual activity was 'always or mostly wrong', with only 11% believing it to be 'never wrong'. Five years earlier, a similar BSAS poll had found that 61% of Conservative and 67% of Labour voters believed homosexual activity to be 'always or mostly wrong'.

Section 28 prohibited local councils from distributing any kind of material, whether that be plays, leaflets, books, etc, that portrayed gay relationships as anything other than abnormal. Teachers were afraid to discuss gay issues with students for fear of losing funding, although breaking the clause did not amount to a criminal offence; no prosecution was ever brought under this provision. However, public fears over the left-wing policies of some local authorities, dubbed the 'Loony Left', stoked concern over the public funding of unheard-of lesbian and gay groups. One case against Glasgow Council in May 2000, in which Section 28 was used, did get to court just weeks prior to the Section being repealed in Scotland. The unsuccessful case was brought by the Christian Institute for the council's funding of an AIDS support charity which the Institute claimed was promoting homosexuality. The reality of Section 28 was that it caused many groups to close or at least to limit their activities. For example, a number of lesbian, gay, transgender, and bisexual student support groups in schools and colleges were closed due to fears by council legal staff that they could be in breach of the Act.

The widespread fear of AIDS was predominantly directed at gays and bisexuals, and these attitudes intensified the existing opposition to school policies and activities which supporters claimed were efforts to be inclusive of sexual minorities, but which opponents deemed to be the promotion of homosexuality.

In 1983 the *Daily Mail* reported that a book entitled *Jenny Lives with Eric & Martin*, a story about a little girl who lives with her father and his gay partner, was provided in a school library run by the Labour-controlled Inner London Education Authority. The then Conservative MP Jill Knight, who introduced Section 28, justified the reasons behind the clause in 1999, adding, 'There was *The Playbook for Kids about Sex* in which brightly coloured pictures of little stick men showed all about homosexuality and how it was done. That book was for children as young as five. I should be surprised if anybody supports that. Another book called *The Milkman's on his Way* explicitly described homosexual intercourse and, indeed, glorified it, encouraging youngsters to believe that it was better than any other sexual way of life.'

On the eve of Section 28 becoming law, on 24th May 1988, several protests were staged by lesbians, including abseiling into Parliament and a famous on-air TV invasion of the BBC's Six o' Clock News, during which one woman managed to chain herself to the desk of Sue Lawley and was sat on by fellow presenter, Nicholas Witchell. This event was all rather comical and slapstick, but it played its part in bringing together all the disparate elements of the gay rights movement and saw the rise of groups such as the Terrence Higgins Trust and Stonewall. While the gay rights movement was united over Section 28, gay issues began to divide the Conservative party, heightening divisions between party modernists and traditionalists. Finally, on 18th November 2003, following Scotland in 2000, Section 28 was repealed in England and Wales, under the Local Government Act 2003.

In 1996 a breakthrough in the treatment of AIDS was made with Highly Active Antiretroviral Therapy or HAART, which was found to significantly delay the onset of AIDS in people with HIV. However, in 2000 fewer than 700,000 people living with HIV in the world had access to this treatment. By 2015 a worldwide UN target was met, giving 15 million people the antiretroviral drugs, they needed. In July 2017, advocates from sixteen countries gathered at the International AIDS Society Conference in Paris to issue the U=U Consensus Statement: 'There is now evidence-based confirmation that the risk of HIV transmission from a person living with HIV (PLHIV), who is on Antiretroviral Therapy (ART) and has achieved an undetectable viral load in their blood for at least 6 months is negligible to non-existent. [Negligible is defined as: so small or unimportant as to be not worth considering; insignificant.] While HIV is not always transmitted even with a detectable viral load, when the partner with HIV has an undetectable viral load this both protects their own health and prevents new HIV infections.'

The Lancet said: "U=U is a simple but hugely important campaign based on a solid foundation of scientific evidence. It has already been successful in influencing public opinion, causing more people with HIV (and their friends and families) to comprehend that they can live long, healthy lives, have children, and never have to worry about passing on their infection to others."

U=U stands for Undetectable = Untransmittable. Suppressing the viral load of someone living with HIV to undetectable levels 'not only saves their lives but prevents them from infecting others. The higher percentage, therefore, of people who are on treatment, in care and who get their viral loads to undetectable, the closer we get to literally ending the epidemic,' says Dr. Anthony Fauci, Director of NAID.

Taking ART medication as prescribed and having an undetectable viral load for over six months means you cannot pass on HIV. If, however, that person stops therapy for two weeks and rebounds, the chances of contracting the virus from them goes up. You are only as virologically suppressed as your adherence to the medication. It takes up to six months before viral growth is completely inhibited, and during that time the use of condoms is highly recommended. Additionally, the HIV negative partner might use antiretroviral drugs as pre-exposure prophylaxis or PrEP, a course of HIV medication taken before sex to reduce the risk of infection. Results in trials have been very successful, with PrEP significantly lowering the risk of becoming HIV positive, and without major side effects. The medication used for PrEP is a tablet called Truvada, which contains tenofovir and emtricitabine, drugs which are commonly used in HIV treatment. Taking PrEP before exposure to HIV means there is enough drug inside you to block HIV if it gets into your body and before it has a chance to infect you.

In clinical trials PrEP has been used in two different ways: taken regularly (one tablet per day) or taken only when required (two tablets, between 2 and 24 hours before sex, one tablet 24 hours after sex and a further tablet 48 hours after sex). This is often called 'on demand' or 'event based' dosing. Both methods have been shown to be very effective.

If you are thinking about getting PrEP from outside the NHS it's important that you talk to an adviser from a sexual health clinic. You will be supported to use the treatment safely and provided with any necessary tests (e.g. kidney function tests).

Had my brother (see introduction) been infected with HIV today, he could have realistically expected to live a full and healthy life with the treatment now available. Unfortunately, for him it came just a few years too late.

In January 2017 the UN issued this statement: '90-90-90, an ambitious treatment target to help end the AIDS epidemic. By 2020, 90% of all people living with HIV will know their HIV status. By 2020, 90% of all people with diagnosed HIV infection will receive sustained antiretroviral therapy. By 2020, 90% of all people receiving antiretroviral therapy will have viral suppression.'

13.
The World Today

There are 195 countries in the world today, or 194 if you discount the Vatican City. Seventy-four have laws against homosexuals and homosexual activity, and most of these are in Africa and Asia. Put another way, 38 per cent of the world's population are living under laws that positively discriminate against homosexuality. In five of those countries, Iran, Mauritania, Saudi Arabia, Sudan and Yemen, and in some states of Nigeria and Somalia, homosexuality is punishable by death. At the other end of the scale are the 99 countries which have signed a General Assembly declaration of LGBT rights or who have sponsored the Human Rights Council's 2011 resolution on LGBT rights which gives gay couples the same legal and marital rights as their heterosexual counterparts. Still, it cannot be ignored that in many countries where anti-discrimination laws do exist, gay people continue to be persecuted both by the authorities and wider societies.

In 2011, the United Nations Human Rights Council passed its first resolution recognising LGBT rights, followed by a report documenting violations against those rights, including hate crime, criminalization and discrimination. In the wake of the report, the UN Human Rights Commission urged all countries which had not yet done so to enact laws to protect basic LGBT rights.

As of November 2017, 24 countries recognise same-sex marriage and grant most of, if not all LGBT rights, including same-sex unions, marriage, adoption rights, serving in the military and anti-discrimination laws, to all their citizens.

Some countries however, are moving towards more punitive laws and strengthening existing penalties. In 2013, India reinstated a 153-year-old colonial-era law criminalising gay sex, and in Nigeria, a country which already bans gay relationships; same-sex marriages, gay groups and any displays of same-sex affection in public have also been outlawed.

The list below contains the countries which uphold anti-gay legislation, subjecting tens of millions of LGBT people around the world to life under regimes and in societies that are at best negative towards homosexuality and at worst where it is a punishable crime:

Afghanistan, Algeria, Angola, Antigua

Bangladesh, Barbados, Belize, Bhutan, Botswana, Brunei, Burundi

Cameroon, Comoros, Cook Islands

Dominica (but no enforcement of anti-gay law)

Egypt, Eritrea, Ethiopia

Gambia, Ghana, Grenada, Guinea, Guyana

India, Indonesia, Iran, Iraq

Jamaica

Kenya, Kiribati, Kuwait

Lebanon, Liberia, Libya

Malawi (enforcement of law suspended), Malaysia, Maldives, Mauritania, Mauritius, Morocco, Myanmar (Burma)

Namibia, Nauru, Nigeria

Oman

Pakistan, Palestine/za, Papua New Guinea

Qatar

Samoa, Saudi Arabia, Senegal, Seychelles (Seychelles does not prosecute anyone under their anti-sodomy law and has promised to repeal it), Sierra Leone, Singapore, Solomon Islands, Somalia, Sri Lanka, St Kitts & Nevis, St Lucia, St Vincent & the Grenadines, Sudan, Swaziland, Syria

Tanzania, Togo, Tonga, Trinidad & Tobago, Tunisia, Turkmenistan, Tuvalu

Uganda, United Arab Emirates, Uzbekistan

Yemen

Zambia, Zimbabwe

It is worth noting that some of the countries on the list are more democratic and liberal than others, and while their laws still uphold homosexuality as illegal, homosexual encounters still occur but at great risk to those involved.

Most Western European countries now have laws making same-sex marriage legal, and Europe can be proud of the fact that it has many gay leaders in the top political roles:

Iceland: Prime Minister Johanna Sigurdardottir 2009-2013
Belgium: Prime Minister Elio Di Rupo 2011-2014
Luxembourg: Prime Minister Xavier Bettel 2013 -
Ireland: Prime Minister Leo Varadkar 2017 -
Serbia: Prime Minister Ana Brnabic 2017 -

Other countries, like Italy, Greece, Switzerland, Croatia, Hungary, Austria, Slovakia, Czechia and Estonia, allow civil partnerships, but it is the Eastern European countries where there is still no legislation for same-sex marriage or civil partnerships, notably Russia, which enacted an anti-gay law in 2013 criminalising any positive mention of homosexuality or 'non-traditional relationships' to minors; homosexuals face the threat of homophobic attacks and discrimination.

For a comprehensive list of those countries with anti-gay laws, go to the BBC's news website and search for 'Where is it illegal to be gay,' an article that shows a map of the world and which countries enforce the death penalty or imprisonment, have different ages for consent or laws against homosexuality and where marriage between same sexes is legal; or 'Commonwealth Summit: the countries where it is illegal to be gay', which lists those Commonwealth countries. For more information visit the Foreign Office: LGBT Foreign Travel Advice.

14.
Where Are the Role Models?

'The extraordinary change in attitudes to homosexuality is unlikely to be undone,' says historian Lucy Delap. 'The criminal sanctions, social contempt and deep distaste for male homosexuality in 19th century Britain – and much of the 20th century – have been significantly eroded.'

The 'significant erosion' Delap speaks of was not something that happened overnight. Though homosexuality was partially decriminalised by the Sexual Offences Act 1967, real change in public attitudes was not visible for another thirty years. The British public's view towards same-sex relationships, according to the British Social Attitudes survey, reported in 1983 that only 17% thought same-sex relationships were 'not wrong at all'. This slumped to a low of 11% in 1987 at the height of the AIDS panic and took nearly three decades to rise, in 2016, to the point where 64% of the population agreed with the statement that same-sex relationships were 'not wrong at all', reflecting the wide social liberalisation that had taken place.

What has changed so dramatically in the public perception of homosexuality?

Methodical knowledge and an increased awareness of the sciences since the late nineteenth century have given psychoanalysts opportunities to challenge ideas of what is 'normal'. Talk of deviance and sin surrounding sexual orientation is now removed from mainstream thinking, as theological, faith-based objections were proven unfounded on scientific information. Fewer people upheld Church and faith as important influencers on their lives, and many of those within the Church began to preach tolerance and understanding towards homosexuals as inclusive members of their congregations – some did not, of course. The traditional family unit changed as well. Since the Second

World War, divorce and single-parent families have become a recognised norm of our society, and different ways of living have been accepted. Women's Lib in the 1960s and 70s also led to the traditional male constraints of hetero-masculinity to be softened. Jobs became interchangeable and sensitivity, child rearing, and their own emotional awareness enabled many men to adopt a new male model or 'metrosexuality' which allowed for a wider range of behaviour, lifestyle and even fashion, to be acceptable. There was a rise in celebrity culture too, in which the traditional fields for homosexuals to work in – the arts, acting, and music – became popularised entertainment through the expansion of television, film, pop culture and social media. Where once the public were only ever exposed to a narrow band of stereotypical character types through the medium of cinema and two or three television channels, soon, through its expansion, every TV programme and film vied for the audience's attention, enabling diversity in individualism and different ideas of what it means to be homosexual to be established.

All these factors and more made the public understanding of homosexuality more real, and empowered homosexuals with a group voice. Slowly, through a lot of activism during the 1970s and 80s and pressure from high-profile individuals and alliances such as Stonewall and Outrage, the time for change gathered apace.

1994 – the age of consent was lowered from 21 to 18.

2000 – the ban on gay and bisexual men and women serving in the British Armed Forces was lifted.

2001 – the last two pieces of unequal law regarding homosexuals were removed. The age of consent was made equal to that of heterosexuals – 16. Group sex between men was also decriminalised.

2002 – same-sex couples were given equal adoption rights.

2003 – Section 28 was repealed. 'Gross indecency' was removed as an offence – this was a cover-all term used for such activities as sex in public and sex in private involving more than two people. Hotels were counted as public spaces and therefore having any gay sex in such an establishment was a criminal offence. Police records for offences of gross indecency rose from 820 in 1969 to a high of 2,022 in 1989. By 2000 this had dropped to just 167.

2004 – a law allowing for civil partnerships between same-sex couples was passed.

2007 – discrimination on the basis of sexual orientation was banned.

2009 – Labour Prime Minister Gordon Brown apologised over the treatment of Alan Turing, and the Opposition Leader for the Conservatives, David Cameron, apologised over Section 28, brought in by PM Margaret Thatcher's third-term Government.

2010 – gender reassignment was added as a protected characteristic in equality legislation.

2014 – gay marriage became legal in England, Wales and Scotland. In the two years following, 60,000 people entered same-sex marriages.

2016 – 40 LGBT MPs sat in the UK Parliament, the highest figure of any Parliament in the world. Prince William appeared on the cover of *Attitude* magazine.

2017 – the Government issues posthumous pardons, known as 'Turing's Law', to 50,000 gay and bisexual men who had been criminalised; among them Oscar Wilde and Alan Turing. A further 15,000 living men were also able to apply to the Home Office for pardon.

As attitudes changed, well-known figures, such as rugby player Gareth Thomas and diver Tom Daley, started coming out instead of being outed by salacious Sunday newspaper stories, and found themselves feted as role models.

In an article 'Being Yourself: LGBT Lives in Scotland', Stonewall Scotland featured some of the role models they work with through different employers, universities, colleges and schools. 'Too many young people are starting their careers believing that their success is reliant on them hiding who they really are,' says Colin MacFarlane, Director of Stonewall Scotland. 'Most of our role models are not celebrities but colleagues, friends, parents or siblings. Being a role model is a choice other people make for you. It is when they see something in you that resonates, something aspirational, or perhaps very normal. Something that says to them, this is possible, whatever this might be. Success means something different to each and every one of us, but we believe that it should never have to come at the price of being able to be yourself.'

When asked about role models in their lives, people typically respond in one of three ways: either they have no role models and are unable to think of a single person who has had any positive influence on their lives; or the reverse, they are overwhelmed with people they consider role models, from primary school teachers to television soap stars; or thirdly, they believe that anyone 'like them' is their role model – in other words, role models are not seen as someone to aspire to, but merely an extension of themselves and all the negativity that implies.

So, what is a role model? What are the attributes that set them apart? As MacFarlane says, they are not necessarily well-known or influential. Precisely how can you quantify the influence of a mentor or role model on people's lives and attitudes? Anecdotal evidence is not the same as observed data, and in the same way that physicists predict the behaviour of millions of molecules working together but are incapable of predicting the behaviour of one molecule, so psychologists can inform on the habits and behaviours of whole populations, but not of individuals. There are, however, certain behaviours that are constant and intrinsic to all human beings. One of the most important in determining our life path is the belief that we do not attempt to achieve anything unless we think it can be done. Seeing someone else succeed at something is far more likely to encourage us to have a go ourselves – it can be done, but we need to see that it can be done by someone like us. The definition of a role model is 'a person who serves as an example of the values, attitudes, and behaviours associated with a role – a person looked to by others as an example to be imitated'. A good role model has a clear sense of what is important to them. They put in whatever effort it takes to reach their goal, which inevitably is to improve or create things that will make a positive difference to others.

Lists extolling the virtues of inspiring role models in the business and entertainment fields, such as the Pride Power top 100 List, might give the impression that these celebrities, politicians, sports personalities and eminent businessmen and women have somehow always been destined to be at the top of their game, that their career paths were ordained from above, their life choices prearranged in some way, and that being 'given' these positions in life make it easier for them to be open about their sexuality, and to voice their opinions and appraisals of society's injustices with impunity. Often every word they utter creates columns of newspaper and magazine space as well as airtime on tv and radio stations. For LGBT causes these spokespeople play an invaluable part. The likes of Stephen Fry, Ian McKellen, Ruth Davidson, Waheed Alli, Owen Jones and many, many others, come from all sorts of backgrounds, socio-demographic walks of life and upbringings, and their only prerequisite in what they choose to do to make a living is their own tenacity and drive to succeed at that. Sexuality is not what makes them successful or even who they are, it is only a part of their makeup. The status of 'role model' thrust upon them, is due to their passion and belief, but as with all of us, self-doubt and worry are still, undoubtedly, a constant internal argument.

Whatever we do in life, one thing is true of all businesses and organisations; that they are built around people who carry out an idea. It is never the other way around – there is no idea too big or too small that doesn't require at least one person to make it happen. It is not uncommon for role models to find it very hard to live up to their own and everyone else's expectations. But in reality, nobody really expects anyone to be superhuman, unflawed and perfect. Here are some qualities most often mentioned as the characteristics and behaviours that people look for in their role models:

1. The ability to demonstrate confidence and leadership. A good role model is someone who is positive, calm, and confident in themselves. Even if they are not feeling positive, calm or confident one day, they are still able to show it. Nobody follows someone who is negative and brings everybody down with them. People admire people who are happy with their achievements but who also continue to strive for bigger and better things.

2. Don't be afraid to be unique. Whatever you choose to do with your life, be proud of the person you've become. Role models do not pretend to be someone they are not.

3. Communicate and interact with everyone. A good communicator is someone who listens as well as talks. People are energized by influencers who explain why and where they are going. Great role models have a consistent message.

4. Show respect and concern for others. You may be driven and successful, but whether you choose to show respect or not to others speaks volumes.

5. Be knowledgeable and well-rounded. Great role models aren't just teachers. They are constant learners and challenge themselves to get out of their comfort zones and surround themselves with people they admire.

6. Have humility and admit mistakes. Nobody is perfect. When a bad decision is made, the good role model lets those who are watching and learning from them know that they've made that mistake and how they plan to rectify it. Taking responsibility and correcting a course of

action is often a painful decision but something the true role model achieves with humility.

7.   Do good things outside the job you are known for. People who put in the work yet still find time for other interests and causes outside of their career, show they are well rounded, willing to learn new things and help others.

The Prince's Trust, partnered with Macquarie, release an annual Youth Index, which analyses the wellbeing of young people across the UK. It shows that in the past few years, wellbeing amongst young people has been decreasing and that happiness and confidence measures are at their lowest levels. Young people increasingly feel that they are not in control of their lives and are trapped by economic, demographic and wider political influences, making them feel anxious about the future. A person's confidence and happiness, irrespective of age, is obviously very dependent on personal circumstances. But the report proves that happiness and wellbeing in several demographic categories: employment, socio-economic status, gender and mental health, are all important factors. Those not in education, employment or training (NEETs) report lower wellbeing scores, as do people who received free school meals (a sign of socio-economic poverty). Women and those who suffer from mental health issues, or do not have significant role models of their gender, also scored low.

'There is substantial evidence that the presence of a positive role model has a significant impact on a young person's mental wellbeing and performance in school' the Youth Index reports. 'Young men without positive male role models are three times more likely than their peers to lack a sense of belonging and three times more likely to suffer from depression. 21% of NEETs without a role model have never had a job, compared to 14% of their peers, and are significantly more likely to stay unemployed for longer than those with a role model.'

The Prince's Trust concludes that 'inclusion should ensure that everyone, regardless of gender, socio-economic or racial background, has access to a role model that can inspire and support each individual to a happy, confident and successful life. The Princes Trust Youth Index shows the importance of this goal, and just how far we are from achieving it.'

The charity *Diversity Role Models* works with schools by going in and talking to students to educate them about homophobic bullying, challenging stereotypes and the use of inappropriate language. 55% of young LGBT people report having suffered homophobic bullying at school, and the impact on individuals can be severe, with increased self-harming, declining engagement in education and even suicide. The in-school workshops run by the charity and facilitated by LGBT and straight ally role models talk directly to the students about their personal experiences. Working in over 200 schools across the country to date, they have reached over 50,000 young people.

Role models, whether they are famous or only known to a few, are people who possess the qualities we would all like to have. We admire their work and aspire to be as brave, intelligent, altruistic or as funny as they are; and those who have most effect on us make us better people.

Part Two

Significant Events

15.
Henry VIII & the Buggery Act - 1533

Henry VIII was the King who introduced the first legislation against sodomy in England under English criminal law, with the Buggery Act of 1533, making buggery punishable by hanging. The Act stated:

Forasmuch as there is not yet sufficient and condign punishment appointed and limited by the due course of the Laws of this Realm for the detestable and abominable Vice of Buggery committed with mankind or beast: It may therefore please the King's Highness with the assent of the Lords Spiritual and the Commons of this present parliament assembled, that it may be enacted by the authority of the same, that the same offence be from henceforth ajudged Felony and that such an order and form of process therein to be used against the offenders as in cases of felony at the Common law. And that the offenders being hereof convict by verdict confession or outlawry shall suffer such pains of death and losses and penalties of their good chattels debts lands tenements and hereditaments as felons do according to the Common Laws of this Realme.

The Act was pushed through Parliament by Thomas Cromwell, Henry's chief minister, in support of the King's plans to reduce the jurisdiction of the church courts. The Act defined the felony without benefit of clergy, meaning that those convicted in holy orders were denied the right to be tried in their own ecclesiastical courts. As well as the death penalty, conviction resulted in the loss of all property to the Crown, thus supporting Henry's policy to seize both power and wealth from the Church. The Act itself states that the reason for its implementation was only because there had been 'no sufficient punishment' before.

However, until the passing of the Buggery Act, all sexual activities except adultery were largely ignored and such cases that did arise were dealt with in ecclesiastical courts.

The first person to be executed under the new statute, along with treason, was Walter Hungerford, 1st Baron Hungerford of Heytesbury, in July 1540. As he was beheaded rather than hanged, it is suggested that his treachery for harbouring a member of the outlawed Pilgrimage of Grace, a group opposing the King's break with the Catholic Church, was probably what cost him his life in the end. In 1541, a cleric, playwright and headmaster of Eton College, by the name of Nicholas Udall, was the first man to be charged in violation of the Act alone. His connections with men in powerful positions of state meant that the sentence was commuted to imprisonment and he was released in less than a year.

Fewer than a dozen prosecutions for buggery are recorded over a hundred-year period, from the Act becoming law in 1533 through to the mid-seventeenth century. In 1570, John Swan and John Lister, a smith and servant of the same master, were charged with sodomy in Edinburgh, and in 1580 Matthew Heaton, an East Grinstead clergyman, was prosecuted at the Sussex Assizes for having a relationship with a boy in his parish. It is not known whether the lack of such cases is due to the scarcity of legal records remaining from the time, or a reflection of the difficulty in proving events in court. For instance, witnesses were not allowed to give evidence if they were seen to profit from a conviction in any way.

The Catholic Queen, Mary I, Henry's eldest daughter, ascended the throne in 1553 and the Act was immediately repealed along with other statutes, giving much of the jurisdiction they had lost back to the Church and its ecclesiastic courts. In 1563 however, the Act was revived by Henry's second daughter, Queen Elizabeth I – a Protestant and staunch admirer of her father's Kingship. The revision of the Act was brought about since:

...ill disposed persons have been the more bold to commit the said most horrible and detestable Vice of Buggery aforesaid, to the high displeasure of Almighty God.

There is no historical evidence to suggest that any such excessive 'boldness' occurred in the interim years of repeal, and the restoration to the old statute was more likely a result of Elizabeth's desire to establish herself as a strong monarch and direct heir to her father, Henry VIII, whom she idolised.

The Act remained in force until it was finally repealed and replaced by the Offences against the Person Act 1828. Buggery remained a capital offence until 1861.

16.
Hanged for Buggery - 1835

The *London Evening Standard* reported on Monday 23rd November 1835: *'the Recorder made his report to his Majesty, at Brighton, of the undermentioned capital convicts under sentence of death in Newgate, convicted at the September and October sessions of the Central Criminal Court:... Robert Swan, 28; for robbery,* (though in the Huntingdon Gazette Robert Swan's conviction is reported as *'extorting money from Thomas Reynolds, a Quaker, under threat of accusing him of a 'nameless offence'*), *John Smith, 40, and James Pratt, 30, for an unnatural crime...* (and others)... *to all of whom his Majesty has extended his royal mercy, except John Smith and James Pratt, who are left for execution on Friday next.'*

Smith and Pratt's fateful assignation took place at the rented room of one William Bonill, aged 68, who lived at a house near the Blackfriars Road, Southwark, London. Bonhill's landlord later stated that he had frequent male visitors who generally came in pairs, and that his suspicions were aroused on the afternoon of 29th August 1835, when Pratt and Smith visited Bonill in his room. Using his ingenuity and guile, the landlord climbed into the loft of a nearby stable building and from this vantage point could see through the window straight into Bonill's room. Horrified at what he saw, he came back into the house, and with his wife went immediately to look through the keyhole, whence upon they both stated they had seen Pratt and Smith in sexual intimacy. The landlord then took it upon himself to break open the door to confront the pair. Bonill was absent at this time, but returned a few minutes later carrying a jug of ale. The landlord then fetched a policeman and all three men were arrested. John Smith and James Pratt were indicted for buggery at the parish of

Christ Church, Surrey, and William Bonill was indicted as an accessory before the fact and sentenced to fourteen years transportation.

The notoriety of this case lies in the fact that John Smith and James Pratt were the last men to be hanged for buggery in Britain.

17.
Reform in the UK - 1861

The United Kingdom Offences against the Person Act 1828, consolidated into a single Act laws relating to offences against the person', meaning in particular, offences of violence. Its introduction was part of a wider process to consolidate criminal law reforms introduced by Sir Robert Peel and known as Peel's Act (Sir Robert Peel 1788-1850 was a British statesman and member of the Conservative Party who served two terms as Prime Minister in 1834-1835 and 1841-1846). Among the laws it replaced was the Buggery Act 1533. In due course, the Offences against the Person Act 1828 was replaced by the Offences against the Person Act 1861. This latest update was significant in that Section 61 of the Act abolished the death penalty for buggery. Instead, a person convicted of buggery could face life imprisonment or any length of sentence, not less than ten years.

Later, Section 11 of the Criminal Law Amendment Act 1885, or the Labouchère Amendment, introduced 'gross indecency' in 'public or private' and categorised consensual activity, aside from sodomy, as a crime in the United Kingdom. Gross indecency per se was never properly defined in the statutes and was instead used in broad terms by the courts to criminalise sexual activity between men where sodomy could not be proven. It was later carried forward onto the statutes of Canada and other British colonies.

Henry Du Pré Labouchère (1831-1912) was a journalist and politician who apparently had an open mind towards the freedoms enjoyed by the general public and society as a whole. He was, however, a strong opponent of homosexuality, and pushed for a penalty of seven years' hard labour to be introduced but was persuaded to opt for the lower 'not exceeding two years, with or without hard labour'. Hard labour meant repetitive manual work such as walking a treadmill or picking apart rope fibres. Oscar Wilde was convicted under Labouchère's Amendment, Section 11, and sentenced to the maximum two years' hard labour in 1895 for 'committing acts of gross indecency with male persons'.

Charges of gross indecency affected so many men during this period that it became known as 'The Blackmailer's Charter', yet it remained in English law until 1967.

18.
The right word for it - 1869

Until the term 'homosexual' first appeared in print in two German pamphlets in 1869, written by Karl-Maria Kertbeny, a journalist and travel writer, there was no recognised categorisation or label for male same-sex love. The term 'heterosexual' was not formulated until almost twenty years later. 'Bisexual' came into effect in the twentieth century, and later other terminologies describing transgender, pangender, asexual and other LBGT groups came into being as enlightened awareness of sexual behaviour and preferences became more widely acknowledged. Other terms were used to describe acts such as masturbation, anal sex and bestiality, also invented by Kertbeny; namely 'monosexualism', 'pygismus' and 'heterogenit', which have all now dropped completely from use.

Karl-Maria Kertbeny spent his youth flitting about Europe, staving off poverty and acquainting himself with various writers and celebrities, such as the Grimm Brothers and Goethe, and getting himself into trouble with the Austrian authorities for not possessing a legitimate passport. His initial writing ambitions seems to have been in the furtherment of Hungarian literature. He himself authored of a number of books, such as *Voices from the Past*, an anthology of Hungarian revolutionary verse, before he later took to writing comprehensively on the subject of male same-sex love. He strongly maintained that his enthusiasm for focusing on this topic was from the point of view of his anthropological interest and intense principles of justice and not his own sexuality. Working at one point in his early life as a bookseller's apprentice, Kertbeny had a close friend who he knew was sexually attracted to men. Tragically, the young man killed himself after being blackmailed and Kertbeny recalled this as a defining moment, saying that it was this episode and his 'instinctive drive to take issue with every injustice' that led him to take such a close interest in the matter of male same-sex love. He continued to claim that he was himself 'normally sexed', a term which in the nineteenth century clearly meant having a sexual appetite that was satisfied by intercourse between a man and a woman, preferably in the marital bed, in the missionary position, and definitely behind closed doors. He never married however, despite stating in a letter to his mother that he was engaged to a rich widowed baroness. What is known of his relationships with other women, through his diaries, is plagued with ambiguity. Researcher Judit Takacs, who has studied his diaries, says that Kertbeny subconsciously reveals himself in his secretive scribblings and notes in the margins; he writes of liaisons with 'beautiful boys', one called 'Hubert' and various others, a 'beautiful barber', and then, 'Horror! The clap again'.

There are no words in Latin that precisely translate to 'homosexuality' or 'heterosexuality', and such concepts in Greek and Roman times would have been unrecognisable. It wasn't until the advances in science and the subsequent requirement for the classification and labelling of almost everything in nature in the nineteenth century that Kertbeny coined the term *Homosexualität*, as a compound of the Greek *homo*, 'same', and the Mediaeval Latin *sexualis*, 'sexual'. Homosexuality, as Kertbeny saw it, was innate and natural, and a matter for consenting individuals over the age of fourteen and not subject to interference from the law. In his new word, *Homosexualität*, he saw a neutral way of referring to same-sex love, a scientific sounding word that counterbalanced other highly charged populist slang words such as 'bugger', 'molly', 'pederast' or 'sodomite', which were loaded with condemnation and shame. It was not immediately taken up by the wider scientific community, however. His primary intention was that *Homosexualität* was to be used as a non-judicial word, devised mainly to serve the needs of a network of gay-identifying German men he'd met and who had been advocating for years the reform of laws, specifically Paragraph 143 of the Prussian Penal Code, which discriminated against them. Shrewdly, Kertbeny did not seek special treatment for this group or the wider homosexual population, who were still a relatively small number with limited powers to initiate change. Instead he promoted the idea that the state should extend the same principles of non-interference in the private lives of homosexuals as it did to all its other citizens.

In a letter he wrote to Karl Ulrichs, the German writer, in May 1868, Kertbeny used this new term for the first time. He used it again for a wider readership in the pamphlets he published in 1869 in Leipzig, when he called for the reform of the Prussian Penal Code.

Karl Ulrichs, who had 'come out' to his family and friends some years earlier, and who had developed his third-sex theory, Uranianism, which he claimed had helped him to discover his own feminine traits within himself, wrote: 'not everyone arrives at a consciousness of this female element. I myself became aware of it only very late, and I might never have arrived at it had I not pondered the riddle of Uranian love or become acquainted with other Urnings [male-bodied persons with female psyches].' He devised Uranianism as an entire classification system based on combinations of attraction and gender, but it proved too difficult and cumbersome to be taken up as the standard.

Later, and much to Ulrichs' annoyance and unease, his theory that homosexuality was congenital was modified in accordance with the popular criminal/medical stance of the day, which emphasized its perversion, sickness and deficiency. Ulrichs summed it up: 'My scientific opponents are mostly doctors of the insane. They have observed Urnings in lunatic asylums and have apparently never seen mentally healthy Urnings. The published views of the doctors for the insane are now accepted by others.'

In the pamphlets of 1869, Kertbeny argued that the Prussian sodomy law, Paragraph 143 (later Para. 175 of the German Empire's legal code, which was used to significant and deadly effect by the Nazis), violated the 'rights of man'. Recalling his friends, the bookseller's apprentice and Karl Ulrichs, who was himself arrested and all his research material removed and sent to the Ministry of the Exterior, including 150 names of Urnings living in Berlin, Kertbeny argued that the law as it stood allowed for blackmailers to extort money from homosexuals, often driving them to suicide. Homosexual men, he said, were not necessarily effeminate, and he pointed to the many great historical figures who were known to have been homosexuals. Astonishingly, this was the first time anyone had put these unfamiliar arguments before the public.

In 1880 Kertbeny contributed a chapter on homosexuality to Gustav Jäger's book *Discovery of the Soul*. The publishers came to the conclusion that it was far too contentious and controversial and left out Kertbeny's section from the final draft. Jäger however, did use Kertbeny's new terminologies throughout the book. Another German sex researcher, Richard von Krafft-Ebing, also used the term 'homosexual' and the then recently invented term 'heterosexual' in his book *Psychopathia Sexualis* (1886), which contained the case studies of over two hundred individuals' sex lives. Krafft-Ebing was so highly influential that the use of these new terms of reference for sexual preferences soon found a wider audience and became the general specification for identifying differences in sexual orientation, nullifying and making redundant Ulrichs' plethora of Uranian terminology, including Urnings.

The term 'homosexual' did not appear in English print until 1891, in John Addington-Symonds' *A Problem in Modern Ethics,* when he described same-sex love as 'homosexual instincts'. Havelock Ellis, the English physician, writer, and social reformer, who studied human sexuality and wrote *Sexual Inversion* in 1897, popularized the idea of 'inversion', that homosexuality was a congenital abnormality. The hope that this reference might gain sympathy and tolerance from the wider public was in vain. What it did was to stigmatise homosexuality still further.

The term 'gay' as we use it to mean homosexuality, and specifically homosexual men, seems to have been in popular use as a reference to general sexual overtones for the past two to three hundred years, according to Rictor Norton, as well as its innocent meaning of joyful and merry. In the eighteenth century, lewd sexual behaviour was part of the 'gay life' and participated in by both men and women. Rakes and hell-raisers, young men who wasted their inherited fortunes on gambling, wine and women, were often called 'gay blades'.

The Oxford English Dictionary's definition of 'gay' is '(especially of a man) homosexual – relating to or used by homosexuals', and a dated use of the word in terms of 'light-hearted and carefree' or 'brightly coloured and showy.' Such exuberant, casual and carefree characteristics were also applied to girls working the streets in the nineteenth century. Consequently, they were called 'gay ladies', and the brothels in which they plied their trade were known as 'gay houses'. As male prostitutes also cruised the same streets and districts, they too acquired the same prefix.

Today the word 'gay' is almost entirely synonymous with homosexuals and homosexuality. Though the word itself is owned by homosexuals to describe themselves, it is also used in derogatory terms to denote anything seen as weak, feeble and/or odd. Not so long ago the terminology for these effete characteristics, or anything that was perceived as 'odd' and not understood, was known as 'queer', which also had undertones of mental deficiency, disorder and abnormality attached to it. Recently, 'queer' has been taken back by many in the LGBT community, who use it to describe their diversity and often fluid sense of being and sexuality.

19.
Oscar Wilde - 1895

1895 is significant in that it was the year 'a love that dare not speak its name' was brought before the courts in the highly-publicised trial of Oscar Wilde. Newspaper headlines from the day need little clarification in revealing the shock that swept through Victorian society about this case: 'Both Guilty. Oscar Wilde and Alfred Taylor Convicted of Unnatural Charges', says one; another headline reads 'Oscar Wilde is found guilty... The Judge regrets that the Law will not permit a more severe penalty.' And this from another paper; 'Moral Lepers of London. English Public Opinion Cries: 'Unclean, Unclean!' Wilde will be punished.'

Born in Ireland in 1854, Oscar Wilde was a playwright, novelist, essayist and poet, and became one of London's most popular playwrights by the 1890s. Renowned for his sharp wit, extravagant style of dress and his dazzling repartee, he was one of the best-known personalities of his day. Today, he is remembered as much for his essays, his novel *The Picture of Dorian Gray* and his plays, such as *The Importance of Being Earnest* and *Lady Windermere's Fan*, as he is for the circumstances which led to his trial, imprisonment, and subsequent early death.

In mid-1891, Wilde was introduced to Lord Alfred Douglas by Alfred Taylor, a young man who inherited a large fortune of £45,000 upon the death of his father, a successful cocoa manufacturer. A private education and a stint in the Royal Fusiliers did nothing for Taylor and the twenty-one-year-old admitted later that since his inheritance he had had no occupation at all and simply lived 'a life of pleasure'. In 1894, Taylor and a female impersonator, by the name of Arthur Marling, were arrested for wearing women's clothing at a party in Fitzroy Street, London.

Alfred Taylor, it is claimed, introduced Oscar Wilde to several young men. One of these was the young, handsome and utterly spoilt Lord Alfred Douglas. Known as Bosie to his family and friends, he was at the time an undergraduate at Oxford. Soon after their meeting, an intimate friendship developed between Wilde and Bosie, and by 1893 Wilde was infatuated and a tempestuous affair ensued.

If Oscar Wilde was renowned for his indiscretions and flamboyant manner, Douglas was positively reckless in his behaviour when he was out in public. Wilde, who at the time was earning up to £100 a week from his plays, indulged Douglas's every whim, material, artistic and sexual, and he soon found himself dragged into the seedy underworld of Victorian London and the joys of rent boys. These sexual assignations were to Wilde 'like feasting with panthers', and the danger of discovery was all part of the excitement.

Lord Alfred's father, the Marquess of Queensberry, who was the inventor of the Queensberry Rules for boxing, was outspoken and brutish, and often fell out with Bosie over the nature of his relationship with the older Wilde. Enraged one day, the Marquess is reported to have told Wilde, 'I do not say that you are it, but you look it, and pose at it, which is just as bad. And if I catch you and my son again in any public restaurant, I will thrash you.' Wilde responded, 'I don't know what the Queensberry rules are, but the Oscar Wilde rule is to shoot on sight.'

On 18 February 1895, the Marquess left a calling card at Wilde's club. It was inscribed, 'For Oscar Wilde, posing sodomite.' Wilde, encouraged by Douglas, yet against the advice of his friends, initiated a private prosecution against Queensberry for libel, since the note amounted to a public accusation that Wilde had committed a crime. Queensberry was arrested for criminal libel, a charge carrying a possible sentence of up to two years in prison. Under the 1843 Libel Act, Queensberry could avoid conviction for if he could demonstrate that his accusation was in fact true, and that there was a 'public benefit' in having openly made the accusation. Queensberry's lawyers thus hired private detectives to unearth evidence of Wilde's homosexual liaisons. They decided on a strategy of portraying Wilde as a depraved older man who habitually enticed naive youths into a life of vicious homosexuality.

The trial opened on 3rd April 1895 amid scenes of near hysteria as the scandalous details of Wilde's private life began to emerge and subsequently appear in the papers. The extent of the evidence massed against Wilde forced him to declare in court, 'I am the prosecutor in this case' as the salacious accusations of his associations with underworld blackmailers, male prostitutes and visits to molly-houses (male brothels) were recorded in various witness interviews. On the advice of his lawyers, Wilde dropped the prosecution. Queensberry was found not guilty and his accusation that Wilde was 'posing as a sodomite' was justified. Queensberry's acquittal meant that Wilde was liable for the considerable costs the Marquess had incurred to mount his defence. Wilde was left bankrupt.

After Wilde left the court, a warrant for his arrest was immediately applied for on charges of sodomy and gross indecency. Alfred Taylor was arrested the following day and both men were charged with offences of gross indecency. To his credit, Taylor refused to give evidence against Wilde. The trial opened on 26th April 1895. Wilde pleaded not guilty. Under cross examination around the content of a poem written by Lord Alfred Douglas, Wilde spoke, at first hesitantly, but then with eloquence:

Charles Gill (prosecuting): What is 'the love that dare not speak its name'?

Wilde: 'The love that dare not speak its name', in this century is such a great affection of an elder for a younger man as there was between David and Jonathan, such as Plato made the very basis of his philosophy, and such as you find in the sonnets of Michelangelo and Shakespeare. It is that deep spiritual affection that is as pure as it is perfect. It dictates and pervades great works of art, like those of Shakespeare and Michelangelo, and those two letters of mine, such as they are. It is in this century misunderstood, so much misunderstood that it may be described as 'the love that dare not speak its name', and on that account of it I am placed where I am now. It is beautiful, it is fine, it is the noblest form of affection. There is nothing unnatural about it. It is intellectual, and it repeatedly exists between an older and a younger man, when the older man has intellect, and the younger man has all the joy, hope and glamour of life before him. That it should be so, the world does not understand. The world mocks at it, and sometimes puts one in the pillory for it.'

This response was counter-productive in a legal sense as it only served to reinforce the charges of homosexual behaviour. However, the trial ended with the jury unable to reach a verdict. Wilde's counsel, Sir Edward Clarke, was finally able to get a magistrate to allow Wilde and his friends to post bail. Edward Carson, Queensberry's counsel, approached Frank Lockwood QC, the Solicitor General and asked, 'Can we not let up on the fellow now?' Lockwood answered that he would like to do so but feared that the case had become too politicised to be dropped.

The final trial was held on 25th May 1895, whereupon Wilde and Alfred Taylor were convicted of gross indecency and sentenced to two years' hard labour. The judge described the sentence, the maximum allowed, as 'totally inadequate for a case such as this,' and that it was 'the worst case I have ever tried.' Wilde's response was thus, 'And I? May I say nothing, my Lord?' was drowned out by cries of 'Shame!' from around the courtroom.

In 1897, whilst in prison, Wilde wrote *De Profundis* – From the Depths – a long letter in which he discussed his spiritually dark journey through his trials. Upon his release, he left immediately for France, never to return. There he wrote his last work, *The Ballad of Reading Gaol* (1898), a long poem commemorating the harsh conditions and daily rhythms of prison life. Destitute and living in Paris, he died in 1900 at the age of just forty-six. He is buried at the Père Lachaise cemetery in Paris. The large tomb by Jacob Epstein was erected in 1914, after it's commission by Wilde's literary executor in 1908.

De Profundis was published in 1905:

When first I was put into prison some people advised me to try and forget who I was. It was ruinous advice. It is only by realising what I am that I have found comfort of any kind. Now I am advised by others to try on my release to forget that I have ever been in a prison at all. I know that would be equally fatal. It would mean that I would always be haunted by an intolerable sense of disgrace, and that those things that are meant for me as much as for anybody else – the beauty of the sun and moon, the pageant of the seasons, the music of daybreak and the silence of great nights, the rain falling through the leaves, or the dew creeping over the grass and making it silver – would all be tainted for me, and lose their healing power, and their power of communicating joy. To regret one's own experiences is to arrest one's own development. To deny one's own experiences is to put a lie into the lips of one's own life. It is no less than a denial of the soul.

'The love that dare not speak its name' is a phrase from the poem *Two Loves* by Lord Alfred Douglas, published in 1894, and used as a euphemism for gross indecency at Wilde's trial.

'...I fell a-weeping, and I cried, 'Sweet youth,
Tell me why, sad and sighing, thou dost rove
These pleasant realms? I pray thee speak me sooth
What is thy name? He said, 'My name is Love.'
Then straight the first did turn himself to me
And cried, 'He lieth, for his name is Shame,
But I am Love, and I was wont to be
Alone in this fair garden, till he came
Unasked by night; I am true Love, I fill

The hearts of boy and girl with mutual flame.'
Then sighing, said the other, 'Have thy will,
I am the love that dare not speak its name.'

-    Alfred Douglas

20.
A Secret Society - 1897

The first organized group dedicated to the culture and spiritual ethos of homosexuals was set up in London by George Cecil Ives in 1897. Ives, a friend of Oscar Wilde's, established The Order of Chaeronea, when aestheticism was at its height in a 'heady mix of art, idealism and politics', to further the cause of same-sex desire through a secret society of homosexual intellects. Knowing that it would not be accepted openly by the public, he structured an elaborate system of communication between its members by the use of codes and passwords. The name 'Chaeronea' was taken from the town in Greece where the remains of an elite army, the Sacred Band of Thebes, were excavated early in the nineteenth century. A great battle that occurred there in 338BC saw the slaughter of a previously-undefeated hand-picked battalion of 300men, 150 older *erastes* (lovers) and their younger male *eromenos* (beloved) partners, before Greece fell to Macedonia.

The mythological status of the Sacred Band of Thebes ascended to new heights when the statue of a lion, reported by Pausanius to have marked the burial ground of the battalion, was discovered and unearthed by George Ledwell Taylor in 1818. Later excavations found a rectangular area with seven rows of 254 skeletons laid out in it.

The Sacred Band of Thebes is a fitting analogy to the legend of King Arthur and the Knights of the Round Table. The Arthurian legend was steeped in homoeroticism and the Gothic revival of Medieval England was very much in vogue in the Victorian era. Ives' secretive system of rituals and ceremonies for his Order of Chaeronea followed a specific philosophy, 'That all real love shall be to you as sanctuary'. The 'Rules of

Purpose' for the group's members stated that the new order was to be 'A Religion, a Theory of Life and Ideal of Duty'. Ives stressed that the Order was not to be used as a venue for men to meet up with other men in liaisons, although this undoubtedly happened. Membership was to be partaken with 'Zeal, Learning and Discipline'. 'We believe in the glory of passion. We believe in the inspiration of emotion. We believe in the holiness of love.'

In 1913, Ives went on to co-found the British Society for the Study of Sex Psychology (later the British Sexological Society) with Edward Carpenter, Magnus Hirschfeld and others. The society's manifesto was to oppose discrimination against homosexuality with scientific studies of sex and sexual conduct, including issues such as birth control, abortion, sterilization, venereal disease and prostitution, as well as homosexuality. Never a group of large numbers, a few hundred at its height, the society continued with minimal finances until around 1941 and the war became a more pressing matter. One society publication was re-issued in 1947 and a 'Sexological Society Library' operated up until 1951.

Ives himself died in Lewisham, London, in 1950. He left a large archive of work, including diaries, papers and correspondence, covering the period 1874 to 1949. The papers were purchased by the Harry Ransom Center at the University of Texas, Austin, in 1977, where they are held today.

21.
Surveys and Statistics - 1904

Magnus Hirschfeld, the German physician and sexologist, was the first person to conduct research and release statistical data on the number of homosexual men in the German population at the beginning of the twentieth century. Hirschfeld centred his work around his collection of material on homosexual behaviour and research into the psychological profile of same-sex desirous personalities. In 1903, in what was the world's first survey of its kind, the Scientific Humanitarian Committee (WhK) sent out approximately 8,000 questionnaires to men: 3,000 to students at a Charlottenburg technical college and 5,000 to metal workers in Berlin factories. He asked a single simple question: was the respondent attracted to women, men, or both?

Of the students who responded, 1.5% said they were homosexuals and 4.5% bisexuals. Of the 5,000 metalworkers, 1.15% said they were homosexuals and 3.19% said they were bisexuals. The survey results were rounded up and Hirschfeld's conclusion was that 2.2% of the whole male German population was homosexual and 3.2% were bisexual.

Hirschfeld's theory was that there was a basic constant proportion of homosexuals living in the population, and that their countries, cultures or indeed, the historical period in which they lived had no bearing on this. This reinforced his belief that the definition of homosexuality was a natural category, intermediate between male and female – a third sex, which many cultures recognise. This overall figure of 2.2% was sensational but proved Hirschfeld's theory that many homosexual men successfully managed to hide their sexual orientation from the outside world. The results were published the following year in the *Jahrbuch für Sexual Zwischenstufen* (Yearbook for the Sexually In-between), which was published regularly between 1899 and 1923 and was the first such publication in the world to focus on the scientific studies of homosexual behaviour.

One disgruntled pastor by the name of Wilhelm Philips of Plotzensee filed charges against Hirschfeld for his distribution of indecent literature, and slander on behalf of six upset students. Hirschfeld had already reported on the many cases of suicide among homosexual men, including one at the Charlottenburg college. He therefore insisted that there was a need for information to better understand the situation of homosexuals and that compassion should be shown towards them. In the end, he was fined 200 marks and the court threw out the charge of indecency Pastor Philips had brought against him.

Another measure by which Hirschfeld sought to document sexual behaviour was via a 'psychobiological questionnaire'. It is said that he collected over 40,000 completed forms, though this cannot be verified, and by today's standards the questions posed were biased and often clichéd. For example, respondents were asked to report on their play behaviour as children: 'Did you prefer to play with boys or girls? Did you prefer boys' games, such as throwing snow balls, play-fighting, hobby-horses, soldiers, etc, or did you prefer feminine child play, such as dolls, cooking, crocheting, knitting?'

The WhK went on to acquire international fame and attracted doctors, researchers, intellectuals and journalists from around the world. Much of the related literature from the period is full of references to the institute. The French journalist Louis-Charles Royer, author of *Love Camp* and other soft-porn erotic literature, described in *L'Amour en Allemagne* (Love in Germany) how he was asked to complete one of the 48-page psychological questionnaires and gave his French readers lengthy detail about Hirschfeld's institute. He described the galleried staircase, displaying photo-portraits of well-known personalities who were inverts or transvestites, and glass cabinets filled with articles of fetishism and material relating to Siamese twins, sadomasochism and hermaphrodites, and a portrait of the Chevalier d'Eon that hung in Hirschfeld's private office. (Chevalier d'Eon was a French diplomat and spy who was famously androgyne in appearance, making him ideal as a spy. In public he presented as a man, but he successfully infiltrated the court of Empress Elizabeth of Russia in 1756 by taking on the persona of a woman. After his death doctors examined his body and concluded that he was a male in 'every respect perfectly formed', but that he also had feminine characteristics.)

According to its annual report, in the year 1919-1920 the WhK carried out 18,000 consultations with a total of 3,500 people, two thirds of whom were men, and of that cohort 30% were homosexuals. Obtaining precise figures on the number of homosexuals within any society is fraught with difficulty for many reasons. Firstly, the society itself plays a huge part in how willing or able a person is in identifying their sexuality. For instance, though same-sex activity between men was illegal in Germany at the time Hirschfeld was conducting his surveys, it was nothing to the anti-homosexual atmosphere of the Nazi period from 1933 onwards. It would have been too risky then to even suggest that you were that way inclined; and indeed, much of the data material Hirschfeld had accumulated in his research was used by the Gestapo to hunt down homosexuals and send them to the concentration camps.

In Britain today, data on sexuality is gathered in the ten-yearly census, but the results are by no means a litmus test of the true sexual make-up of the nation, as so many leave that particular question blank or lie, for many different reasons. Secondly, studies also tend to pose two sets of questions, one examining same-sex sexual experiences and/or attraction, while another examines data surrounding personal identification as homosexual or bisexual. Add to this the quandary that being 'gay' is not a term that would necessarily be recognised by all men who have sex with other men (MSM). In 2017, a nationally representative study carried out by Kantar TNS concluded that 87% of British men aged 18 to 30 years identify as heterosexual, 7% as homosexual, 5% as bisexual, and 2% as other – statistics that show a much greater percentage identifying as homosexual than Hirschfeld determined from his research of German students and metalworkers back in 1903. This could indicate the progress Western liberal society has made over the past hundred or so years but is by no means conclusive.

22.
Gay Love on Film - 1919

The first silent movie to have gay love as its central theme, was *Anders als die Andern* (Different from the Others), a German-produced film released in 1919 during the time of the Weimar Republic. It starred Conrad Veidt and Fritz Schulz and was co-written by Richard Oswald and Dr. Magnus Hirschfeld, the physician and sexologist, who helped fund the film's production through his institution, the WhK. The aim of the film was to present the story of tormented same-sex love interspersed with documentary-style commentary by Hirschfeld via the intertitles, as a persuasive argument against the Paragraph 175 ruling, which made homosexuality a criminal offence in Germany.

The film's plot revolves around a violinist, played by Veidt, who falls in love with one of his pupils, Kurt Sivers, played by Fritz Schulz. It opens with the violin teacher, Paul Korner, reading the obituaries column in his daily newspaper, which are filled with the vaguely-worded and unexplained suicides of several men. Korner believes they are linked to the terrible law of Paragraph 175 which states: 'Unnatural fornication, whether between persons of the male sex or of humans with beasts, is punished with imprisonment, with the further punishment of a prompt loss of civil rights.'

Sivers approaches Korner in the hope that he will agree to give him violin lessons. Their passions for music and one another seem to be a perfect match, and they spend more and more time together. Sivers' parents suspect something is wrong and become worried about their son's infatuation with the violin teacher. Korner appears to have no interest in getting married or starting a family, and his mother and father, with their suspicions raised, go to see the family doctor, played by Magnus Hirschfeld.

'You must not condemn your son,' the doctor tells them, speaking directly to camera and the film's audience via the intertitles. 'Because he is a homosexual, he is not to blame for his orientation. It is not wrong, nor should it be a crime. Indeed, it is not even an illness, merely a variation, and one that is common to all of nature.'

After a failed session of hypnotism and in despair of his homosexual feelings, Korner visits the doctor himself, who tells him and the watching audience: 'Love for one's own sex can be just as pure and noble as that for the opposite sex. This orientation is to be found among many respectable people in all levels of society.' With the gravest sincerity he tells Korner, 'Only ignorance or bigotry can condemn those who feel differently. Don't despair! As a homosexual, you can still make valuable contributions to humanity.'

The film closes with a brush stroke crossing through the dreaded Paragraph 175. *Anders als die Andern* was not only pioneering in its choice of topic but also for creating one of the first films to directly engage the public and educate them on homosexuality. Its premier in May 1919 was followed by an initial flurry of success, but shortly afterwards, conservative religious and right-wing groups started turning up at cinema screenings to cause disruption and embarrassment to audience members. At the time, the Weimar Republic was a supporter of freedom of speech and individual expression, and it was even written into the constitution that 'No censorship will take place', though The Film Assessment Headquarters, set up in Berlin, already regulated pornography. The release of *Anders als die Andern* prompted further debate on censorship, for although the film was not pornographic its subject matter was considered biased in respect of Paragraph 175, and it was feared that its presentation of homosexuality could have been confusing to a younger audience or persuade viewers to turn homosexual. The Film Assessment Headquarters panel, made up of opponents of Hirschfeld and his advocacy towards homosexuality, finally advised that the film should be banned from public screening in October 1920. The film was only allowed to be shown in private, and for educational purposes to medical professionals. In the end, the only place it was screened was at Hirschfeld's institute offices.

When the Nazis came to power all known copies of the film were destroyed. Fortunately, Hirschfeld had already included forty minutes of the original footage in a scientific film called *Laws of Love*, which was shown in Russia in the late twenties and early thirties and remained hidden in archives there for decades afterwards. In 2011, UCLA Film and Television Archive purchased a fine-grain master positive (a high-definition print used to create additional film negatives) from the Russian film archive, with the aim of creating a feature out of the forty minutes of film that was both faithful to the original story and which a modern audience could relate to.

23.
The Nazis and the Night of the Long Knives - 1933

Throughout the last decades of the nineteenth century and continuing into the twentieth, German physicists, sexologists and writers continued to investigate and present homosexuality not as an abomination, but as an alternative way of being. They led the world. From Karl Ulrichs to Dr Magnus Hirschfeld, German academics were at the forefront of investigative research into the subject.

Magnus Hirschfeld founded the Scientific Humanitarian Committee, the first-ever official organization to campaign for the social recognition of homosexuals, bisexuals and transgender men and women, and sought to repeal Paragraph 175 under German legislation, which made homosexual acts between men a crime. At its peak the organization, known by its German acronym WhK, had 500 members and branches in more than 20 cities across Germany, Austria and the Netherlands.

Another advocate for the homosexual cause was Adolf Brand, the writer, activist, and publisher of the early German gay periodical *Der Eigene* – The Unique – (1896). A huge scandal erupted in 1907 when he published an article outing the then Chancellor, Prince Bernhard von Bülow, for having a long-standing homosexual relationship with the Privy Councilor, Max Scheefer. The Prince sued Brand for libel and won. Brand spent eighteen months in prison, but steadfastly maintained, 'When a person joins a party that raises such an indecent view to a program and would like to set in the most damaging way, the intimate love contact of others under degrading control, in that moment his own love life has ceased to be a private matter and forfeits every claim to remain protected henceforward from scrutiny and suspicious oversight.' Brand was adamant that these swindlers of political hypocrisy, who proclaimed anti-homosexual rhetoric while continuing themselves to have same-sex relations and liaisons with rent boys should be outed. Brand curbed his activities during the First World War and Der Eigene did not appear again until 1919.

This movement of political awareness and scientific research into homosexuality came to a crashing halt however when the Nazis took power and Adolf Hitler was appointed Chancellor in 1933. In February of that year, the Nazis launched a purge on homosexual clubs and bars in Berlin, outlawed sex publications and banned organised groups that promoted homosexuality. Known homosexuals were jailed and later sent to concentration camps. If they survived, they did so only after suffering extreme cruelty.

In May 1933, a series of public book burnings was organised, targeted at academic and literary works the Nazi party viewed as 'un-German'. They were attended by huge crowds. Hirschfeld's extensive library at the Institute for Sexual Research was ransacked and the entire contents, including the research archive, were hauled out onto the Opernplatz and burned. An estimated 20,000 books and journals and 5000 images, were destroyed. More worrying were the extensive lists of names and addresses of those who had taken part in the research, which were seized by the Gestapo, along with the building. Hirschfeld himself had fortuitously left Germany on a speaking tour and was in Switzerland at the time. He never returned, but instead went into exile in Paris, where he endeavoured to re-establish the Institute. In 1935, however, he died in Nice from a heart attack before this was ever realised.

Adolf Brand gave up homosexual activism in the early 1930s after constant harassment from the Nazis, who had already shut down Der Eigene and destroyed his life's work, leaving him in financial ruin. He continued to make a stand for five months after the book burnings, but in November 1933 he was forced to publish a letter to all his supporters announcing the end of the movement. He remained in Germany, and he and his wife were killed in a bombing raid by the Allies on 2nd February 1945.

Hitler's determined pursuit and eradication of homosexuals continued, and on 30th June 1934, in what became known as the Night of the Long Knives, the leader of the SA, Ernst Rohm, was arrested and later executed. Rohm was known to be a homosexual and on the night of the raid at the Hotel Lederer am See in Bad Wiessee, where he and other SA leaders were staying, the SS also found, amongst others, the SA leader for Breslau, Edmund Heines, in bed with an eighteen-year-old male senior SA troop leader. Both were taken outside and summarily shot.

The Night of the Long Knives was infamous for the murders of many of Hitler's opponents and was followed by even stricter laws on homosexuality and an increased crackdown on what Goebbels described as part of a 'moral turpitude'.

The pink triangle symbol denoting a prisoner as homosexual was first introduced in Nazi concentration camps in 1937. It was one of many different coloured triangles of material that made up a classification system and were sewn onto prisoner's uniforms as a means of identification. Homosexuals wearing the pink triangle were on the bottom rung when it came to camp hierarchy. While the number of homosexuals imprisoned by the Nazis is hard to estimate, Richard Plant, who was himself a gay Jewish émigré and who fled persecution to Switzerland in 1933, estimates the number of men convicted for homosexuality by the Nazis between 1933 to 1944, 'at between fifty to sixty-three thousand.' Following his retirement in 1973, and inspired by the growing Gay Liberation Movement, Plant wrote a book, *The Pink Triangle: The Nazi War against Homosexuals*, which was published in 1986.

24.
Germany - 1945

Estimates range between 50,000 and 100,000 men were arrested from 1933 to 1945 by the Nazis for violating their stringent laws against homosexuality. Of these, approximately 50,000 were given prison sentences. An estimated 5000-15,000 men were further sent on to the concentration camps, where an unknown number of them perished. In 1934, the Gestapo instructed local police forces to keep lists of all men engaged in homosexual activities. This practice had already been commonplace for the police in many parts of Germany for years. The Nazis then used these 'pink lists' to hunt down individuals during their police actions.

On 28th June 1935, the German Ministry of Justice revised Paragraph 175, which made homosexual acts between men a crime. The revisions provided a legal basis for extending the Nazis' persecution of homosexuals in their quest to eliminate them from the Aryan race. The Nazis saw homosexuality as a disease that should be eradicated from society in order that every male succeeded in his potential to father children. Ministry officials expanded the category of 'criminally indecent activities between men' to include any act that could be construed as homosexual. The courts later advocated that even intent or thought was enough guilt to warrant a prison sentence.

On October 26, 1936, Himmler formed a new department within the SS; the Reich Central Office for Combating Abortion and Homosexuality. The new expansive law and the increased power of the police gave them the right to hold in 'protective custody' or 'preventive arrest' those deemed dangerous to Germany's moral fibre, jailing for indefinite periods and without trial anyone they wanted. Homosexual prisoners who were released from jail after having served their sentences were often immediately re-arrested and sent on to concentration camps under the supposition that it was thought likely that they would continue to engage in homosexual acts.

In the concentration camps, prisoners were categorised and identified by the wearing of a badge on the tunic of their striped uniform. Criminals wore green inverted triangles, political prisoners red, while 'a-socials', including nonconformists, vagrants and other groups, wore a black triangle. Roma people wore black or brown, Jews wore the yellow Star of David, and so on. Homosexuals wore the pink triangle. Prisoners marked by pink triangles were treated severely in the camps. According to many survivors' accounts, homosexuals were among the most abused groups. Rudolf Hoess, commandant of Auschwitz, segregated them to prevent homosexuality from spreading to other inmates and the guards. The Nazis' belief that homosexuality, like any other disease, was contagious, seems to have been widely held. As with other clinical diseases, finding a 'cure' for homosexuality was of paramount interest, and with a captive and expendable group at their disposal, medical experiments on inmates soon included homosexuals. These experiments often caused illness, mutilation and death, and produced no scientific data or practical knowledge. If they survived the experiments, inmates would simply report that they had been 'cured' just so that they could be moved back to the main camp.

Though individual homosexual inmates could secure a measure of protection in some ways, for example by ingratiating themselves with their barrack Kapos as batmen and sex-slaves, as a group, homosexual prisoners did not enjoy the support network that was common amongst other inmates. Without this help in moderating the barrage of abuse and brutality, their survival rates were, on average, no longer than two months. Many died from the beatings they received from the SS guards and their barrack Kapos, and some as a result of the violence inflicted on them by their fellow prisoners. While it is difficult to ascertain actual figures, it is estimated that 60% of homosexuals sent to the concentration camps died there; this, compared to 41% of political prisoners and 35% of Jehovah's Witnesses. Though for the Jews and the Roma the official Nazi policy was extermination, this was not the case for homosexuals. The goal to eliminate them from society was to do so by means of 're-education' either through hard work and forced labour, or 'reverse' sexuality through medical experimentation and castration.

At the Nuremberg trials that followed the Allies' victory, and the liberation of the concentration camps, no mention was made of the crimes the Nazis and the SS committed against homosexuals. No SS official was ever tried for specific atrocities against homosexual prisoners, and many of the known SS doctors who had performed grotesque operations on homosexuals were never held to account for their actions. One of the most notorious of those was Danish SS Major Carl Peter Vaernet, who performed numerous experiments on homosexual inmates at Buchenwald concentration camp where he tried to 'cure' inmates' homosexuality by injecting synthetic hormones into their testicles. He was never tried for his crimes and escaped to South America, where he died a free man in 1965.

After the war, homosexuals who survived the concentration camps were not acknowledged as victims of Nazi persecution. Hundreds of thousands of prisoners were liberated, and the Allied Military Government of Germany revoked countless laws and decrees in the following months and years. Left unchanged, however, was the 1935 Nazi revision of Paragraph 175. Some homosexuals were even forced to serve out their prison terms regardless of the time they'd served in the concentration camps. Survivors could also be re-imprisoned for repeat offences and their names kept on modern pink lists of 'sex offenders'. Reparations and state pensions that were available to other groups were refused to homosexuals under the guise that they were still classified as criminals.

The 1935 version of Paragraph 175 remained in force in West Germany until 1969, when finally, the law was revised by the Bundestag and homosexual relations between men over the age of twenty-one was decriminalised. The first gay bar in post-war Berlin opened in the summer of 1945, and the first drag ball took place in the American sector that autumn.

Many liberated homosexuals who had survived the camps and were not subjected to further prison terms found themselves ostracised from society. Some were not welcomed back to their homes or communities for the shame they brought on their family's reputation. Those that did return often kept their experiences to themselves, fearing that the sensitive nature of the horrors they had experienced would bring further distress to family members. Many never spoke of their suffering again.

The Nazis' anti-gay policies and their destruction of the early German gay rights movement were generally not considered suitable subject matter for Holocaust historians and academics to pursue. It wasn't until the 1970s and 80s that there was any mainstream exploration of the subject, and only then when Holocaust survivors began writing their memoirs. The play *Bent* (1979) by Martin Sherman, about the persecution of homosexuals in Nazi Germany, which takes place during and after the Night of the Long Knives, signalled a wider interest, and more historical research and documentaries began to be published.

Recognition did eventually come, but half a century too late for many of the homosexual victims and survivors, who, in the eyes of the law, lived the rest of their lives as criminals. While memorials were erected to remember the millions of other victims of the Holocaust, it was fifty-four years before one such memorial included homosexuals. In January 1999 Germany finally held its first official memorial service for homosexual victims at the former Sachsenhausen concentration camp, where the largest number of homosexuals were murdered.

It wasn't until December 2000 that an apology came from the German government, when it issued an admission of guilt for the prosecution of homosexuals in Germany after the war and agreed to recognise homosexuals as a specific group of victims of the Nazis. Survivors were encouraged to come forward and claim compensation for their treatment during the Holocaust. Claims had to be registered before the end of 2001. On 17th May 2002 the process was completed as thousands of homosexuals who had suffered under the Third Reich were officially pardoned by the German government. About 50,000 men were included. The justice minister, Hertha Daeubler-Gmelin, told the German parliament, 'We all know that our decisions today are more than fifty years late, they are necessary nonetheless. We owe it to the victims of wrongful Nazi justice.' A memorial to the homosexuals who died in Nazi concentration camps was unveiled in May 2008 opposite the main Holocaust memorial for Jewish victims in Tiergarten Park in Berlin.

25.
Purges and Police Raids - 1954

Police enforcement of laws against homosexuality was rigorously pursued in the 1950s. By the end of 1954 there were 1,069 homosexual men held behind bars in England and Wales, with an average age of 37. The prevailing atmosphere homosexual men experienced at the time amounted to a sanctioned witch-hunt against them, as the number of incidents brought before the courts during the 50s doubled that of the interwar years. With the increasing police activity around establishments that attracted homosexuals, the proprietors and other 'masculine' gay men who frequented these places became less willing to accept the overt flamboyance of camp gay men, known as 'queans', who always attracted a flurry of unwanted interest. At the same time, the public started to become aware of the 'modern medical causes' of sexual differences. Rather than being a caricature of 'womanhood', homosexuality was seen, for the first time, as a choice of sexual partner for some men. The morality of that was still in question, but it was no longer about men trying to be women. If those queans wore drag, they did so only in particular venues. Mostly, they lived their everyday lives as men. The quean soon became a rapidly declining minority.

During the 1950s a range of treatments were developed to change homosexuals into heterosexuals. These treatments, the most common of which was aversion therapy, were not based on any evidence of their effectiveness. Participants of a study into the effects of such treatments given to many homosexual men in the period between 1950 and 1970 often comment on the extreme negativity of the British media at the time. 'There were no positive role models and the newspapers were full of the most vituperative filth that made me feel suicidal...

I felt totally bewildered that my entire emotional life was being written up in the papers as utter filth and perversity,' said one man. Some men did take tentative steps to try to understand, and in some way resolve, their situations, by requesting help from mental health professionals. Others, knowing that they could not live the rest of their lives in a constant state of anxiety and unfulfillment, contacted their GPs about their homosexual feelings. However, doctors often lacked any knowledge of the subject. One man quoted his doctor's reaction, 'He said he'd never had any experience with this and no one had ever raised this before. He said, "if you come back next week I'll do some research." I went back to see the GP and he said, "well, I've been in touch with colleagues. Obviously, you can't go on living with the stress and the way you are – it's wrong, it's perverse, it's a sickness."'

The general outcome for men who talked to their GPs about their homosexual feelings, was to be referred on to NHS professionals. The age range for treatment was 13-40 years. Most of the cases quoted in the study were treated in their late twenties. Treatments were mainly administered in NHS hospitals throughout Britain, the most common being behavioural aversion therapy with electric shocks. In this treatment, electrodes were attached to the wrist or lower leg and shocks were administered while the patient viewed photographs of men and women in various stages of undress. The aim was to encourage avoidance of the shock by moving the patient towards photographs of the opposite sex. It was hoped that arousal to photographs of the same sex would reduce, while relief arising from shock avoidance would increase interest in the opposite-sex images. Patients would recline on a bed or sit in a chair in a darkened room, either alone or with a professional behind a screen. Each treatment lasted about 30 minutes. Some participants were given portable electric shock boxes to use at home while they induced their own sexual fantasies. Another therapy was prescribed apomorphine, a strong dopamine administered through injection or by infusion pump. Patients were often admitted to hospital due to side effects of nausea and dehydration and the need for repeated doses, while those receiving electric shock aversion therapy attended as outpatients for weeks afterwards, or in some cases up to two years post treatment. Other forms of treatment included oestrogen to reduce libido, psychoanalysis, religious counselling and discussions around the evils of homosexuality, and desensitisation to an assumed phobia of the opposite sex. Psychodrama, in which patients were encouraged to act out past events, and the release of repressed emotions through suggestion and hypnosis, were also used. Even dating skills were sometimes taught, and occasionally men were encouraged to go out and find a prostitute or a willing female friend with whom they should try to have sexual intercourse.

The contrast between the depth of their sexual feelings and the simplicity of the treatment made many doubt the wisdom of the approach. Most became disillusioned and stopped the treatments themselves. One former patient in the study was quoted as saying: 'I said, "when am I going to find a breakthrough? You keep saying things will change and everything's going to be OK." She [the psychiatrist] said, "well, I'm going to have to tell you now, I don't think we are going to get anywhere. To be quite honest I never expected we would in the first place. You're going to have to go home and tell your wife that you're gay and start a new life."'

These men were not criminals; they had not been convicted of any crime but had simply tried to seek help. One respondent reported that his brother had died from the side effects of apomorphine, usually given these days to people with advanced Parkinson's who do not respond to other oral drugs. Several men in the study sought out further treatment, usually private psychoanalysis, but none of them continued with further behavioural treatments. 'From a guilt-ridden Christian point of view,' one man said, 'the treatment meant that at least I had tried to do something, and it had proved not to work. I'd done my bit to try and deal with the problem and I found that comforting.' None of the participants who had undergone any of these treatments believed that there were any benefits, and for many, it simply reinforced the emotional isolation and shame they felt, which had been a constant feature of their childhoods and adolescence. Occasionally, it meant they were finally able to accept their sexuality, but many also retained a sense of 'loss and unease'.

Antony Grey, who later became secretary of the Homosexual Law Reform Society (HLRS), describes in a *Guardian* interview how living with a man in the 1950s was 'a dangerous business'. After a drunk coach driver crashed into their parked car outside their house in the middle of the night, 'the first thing we had to do was make up the spare bed. We knew from experience that if you called the police and they suspected you were homosexual, they would ignore the original crime and concentrate on the homosexuality.'

The mathematician Alan Turing, now famously celebrated and remembered for his work in cracking the Germans' Enigma code during the Second World War, was a victim of just such misplaced criminalisation when, in 1952, he also reported a break-in at his house to the police. Turing had started a relationship with Arnold Murray, a 19-year-old whom he'd met just before Christmas. A few weeks later in January, Turing's house was broken into. Murray said he knew who the burglar was. Turing immediately reported it. During the investigation he acknowledged that he was having a sexual relationship with Murray, and subsequently both men were arrested and charged with gross indecency. A trial followed at the end of March. Turing did not argue or provide evidence against the allegations and was therefore convicted of the offence and given a choice between imprisonment and probation, which was conditional on his agreement to undergo hormonal treatment designed to reduce libido, or treatment by injection of a synthetic oestrogen for the course of one year. Turing opted for the latter, which left him impotent and with enlarged breasts. Eloquently, Turing predicted: 'no doubt I shall emerge from it all a different man, but quite who, I've not found out'. Murray, meanwhile, was given a conditional discharge.

Turing's conviction led to the removal of his security clearance and barred him from continuing with his cryptographic consultancy for the Government Communications Headquarters, or GCHQ, though he kept his academic job. The trial was not widely reported at the time and his work at Bletchley Park during the war was not spoken of until it became declassified in the 1970s.

On 8th June 1954, he was found dead by his housekeeper. The post-mortem examination found that the cause of death was cyanide poisoning. When his body was discovered, a half-eaten apple lay beside his bed, and although the apple was not tested for cyanide, it was speculated that this was the likely means by which he had consumed the fatal dose. Consequently, the inquest determined that he had committed suicide. There have since been some questions raised about Turing's intention to take his own life, such as that from Professor Jack Copeland, who suggests that the cause might have been the accidental inhalation of cyanide fumes from an apparatus for electroplating gold onto spoons, which uses potassium cyanide to dissolve the gold. Turing had just such a contraption set up in a tiny spare room. Copeland noted that the autopsy findings were more consistent with inhalation than with the ingestion of the poison. Turing was also habitual in eating an apple before bed, and it was not unusual for the house-keeper to find a half-eaten one discarded nearby in the morning. Also, Turing had reportedly borne his legal setbacks and hormone treatment, which had finished a year before, and shown no sign of despondency prior to his death, to the point that he had written a list of tasks to be completed on his return to his office after the holiday weekend. Turing's mother also believed that her son's poisoning was accidental and probably as a result of his 'careless storage of laboratory chemicals'.

Undercover 'pretty' police officers were often used as 'agents provocateurs', posing as homosexuals importuning for sex in public places. In 1953, the actor John Gielgud was arrested for cruising in a public lavatory in Chelsea. Gielgud was fined, and the ignominy of the court case was, he thought, going to be the end of his career. Starring in the pre-West End run of the play, *A Day by the Sea*, in his first appearance since his arrest, he was too paralysed with nerves to take his cue and go on, knowing that the entire audience knew of his shame. His co-star, Sybil Thorndike, whispered encouraging words and took him by the hand, 'Come on, John darling, they won't boo me' she said, and she led him out on to the stage. To everyone's astonishment the audience began to clap and cheer and gave Gielgud a standing ovation. The message was clear: the public didn't give two hoots about their beloved favourite actor's private life.

Despite the adoration and confirmation of the public's respect for him, Gielgud suffered a nervous breakdown a few months later. He never spoke of the episode and it was forever politely ignored by journalists and writers. In later life he commented to fellow actor Simon Callow, 'I do admire people like you and Ian McKellen for coming out, but I can't be doing with that myself.'

The police continued their McCarthy-esque purge, known in the U.S as 'the Lavender Scare', after mass firings of homosexuals from Government posts. Here they targeted homosexuals from wealthy society backgrounds, and high-profile cases were increasingly reported in the national newspapers.

Edward Montagu, third Baron of Beaulieu, Conservative Member of the House of Lords from 1947 and later founder of the British National Motor Museum at Beaulieu, was, after his arrest for gross indecency, labelled 'one of the most notorious public figures of his generation'. In the summer of 1953 Montagu offered the use of a beach hut near his country estate at Beaulieu to his friend Peter Wildeblood. Wildeblood brought with him two young RAF servicemen, Edward McNally and John Reynolds. They were joined by Montagu's cousin, Michael Pitt-Rivers. They were arrested in January 1954 for 'conspiracy to incite certain male persons to commit serious offences with male persons' (buggery). At the trial in March, the two airmen turned Queen's Evidence against Pitt-Rivers, Montagu and Wildeblood, claiming that there had been dancing and 'abandoned behaviour' at the beach-hut party. Wildeblood said that in fact it had been 'extremely dull' and Montagu stated that it was all remarkably innocent, saying, 'We had some drinks, we danced, we kissed, that's all.' A frenzied circus of salacious newspaper reporters followed the trial at Winchester Assizes, and after eight days, Pitt-Rivers and Wildeblood were sentenced to 18 months imprisonment and Montagu, 12 months.

For all that the law was draconian, it was also mostly unenforceable. As a result, arrests were often arbitrary and random. One public lavatory used for cottaging was well known to police and magistrates in 1958, yet there hadn't been an arrest or conviction citing this place in thirty years. On the other hand, sporadic trawls through known homosexuals' address books resulted in up to twenty men at a time appearing in the dock, accused of being part of 'homosexual rings', even though many of them might never have met any of the others before.

The case of Pitt-Rivers, Wildeblood and Montagu eventually led to the Wolfenden report, which in 1957 recommended the decriminalisation of homosexual acts in the United Kingdom between consenting adults in private. It did not argue against the idea that homosexuality was immoral, only that the law as it stood was impossible and impractical to enforce. The age of consent, they decided, was to be set at 21, which was, in the committee's view, preferable to that of 16 as for heterosexuals, because young men often left the parental home to go to university or into the forces after finishing school, and therefore were deprived of the guidance and control of their parents.

There is a myth that the Wolfenden report was a turning point. It was more a stepping-stone, for the vote against it in the House of Commons was overwhelming, and it took a further ten years before it was passed into law with the Sexual Offences Act 1967.

26.
The Sexual Offences Act - 1967

The fiftieth anniversary of the Sexual Offences Act 1967 has recently passed. It was celebrated and marked as an historical milestone in the LGBT struggle for equality. It was a point of modern British Parliamentary law-making worth celebrating, but was it the beginning of a period of openness and tolerance of diversity?

After the Wolfenden Report of 1957, the lobby for reform of the laws surrounding homosexual behaviour gained momentum. Though it did not immediately change the law, what the report did was to provide an authoritative framework on which to focus attention, something which until then had been sorely lacking. A flurry of correspondence about the report in *The Times* newspaper in March 1958 led to the Homosexual Law Reform Society (HLRS) being founded. Its mandate was to engage those who had a growing political awareness of the law in respect to homosexuals, progressive medical experts and liberal public and artistic figures of the day, to debate the Wolfenden Report and to bring about changes in the law. A new Sexual Offences Bill was proposed, drawing heavily on the recommendations made in the report. After a series of failed attempts, the Sexual Offences Act 1967 was finally made law. It covered England and Wales only and did not include men serving in the armed forces or the merchant navy. Critically, it did not mark a transformation in public attitudes towards homosexuals and homosexuality. For most people the new law simply made no difference at all to the lives.

A woman interviewed on the BBC's *Man Alive* programme: *Consenting Adults – Men*, which was aired in June 1967, a few weeks before the Sexual Offences Act was given Royal Assent, told of how she had married a man who had turned out to be a homosexual. Much to the interviewer's incredulity, the woman said she had had no prior knowledge of her husband's homosexual tendencies. She was brave and way ahead of her time when she said 'there was never a question of a homosexual man being different. A homosexual is the same as any other man, except there is one particular thing – this particular thing – that is slightly different.' What surprised her so much was other people's attitudes. She looked to one side briefly, recalling an incident – it was written on her face. 'There was something they simply could not understand; that somebody could be gifted, talented, charming, loveable, and at the same time [her voice drops in despondency] homosexual.'

Twice her husband was arrested for importuning in public lavatories. After the second time, he killed himself rather than face the punishment of the court and the disgust of his friends. The programme fully recognised that a change in the law did not necessarily mean a change in attitude 'by the rest of us.' That attitude is epitomised by Jeremy James, the interviewer, as he calmly and reassuringly tells the audience in his best soft Etonian accent, 'For some of us, this is revolting – men dancing with other men.' The scene shows men, not in close bodily contact, but rather dancing around one another in a well-lit room, quite tamely.

Next, a forty-something-year-old male hairdresser is introduced. 'Do you think you can be born homosexual? Can you be cured of homosexuality? Would you like to be cured? Why not?' he asks.

Of an elderly, well-spoken doctor, James asks, 'I suppose some people might be appalled to think of their doctor as homosexual, especially if they were taking their young sons to see him. Do you think parents ought to worry about that sort of thing? Why not?'

The new legislation brought about the repeal of the maximum penalty of life imprisonment for anal sex. The age of consent, however, was set at twenty-one, five years above that for heterosexual men. Conviction for 'buggery' with another man between the age of sixteen and twenty-one was ten years; five years if the younger man consented. Though the onus of proof was on the prosecution, homosexual sex outside of a rigid doctrine still remained a prosecutable offence if it did not take place within the privacy of the home, between two consenting adults with the curtains drawn, and with no other person present in any part of the house. Hook-ups in hotels for gay sex were also illegal, as they were deemed public space, and sexual activity of any kind in a public lavatory still remains an offence for both gay and straight couples. For those who would not conform to the Act's unyielding model of 'respectable' homosexuality as an archetype of heterosexual marriage and citizenship, it was disastrous and at best irrelevant, for how many homosexual men could aspire to such a lifestyle when the chances of ever meeting a kindred spirit and settling down were so utterly remote?

In the years after the Sexual Offences Act was passed, recorded cases of indecency between men doubled, peaking in 1974 at 1,796 compared to 820 in 1969. The number did then start to fall but hit another high in 1989 amidst the panic of AIDS, with 2,022 arrests. Overall, the numbers from 1967 to 1989 rose by 40 percent as a direct result of increased vigilance by the police.

In 2012 the Government introduced a scheme to allow those who had fallen foul of the outdated gay sex laws to have their convictions removed from the police and court records. There were approximately 50,000 such convictions between the 1950s and 2000. Some 16,000, of those men were still living in 2012 and of those, 242 applied to have their records wiped clean. Not all of these were eligible for various reasons, including non-consensual sex, sex with someone under the age of sixteen, or other activities which would still be an offence likely to lead to arrest today, such as having sex in a public toilet or open space. According to the Home Office, just 83 applications were granted. In 2016 family members were able to apply for posthumous pardons.

27.
David Bowie - 1972

'I met Bowie in his publisher's office, high above Regent Street. He was dolled up as Ziggy, before the world knew of rock stars from outer space. Skin-tight pantsuit, big hair, huge, red plastic boots – dazzling,' so the journalist Michael Watts told Dylan Jones in his book David Bowie: A Life, about the interview with Bowie he did for *Melody Maker* in January 1972. He went on, 'He was charming, slightly flirtatious, but made me uncomfortable with myself. 'Camp as a row of tents,' I wrote - did I invent that phrase? - when I wanted to be unmanly and shout: he is unreservedly fabulous.'

David Bowie's career at that point was beginning to show signs of taking off after years of trying things out and not quite making it. In September 1971 he went to New York with a small entourage and signed a record deal with RCA. Tony Zanetta, who at the time was an underground theatre actor who'd met Bowie after playing in Andy Warhol's *Pork* at the Roundhouse in London a few weeks earlier, says: 'David Bowie wasn't a sex hunter, he wasn't going out looking for sex all the time, but sex was always a little part of the equation. A lot of people might've ended up in bed with him because he was so seductive.' It was Zanetta who introduced the then long-haired and languid looking Bowie to Warhol, at the artist's Factory in New York. The 'Greta Garbo' image of Bowie as a troubled, star-gazing artist, made the cover of his next album, *Hunky Dory*, which was released by RCA in December 1971. But already, that look had been ditched and Bowie was busy recording material for a new album and at the same time creating Ziggy Stardust.

As he freely admitted himself, Bowie was a vaudeville showman, much more interested in the whole theatrical performance of his music than simply the sound it made.

By the standards of every other musician and music journalist of the day, this was genuinely considered inauthentic musicianship.

Watts wrote in the *Melody Maker* interview, 'David's present image is to come on like a swishy queen, a gorgeously effeminate boy,' implying that it was all just a pose, like the Garbo gaze Bowie had copied for the cover of *Hunky Dory*. What got the interview onto the front page were two words that would reverberate for many years to come: 'I'm gay.'

It was these two explosive words that finally ignited Bowie's career. For a generation of teenagers, the fact that someone whose entire profession depended on the public adoring him, and who could openly admit this to the world, adding; 'and always have been, even when I was David Jones,' was like a giant door being swung open on a whole new realm of possibilities.

'In truth, I felt lucky,' recalled Watts some years later. 'Did his admission matter? Well, laws on homosexuality had been reformed only five years previously. After Bowie came *le déluge*. He had shrewdly calculated the consequences, however. Busting taboos stokes the star-maker machinery. He was also just being honest. Sometimes, even in pop, honesty pays.'

Much debate has gone on over the years surrounding Bowie's 'coming out'. Was it for real or was it a pose? What is evident is that Bowie saw sexuality as a fluid emotion, one that could change and morph to the situation and the person you're with, in much the same way as he saw himself playing different parts and roles, both on and off stage. Sexual fluidity was a forward-thinking idea, and one voiced by Alfred Kinsey in the late forties, but this was generally not a popular attitude in the 1970s. What Bowie didn't do was align himself with the cause of the Gay Liberation movement, and for a lot of the gay community that was a sure sign, albeit a cynical one, that he was playing the gay card simply to attract that audience.

Whatever the case, anyone watching him perform *Starman* on the BBC's *Top of the Pops* show in July 1972 had no doubts, when he slung his arm lasciviously around the shoulders of Mick Ronson, his guitarist, with his other hand slammed firmly on his jutting hip, that there was an unspoken message about same-sex desire being broadcast into the living rooms of millions of eager teenagers, who believed that Bowie really was 'picking on them' when he pointed his finger down the camera lens.

Michael Watts concedes that the Melody Maker interview made 'good copy' and that Bowie 'was certainly aware of the impact it would make. He understood the news value of something like that.' What followed however, was a cultural shift towards homosexuals, which was due in no small part to the allure of Bowie and his transition from mere rock star to cultural icon. His effect on music, fashion and attitudes towards sexuality made him one of the most influential personalities of the latter half of the twentieth century. Bowie paved the way for other musicians to explore sexuality and the blurring of lines between gender. Androgyne became the byword of the age.

28.
Coming Out in the Forces - 2000

In the 1960s, the Royal Navy feared that half its personnel were either practising or 'rehearsing' homosexuals. Proof, if any were needed, that the Navy was, as it had always been, an obliging cruise-line for over-sexed, uninhibited young men seeking adventure and to see the world. But if any of the British armed forces deserves to be decorated for its services to homosexuality above and beyond the call of duty, it should be the Army. From the Household Cavalry's renowned nocturnal activities over the centuries in St James's Park to scandals involving such heroes as the Victorian General Hector MacDonald, whose image is still used to market Camp Coffee, and the S & M predilections of T. E. Lawrence (of Arabia), or more recently, James Wharton, the army's poster-boy for being the first out gay soldier, and numerous others, the Army can safely say that they outstrip the Navy when it comes to gays within the ranks.

This is as it may be, but the official Armed Forces Policy and Guidelines on Homosexuality, until as recently as the turn of the twenty-first century, stated that a homosexual lifestyle was incompatible with 'the good order and discipline' of military life, because of the 'close physical conditions in which personnel often have to live and work, and also because homosexual behaviour can cause offence, polarise relationships, and damage morale and unit effectiveness'. A 1996 report by the Homosexuality Policy Assessment Team, asserted that allowing homosexual servicemen (and women) in the armed forces, would not only be detrimental to morale, but also leave them vulnerable to blackmail from foreign intelligence agencies.

Around 60 people were dismissed annually from the services for being gay, but in 1999 this rose dramatically to 298. On a Radio 4 programme titled 'Cleaning Out The Camp', Wing Commander Phil Sagar, who ran the Armed Forces' Joint Equality and Diversity Training Centre at Shrivenham, Wiltshire, recalled his experiences in 1985 of barrack raids by the police, who undertook special investigations on suspected gay men and women to 'clean out homosexuals'.

'I appeared in the appropriate barrack block to find four provost senior NCOs – and for some reason best known to them, a dog – cutting the padlock of a young serviceman's locker, search through all his material, read all his letters, search all his belongings; purely on the suspicion that he was gay,' stated Wing Commander Sagar. 'At the time, I didn't see anything wrong with that. I stood there as a serviceman doing my duty in accordance with the rules, regulations and culture of the time.' Sagar went on to apologise: 'Of course we're sorry for anyone who's suffered personal trauma. We can't change the past and what's happened has happened. But if, as I'm sure you have, you've got testimony from people who feel that their lives have been ruined from this, then clearly that is not a good place to be.'

Warrant Officer Robert Ely, a bandsman who joined the army aged seventeen, had served for twenty years before he was dismissed after the discovery of a letter which led to his sexual orientation being investigated and subsequently his being thrown out of the army for his homosexuality. He set up a group for armed forces gay men and lesbians in 1991, called Rank Outsiders. The group's remit was to seek an independent review of homosexuality within the armed forces, because, they argued, the Ministry of Defence had not produced evidence to substantiate its claims that homosexuality caused tension and damaged cohesion. 'It remains the case that once identified, a gay man or lesbian woman has their life closely scrutinised, investigated and often ruined,' Ely said.

Ely approached Stonewall, the charity founded in 1989 by the actors Ian McKellen and Michael Cashman among others to campaign and lobby against Section 28 of the Local Government Act. Together with Stonewall, Ely brought evidence before the Armed Forces Select Committee about the position of gay men and women serving in the forces and recommended its decriminalisation. In 1995, the first legal challenge was mounted in the high court by an RAF nurse and three servicemen. They were Jeanette Smith from Edinburgh, who was discharged in 1994 after her relationship with a female civilian was reported to her superiors; Graeme Grady, an RAF Sergeant from London with two children, also discharged in 1994 after attending a counselling group for married gay men in Washington DC where he was posted as chief clerk at the British defence intelligence liaison office, with a high level of security clearance; Duncan Lustig-Prean, a naval lieutenant commander on HMS Newcastle, who was about to be appointed as a military adviser to PM John Major when he too was discharged in 1994 after a reported blackmail attempt; and John Beckett, a weapons engineering mechanic on board HMS *Valiant*, a nuclear submarine. Beckett had signed on for 22 years' service in 1989 but was discharged in 1993 after he reported a homosexual relationship he had had with a civilian to both his commanding officer and his chaplain. The group of four asked Stonewall to arrange legal representation and a long court battle ensued. In the High Court, Lord Justice Simon Browne ruled that the ban was not unlawful and could not therefore be overturned, but it was, in his view, without merit and based solely on prejudice. 'The tide of history is against the Ministry,' he said, and advised that the MoD should review the ban and examine the experience of the growing number of countries who had lifted such bans on their military personnel.

Having lost the case in the British High Court and Court of Appeal, the four appealed to the European Court of Human Rights in Strasbourg. In September 1999 the European Court ruled that investigations by military authorities into a service person's sexuality breached their right to privacy. As a result of this ruling, which applied to the militaries of all EU member states, the MoD capitulated and was forced to lift the ban. It subsequently began allowing homosexuals to serve in the armed forces from January 2000. According to a National Opinion Poll published a week before the European Court ruling, the MoD's position on the banning of homosexuals serving in the military was opposed by 68% of the population.

Before 2000, dozens of servicemen and women were discharged each year because of their sexuality. The actual number affected, however, is hard to ascertain. The Royal Navy, for instance, recorded such discharges as being due to 'medical reasons'.

Figures for the number of serving homosexuals were not available until 2015. Since then new recruits have been asked about their sexuality, with the proviso that they can answer the question with a 'prefer not to say' if they so wish. In a complete shift in their moral standpoint, however, the Ministry of Defence says, 'Service personnel are now encouraged to declare their sexual orientation. Although this is not mandatory, collecting the data will give us a better understanding of the composition of our armed forces and help ensure our policies and practices fully support our personnel. The MoD proudly encourages diversity at all levels.'

Lieutenant General Patrick Sanders says: 'Under fire, no one cares if someone is black or white, gay or straight, because they value the individual for who he or she is, what he or she can do, and because they are so utterly dependent on him or her. But this experience is not universal. Away from the cauldron of operations or training, lazy or ingrained prejudice remains, ranging from outright bullying and discrimination to the sort of casual but hurtful remark that refers to ice cream as "gay". I am proud to be the Army's LGBT champion and a straight ally. I celebrate your service as LGBT members of the army and I cheer the fact that we are recognised as a top LGBT employer. As Commander Field Army, I will make sure everyone understands that diverse teams are stronger and more effective than homogenous teams. I want us to live all the values and standards that define us: selfless commitment, courage, discipline, integrity, loyalty and respect for others. These qualities I saw daily in dusty compounds in Afghanistan and in my battle group in Basra should extend everywhere until we have expunged the last dregs of prejudice and intolerance. I don't want more for the LGBT community – I just want the same that any soldier has the right to expect: respect.'

Commander Douggie Ward, who was awarded an MBE in the Queen's Honours List in 2016 for his services to diversity in the Royal Navy, shared his experience of being out in the Forces:

I joined the Royal Navy as a logistics officer in 1997. My grandfather had also served in the Fleet Air Arm on the aircraft carriers in World War Two, and the brother of one of my very good friends was also in the Navy. I used to hear his tales of all the things he got up to and I thought I could do that. I have always wanted to put something back into the community, and society in general, and the more I read about the Royal Navy, the more I liked the idea. At the time I joined and for a long time after, I was living as a straight man, and I even got married to a woman in 2003. I didn't know then that I was a gay. I really, honestly did not know. It was only as time went on that I realised something deep inside me wasn't right. By my mid-thirties I was married, I had two children, a lovely home in Rosyth and a good job. I'd served in the submarine service and qualified as a barrister, and worked in the Middle East, Afghanistan and Iraq. But I wasn't happy, something was wrong. Attitudes towards gay people weren't something I noticed much. I did know people who were serving and gay even before 2000 when the policy changed. Officially, anyone who knew of someone who was gay had a duty to inform the service police. It was very difficult for everyone involved.

After a lot of soul-searching, finally, in 2010, I reached out to the Royal Navy's LGBT organisation, knowing by then that my problems were to do with my sexual orientation. I realised I was gay but for some time I didn't do anything about it. Until one day, a woman I shared an office with was listening to a radio discussion about a politician's private life – was he gay or was he not? My colleague chirped up 'people don't really care who you are, as long as you are happy in yourself and honest with everybody else'. As a lawyer, my job is about not misleading people, so I realised I had to be honest. I also wanted to be honest for my wife, because I wanted her to have the opportunity of finding happiness and moving on. I drove home that evening with the words of my colleague ringing in my ears – I knew I was not being honest with myself or with other people. I had to make the decision; whether to stick a grenade under my world or to say nothing and be the person I knew at that stage, I was not. That evening I came out to my wife. It was very emotional, but she was, and is still, incredibly supportive, and it felt like the world had been lifted off my shoulders.

Once I had made the decision to come out, the next day I sent an email to the other barristers in the Royal Navy – there are only thirty-two of us, so it's a small community. I told them that I was gay, but I hoped it wouldn't change anything between us. In the Navy, you go through a lot together. Your colleagues are also your best friends. If I hadn't have told them, people would have asked me why I'd left my wife, so I had the choice either to live with another lie or to tell them the whole truth. The response I got was nothing but supportive. There were some whom I thought might have been, at best, indifferent, but the feedback generally was, "we thought you were going to tell us something important, like you were resigning. Of course, it doesn't change how we see you." Every time I join a new team there's always the question of coming out again, but LGBT people make that call in all walks of life.

In 2012 I was deployed to Afghanistan, working in an office, advising a US General. It was shortly after the 'don't ask, don't tell' policy in the US was repealed. This was the policy the American government introduced to overcome the question of homosexuals serving in their forces. I wasn't sure how me coming out to them would play out. One day the guys in the office were asking me who my favourite actress was. I said I didn't really have favourite actresses, but I did have favourite actors. It wasn't an issue at all. The reactions I've had from colleagues, friends and family, and even my wife's family, have always been amazingly positive. My daughters don't see it as an issue either.

You live cheek by jowl in the Navy and the only way you can ever live in such confined quarters is by accepting everyone's differences. We have a very strong team spirit and ethos, and the most important thing is that you are an effective part of the team, and by being yourself you can be more effective. It is also important to show society that we are their Royal Navy, that we represent and reflect society in all its aspects, and in doing so we need to be just as diverse. For me, personally, it is so much easier being out at work, because I don't have to hide, or lie, or make up stories.

When the Navy was looking for a new chair for its LGBT network, I immediately volunteered. The response to my coming out had been so wonderful I wanted everyone to have the same reception I had. I never hear of any negativity, but we do live in a culture of banter, so people might say things like "that's so gay". It's low-level stuff and not unique to the Navy, but I always challenge it when I hear it.

Since 2000, the Royal Navy has led the way in embracing diversity and was the first defence organisation to join Stonewall as a Diversity Champion in 2005, and it continues to develop its own network for LGBT+ personnel called Compass. The Co-Chair of Compass, Surgeon Lieutenant Commander Mike Hill, joined the reserves in 2002 as a medical doctor deployed with the Submarine Service and Fleet Air Arm. 'Prior to the ban being lifted, I didn't even consider a career with the military,' he says. 'Why, as a gay man, would I join an organisation that didn't appear welcoming?' A car journey to his first interview with his mother summed it up, 'She was concerned that while the law may have changed to allow people who are gay to serve, attitudes wouldn't have.'

The interview was unsuccessful, partly because he froze when the panel asked him about his 'girlfriend'. 'Fortunately, I wasn't deterred and successfully reapplied. I had one colleague who found out I was gay and tried to out me, but otherwise I've had no issues. Thankfully attitudes have changed.'

Submariner Engineering Technician Robert Morrison joined up fourteen years after the ban was lifted. He had not come to terms with his sexuality at the time, but he found he was fully supported and never experienced any negativity. 'People are naturally curious, and in an organisation where banter helps with team cohesion, there are jokes, but nothing offensive or said with malice.'

Royal Marine Michael Johnson echoes this feeling, 'Those who are openly homophobic, transphobic, or racist or sexist are not welcome to bring their views into the Service,' he says.

'If you can be authentic then you will be able to concentrate on the job in hand,' concludes Commander Ward. 'People know when you're not being honest with them, and when people come out, it enhances the bond in the team because you're not hiding anything. What's important in the Royal Navy is that you are part of a team, and that you can do your job – nothing else matters.'

Today, all service personnel are given diversity training, and all three UK Armed Forces positively recruit from the LGBT community. Each has an active forum dedicated to LGBT colleagues and since 2008, all military personnel have been permitted to march at Pride festivals, in uniform.

Epilogue

In an article for *The Holy Male* online magazine, Toby Johnson advocates the idea that modern gay men are the essence or the reincarnated lives of all homosexuals of the past, and that everybody's lives, whether they be gay or straight or anything else, are based on myths we create about ourselves. Whether we know it or not, we construct a façade built on myth to appease, excite or sometimes to repulse our own exclusive audience. Johnson reiterates the age-old belief that we make sense of our personal life experiences through the lessons we learn and inherit from the past.

'The myth of karma and reincarnation is not about the course of individual souls as a popularised escape from mortality,' he says, 'but as a mythological presentation of evolution; that each generation improves because it learns from the past. It is a metaphor for the greater collective mind of the planet – of the 'God' that lives on beyond all its incarnations. We all dance to the music of the common band... with old steps and new.' In Johnson's hypothesis we subconsciously invent ourselves. 'We are not the objects of the process. We choose to resonate with the patterns of the lives of those before us and the ways they experienced life. We reincarnate them in the way an actor impersonates a real person. In essence, we are the reincarnation of everybody whose patterns we resonate with.'

This may be true enough for every human being, but what homosexuals profoundly lack in Western culture is a mythos or a cultural anchor of reference. For homosexuals there is no past. How can we create a narrative that reflects our situation with any honesty when mythical stories do not exist for the homosexual man? In his book *The Missing Myth: A New Vision of Same-Sex Love*, Gilles Herrada concurs with this point 'that modern homosexual consciousness is absolutely deficient of any sort of explanatory mythology'. Talking in an interview with the life coach YouTuber Jordan Bach, in 2013, Herrada describes why it is so difficult for us to understand homosexuality, 'Modern homosexuality has no meaning other than its bio-medical definition. Thus, homosexuality today is symbolically empty, still absent from the mythos and still disconnected from the sacred. As a matter of fact, modern homosexuals live today merely in the same mythic context as the sodomites of the middle ages. From a psycho-cultural view point, this isn't just uncomfortable, this is torture.' The truth of this is well-known and comes with a warning. 'Without a positive representation in the mythos to consolidate its socio-cultural existence, homosexuality remains completely vulnerable to a resurgence of homophobia and scapegoating.'

Where are the positive narratives from the past millennia, the iconic figures of legend, the tales of the good homosexual handed down from generation to generation? The Western world is devoid of them, and the roots of this absence is in the ancient Greek and particularly the Roman societies upon which our culture stands.

The Greco-Roman philosophy on homosexuality was based on penetrative dominance, of age over youth, of class status, and of the power of semen to pass wisdom and knowledge down the generations. This viewpoint is archaic and outdated. Today's homosexuals champion something entirely different: equality and mutual affinity. It is worth pointing out that homosexuality has evolved, and particularly so since the Second World War. Homosexual relationships today can be an equitable partnership where each person is equal in age, income, background, and status, and where either, or both, can be the penetrator and the passive partner at any given time, or choose not to include penetration at all. This attitude and way of living, as sexual beings on a par with one another, was unthinkable even as recently as the late 1960s and early seventies. Herrada says, that the consequences of social change first started in the 1930s, means that, 'now is the time to establish a positive mythos and ideology for the future'.

Our culture provides heterosexual men and women with a vast tradition and depth of lore about what it means to be straight. Women grow up with the myths of Eve, Gaia and the Virgin Mary, while men have Adam, Mars, Zeus and the great religious prophets to identify with. Imagine a world for instance without the representation of women anywhere; a fictious world in which there are no positive images or examples of women in the church, in government, in film, books or on TV, or indeed of playing any meaningful role throughout history. It is unbelievable, yet this has been the way homosexuals have lived without any gay male archetypes. Because of the lack of backstory, every new gay-themed film, TV show or book that appears, every new celebrity, personality or politician who comes out, is so significant to our collective gay story that we jump on it voraciously. Often, this causes a backlash and straight people can be heard saying things along the lines of 'They've got equal marriage, they can join the army, there are no anti-gay laws anymore, what more do they want? Why do they have to keep harping on? Why can't they just be quiet and accept that they're equal now?'

Growing up without proper foundations of myth, gender diverse references or role models, is not equality, so every single gay story is as important today as it ever was, even when we have come so far. Story-telling is a fundamental building block of any society. It is what makes us human – passing on our traditions, our wisdom, our folklore and myths from one generation to another. But instead of relying on a passive view of Western culture in which homosexuals are largely airbrushed out, we unequivocally need to create a new narrative, and to do that we need to find a commonality – a singular truth.

The most powerful force for truth in the last 200 years has been scientific research. Ever since the Age of Enlightenment in the eighteenth century, and the advances

236

in technology, medicine and psychology in the nineteenth century, reason and science have shown us a path to certainty. When observing our world, we can see that it is shaped by opposing forces; magnetic poles, male and female, and the micro-world of protons, neutrons and electrons. There is another force at work, inexorably drawing opposing forces together. That force is gravity, and without it our world would not exist. Hold that thought.

In Chapter 20, we learned that a possible reason for the evolutionary existence of homosexuals was a means to defend their mothers and siblings by bringing special skills and talents to the family unit that might otherwise be lacking in the other sons. We learnt also that another factor in the propensity to bear a gay son might be a traumatic event endured by the mother during pregnancy, thus creating the correct hormonal environment for the unborn male foetus to develop more caring, nurturing traits that would be necessary to safeguard the mother's future well-being. What can be seen in both these scenarios is the requirement for the son to have empathetic and nurturing skills, but also to be a character who can negotiate and reconcile situations when for instance, food and resources essential to the family are in limited supply. The homosexual, though often portrayed in the guise of the stereotypical drama queen, the self-centred narcissist or the vitriolic one-line bitch, more often than not possesses the antitheses of these less desirable character attributes, with an abundance of softer, more compassionate and supportive qualities. This idea of drawing people together, of reconciling, co-operating, and understanding opposite points of view, is familiar to the homosexual character, and it is this mythos we should research, explore, refine and tell.

What, for instance, would have been the effect on mankind if the greatest emissary in Christendom had been 'one of us'? Supposing God had sent His Son to save mankind and teach the lost the way of His word; what a difference it would have made if Jesus had been gay. It would have made perfect sense to the story if he had been. Could not a homosexual Jesus have displayed the ideal virtues of love based on respect and equality, as well as the character traits of someone whose job it was to draw people together; to act as the gravitational pull between them? It is certainly food for thought.

As discussed in Chapter 6, sexual orientation as a concept is a relatively new idea and until the late 19th century same-sex sexual behaviour in the Christian world was regarded much in the same way as other sins such as gluttony and wrath – a vice that anyone might be prone to or succumb to, but not something that defined their entire character. World religions inevitably draw their traditions from the time-frame in which their faiths were written down in their holy books, and it is understandable how, in times of epidemics, starvation and the utter reliance upon nature to provide, that men who preferred to have sex, particularly anal sex, with other males were vilified and condemned for 'going against nature' and sinfully spilling God's seed. Had there been homosexual faith leaders who performed the vital roles of drawing people together in times of their greatest need, then same-sex love would not have been seen as a sin but rather, as the Two-Spirits of the American Indian tribes are, venerated as special and a necessary cohesive part of society.

Nature's force of gravity, which inextricably brings objects together, is the same force that in humans is characterised by traits such as caring and compassion. But gravity also holds a different meaning – that of extreme importance and seriousness. Sir Isaac Newton, who is recognised as one of the most influential scientists of all time, did not invent the word 'gravity' to explain the force he'd discovered – the word existed in language long before that, but he was the one who first used it in this new meaning. Before then, gravity denoted a quality rather than a force. It came from the Latin *gravitas* (*gravis* meaning heavy), and has subsequently come to mean something of heaviness, significance or of dignity. Homosexual men are more often than not blessed with an innate sensitivity to others, and while most of us do not wield great power and are relatively small in comparison, the forces of gravity work just the same in each of us, no matter how tall or rich we are.

Let us take then these two ideas: that of the boys born to aid the family unit and protect their mothers, and the force of gravity that draws objects/people together. Given this hypothesis, can it be denied that homosexuals hold a special place in society and in the greater scheme of things? Surely this is fact.

To enable us to build a modern gay mythos, we need to own the past. We need to reveal our stories and tell those of other homosexual men who, throughout history, have pulled their communities together, who have given of themselves in all walks of life and without whom our world would be a lesser place. Our task has just begun.

It has been my immense privilege to unearth some of the stories of men such as Karl Ulrichs, Karl-Maria Kertbeny, Oscar Wilde, Gaius Petronius and Catullus, Jack Saul, George Cecil Ives, Ian Gleed and Alan Turing, among others. I have discovered so much through my research about gay culture and history that I had no idea of – that had been denied me for far too long. I hope, having read *This Forbidden Fruit*, that you will take from it a continuing desire to scrutinise and explore further our gay history and culture for yourself.

~

Source Notes & Citations

Introduction

Marriage (Same Sex Couples) Act 2013 – Fully in force since 13th March 2014

BBC news 20.10.15 'The Office for National Statistics (ONS) confirmed a total of 15,098 couples had legally married since 2014.'

Gov.UK Same Sex Marriage Becomes Law, Grounds For Divorce

On Civil Partnerships: ONS 2011 data quoted in Guardian Datablog – 53,417 couples in the first 7 years (over 100,000 individuals).

Family Law in Partnership Same Sex Marriage & Civil Partnerships

Civil Partnerships – Office for National Statistics 'The Act came into force in the UK on 5 December 2005, the first day that couples could give notice of their intention to form a civil partnership. Couples could first form and register a partnership on 19 December in Northern Ireland, 20 December in Scotland and 21 December in England and Wales.'

Huffington Post – The Pink Pound, Edward Johnson, Dec 2016

Part 1. Chapter 1

George Nash *The Subversive Male: Homosexual & Bestial Images on European Mesolithic Rock Art*

Psychology Today – The Oldest Gays in History, Neel Burton, Jul 2017

Wikipedia – Khnum-hotep and Nyankh-khnum

Ancient Origins – The Importance of Evidence in the Heated Debate on Homosexuality in Ancient Egypt, Nov 2015

Wikipedia – Cretan Pederasty

Concise Oxford Dictionary – Paedophile

Higher Love – Elitism in the Pederastic Practice of Athens in the Archaic & Classical Periods, Caitlin Deegan, Apr 2012

Ancient Origins – What was the Real Relationship Between Alexander the Great and Hephaestion?, Natalia Klimczak, Jul 2016

Heritage Daily – Roman Sex, Sexuality, Slaves and Lex Scantinia, Marcus Milligan, Jan 2018

Ancient Origins – Roman Law and the Banning of 'Passive' Homosexuality, April Holloway, Sep 2013

Wikipedia – Homosexuality in Ancient China and Japan; Emperor Ai of Han; The Cut Sleeve; Don Xian

Making Queer History – The Bitten Peach & The Cut Sleeve, Laura Mills, May 2016

MailOnline – Hidden World of the Hijras: Inside India's 4000-year-old Transgender Community, Jefferson Mok & Stephanie Linning, Jun 2015

Wikipedia – Hijra

Indian Country Today – 8 things you should know about two-spirit people, Tony Enos, Mar 2017

Wikipedia – Two-Spirits; History of Homosexuality: The Ameicas

Stephen Murray & Will Roscoe *Boy-Wives and Female Husbands: Studies of African Homosexualities*

The Guardian – If you say being gay is not African, you don't know your history, Bisi Alimi, Sep 2015

American Anthropologist – Sexual Inversion Among the Azande, E. E. Evans-Pritchard

James Neill *The Origins and Role of Same-Sex Relations in Human Societies*

Stephen O. Murray *Homosexualities*

Enze Han & Joseph O'Mahoney *The British Colonial Origins of Anti-Gay Laws*, Oct 2014

Wikipedia – LGBT rights by country & territory

Chapter 2

Fordham University – The Experience of Homosexuality in the Middle Ages

Fordham University – The Medieval Sourcebook:

Wikipedia – Peter Damian

E-RI – It's A Man's World: The Effect of Traditional Masculinity on Gender Equality, Aydon Edwards, Mar 2015

William Burgwnkle *Sodomy, Masculinity & Law in Medieval Literature*: Imagining Sodomy, Peter Damian, p53

PBS Frontline – Inside the Mind of People Who Hate Gays, Karen Franklin

Gov.UK – Hate Crime, England & Wales 2011-2012: of 43,748 hate crimes recorded by the police, 4,252 (10%) were concerning sexual orientation.

Home Office Report – Hate Crime, England & Wales 2016-2017: of 80,393 hate crimes recorded by the police, 9157 (11%) were concerning sexual orientation.

Wikipedia – Biology, XY Sex Determination System, Gender, Human Sexuality, Psychosexual Development

Kinsey Institute – The Kinsey Scale

Concise Oxford Dictionary – Personality definition

Homosapiens Podcast – Owen Jones

Gay Dad – Linda Riley: We've Come A Long Way, But These Are Just The First Steps

Chapter 3

Wikipedia – Gay Literature

Wikipedia – Symposium, Plato

Sparknotes.com – The Symposium: Overall Analysis & Themes

The Metropolitan Museum – The Symposium in Ancient Greece

Pride.com – 52 Queer Gods Who Ruled Ancient History

Wikipedia – Satyricon, Gaius Petronius

GLBTQ.com – Petronius, Raymond Jean-Frontain

Claude J Summers – Gay & Lesbian Literary Heritage

Fordham University – The Experience of Homosexuality in the Middle Ages, Paul Halsall, 1988

Rictor Norton – Gay History & Literature: My Dear Boy: Gay Love Letters Through the Centuries; Saint Anselm & Gundulf & William; Baudri of Bourgeuil & Various Others; Alcuin of York, Marbod of Rennes & Walafrid Strabo: Best Beloved Brother

R Zeikowitz *Homoeroticism & Chivalry: Discourses of Male Same-Sex Desire in the 14th Century* p.35

Gay Art History – Nobody Told Us Hercules Was Gay

Wikipedia – Richard I

Francoise H M LeSaux *Amys &*

Anna Klosowska Roberts *Queer Love in the Middle Ages* p.143

Wikipedia – The Renaissance

Rictor Norton – The Homosexual Pastoral Tradition: An Era of Idylls/Affectionate Shepherds

Rictor Norton – Pastoral Homoeroticism & Richard Barnfield, The Affectionate Shepherd

Rictor Norton – Gay History & Literature, Critical Censorship of Gay Literature

Wikipedia – Michelangelo

Rictor Norton *Myth of the Modern Homosexual: Queer History & the Search for Cultural Unity* p143

Rictor Norton – A History of Homoerotica: England's First Pornographer

Wikipedia – John Wilmot, 2nd Earl of Rochester

Oxford Reference – Declaration of Indulgence

Wikipedia – Age of Enlightenment, Immanuel Kant, Nicholas Chamfort

Rictor Norton – Gothic Readings: The First Wave 1764-1840, p.169

Rictor Norton – A History of Homoerotica: A History of Gay Sex

Rictor Norton – Homosexuality in 18th Century England, Newspaper Reports, 1772 (The Craftsman, Say's Weekly Journal).

Revolvy – A Year in Arcadia: Kyllenion

Literary Hub – The Evolution of the Great Gay Novel

Wikipedia – A Year in Arcadia: Kyllenion, Rebecca Brill, Jun 2015

Warm Brothers – Queer Theory & the Age of Goethe, Robert Deam Tobin

S. Brady *Masculinity & Male Homosexuality in Britain, 1861-1913*, p.121

Oxford Bibliography – John Addington-Symonds, Howard J. Booth

Wikipedia – John Addington-Symonds, Havelock Ellis

University of Columbia – Havelock Ellis' Search for the Sacred: Sexology, Spirituality, & Science in Turn-of-the-Century Britain, Catherine Paul, 2004

Attitude – The Sodomite Rent Boy Who Scandalised Victorian London, Glenn Chandler, Apr 2016

Wikipedia – John Saul (Prostitute)

The Graduable – Victorian Pornography Part IV: Jack Saul, Justin O'Hearn, Apr 2013

Wikipedia – James Campbell Reddie

The Erotica Bibliophile – James Campbell Reddie, Sheryl Straight, 2010

Wikipedia – Simeon Solomon

Simeon Solomon Research Archive, Robert C Ferrari & Carolyn Conroy, Feb 2010

Revolvy – William Simpson Potter

Wikipedia – William Simpson Potter
Wikipedia – Cleveland Street Scandal
Notches – Uncovering Cleveland Street: Sexuality, Surveillance & Late Victorian Scandal, Katie Hindmarch Watson, Dec 2014
Wikipedia – Thomas Mann, Death in Venice
Wikipedia – E. M. Forster, Maurice
Central Gutenburg – Gay Literature
Wikipedia – Gay Literature
Wikipedia – Christopher Isherwood, Berlin Stories
John Henry Mackay *The Hustler: The True Story of a Nameless Love from Friedrichstrasse*, p.296

Chapter 4

Gay Art & History.org
Homoerotic Museum.net
Concise Oxford Dictionary – definition of homoerotic
The British Museum – The Warren Cup
QSpirit – St Sebastian: Gay Icon
Encyclopedia Britannica – St Sebastian: Christian Martyr
Wikipedia – Saint Sebastian
Matt Houlbrook *Queer London: Perils & Pleasures in the Sexual Metropolis, 1918-1957* p177 'institutionalised erotic trade …'
Richard Viven *National Service: A Generation in Uniform 1945-1963*
Brian Lewis *Wolfenden's Witnesses: Homosexuality in Post War Britain*
The National Gallery – The Hay Wain
The Telegraph – Viewing Art Gives Same Pleasure As Being In Love, Richard Alleyne, May 2011
Professor Semir Zeki (UCL) – The Neurology of Beauty (video)
AAAS.org – How Engaging with Art Affects the Human Brain, Kat Zambon, Nov 2013
New York University – Futruity, Science & Technology When Art Touches a Nerve, the Brain Lights Up, James Devitt, Apr 2012
The Telegraph – Brain Scans Reveal the Power of Art, Robert Mendick, May 2011
On Psychology & Neuroscience – This is Your Brain on Art, Mar 2015
Wikipedia – Mannerism, Tenebrism
Wikipedia – Young Sick Bacchus, Caravaggio

Leo Bersani & Ulysse Dutoit *Caravaggio's Secrets*
Salt & Light Media – Catholic Focus Caravaggio: A Catholic Artist? Nov 2011
Artible.com – Caravaggio
The Guardian – The Complete Caravaggio Part 2, Jonathan Jones, Feb 2005
Wikipedia – The Madonna of Loretto
Wikipedia – Simeon Solomon
Simeon Solomon Research Archive
Guy Burch – Queer British Art 1800-1899
Arte Fuse – Nude in Public: Sascha Schneider, Homoeroticism & the Male Form circa 1900, an exhibition by the Leslie Lohman Museum of Gay & Lesbian Art, New York, Sep 2013
Art History Teaching Resources.org – Queer Art 1960s to Present
Wikipedia – Paul Cadmus
Matthew Stradling.com
Cody Furguson.com
NAMBLA.org – Wilhelm von Gloeden
Wikipedia – Wilhelm von Gloeden, Vincenzo Galdi
Numero – Who is James Bidgood, the Pope of Queer Culture? Marion Ottaviani
Wikipedia – Arthur Tress
Mapplethorpe.org
Wikipedia – Robert Mapplethorpe
Smh.com.au – Homoeroticism: The Essence of all Friendship, Sam de Brito, May 2010

Chapter 5

Wikipedia – History of the Royal Marines
Royal Navy – Royal Marines 353 Years
Hans Turley *Rum, Sodomy and the Lash: Piracy, Sexuality and Masculine Identity*
B R Burg *Gay Warriors: A Documentary History from the Ancient World to the Present*, p.103
B R Burg *Boys at Sea: Sodomy, Indecency and Courts-Martial*
Wikipedia – The First Mutiny Act
Stephen Stratford *British Military and Criminal History 1900-1999*
Soldiers of Misfortune – Homosexuality: Brotherhoods of Warriors
British Tars – British Tars 1740-1790

N A M Rodger *The Wooden World: An Anatomy of the Georgian Navy*

Marie H Loughlin *Same-Sex Desire in Early Modern England, 1550-1735: An Anthology of Literary Texts and Contexts* – the trial of Captain Rigby p.121

Rictor Norton – Homosexuality in 18th Century England; The Trial of Captain Edward Rigby

Lawrence James *Warrior Race: A History of the British at War*

Genius – Richard Burton Terminal Essay, from his translation of The Arabian Nights 1885

Richard Phillips *Sex, Politics and Empire: A Postcolonial Geography* p.167

Ruth Vanita *Queering India: Same-sex Love and Eroticism in Indian Culture* p.17

The Telegraph – Love and Lust in India, Sally Howard, Dec 2013

Chapter 6

International Encyclopaedia of the First World War – Sexuality, Sexual Relations, Homosexuality, Jason Crouthamel, Oct 2014

East Sussex WW1 – Homosexuality in the First World War, Beth McGhee

Vada Magazine – Hatred and Homosexuality: Queer Men in the First World War, Gaz Morris, Feb 2014

The Guardian – First World War: Another Battlefront, Joanna Bourke, Nov 2008

Wikipedia – Harden-Eulenburg Affair, Noel Pemberton Billing

Academia Edu – The British Society for the Study of Sex Psychology: Bloomsbury and the Medicalization of Same-Sex Love, Eileen Barrett

Pink News – The Hidden Origins of the Modern Gay Rights Movement in WW1, Laurie Marhoefer, May 2017

Chapter 7

Matt Cook *A Gay History of Britain: Love & Sex Between Men Since the Middle Ages*, p.45

Time Out – Gay London in the 20's, Matt Cook, May 2007

Lay Readers Book Review – The Dilly: A Secret History of Piccadilly Rent boys by Jeremy Reed, Oct 2016

Matt Houlbrook *Queer London: Perils & Pleasures in the Sexual Metropolis 1918-57*, p.76-p.80

London Review of Books: Join the Club – Queer London: Perils & Pleasures in the Sexual Metropolis 1918-57 by Matt Houlbrook, Richard Hornsey, Sep 2006

Paul Pry *For Your Convenience*

Bryars and Bryars – For Your Convenience: The First Queer City Guide? Sep 2016

Wikipedia – Thelema

Queer Music Heritage: J D Doyle – Masculine Women, Feminine Men

YouTube – Masculine Women, Feminine Men (1926), sung by Irving Kaufman

Backlots – The Happiest Marriage in Hollywood: The Story of William Haines and Jimmy Shields, Jun 2014

Wikipedia – William Haines

Wikipedia – The Caravan Club

The Guardian – Revived: The 1930's London Gay Members' Club Raided by Police, Mark Brown, Feb 2017

Wikipedia – Emergency Powers Defence Act 1939

Chapter 8

BBC – WW2 People's War: Fact File: Commonwealth and Allied Forces

National Survey of Sexual Attitudes and Lifestyles 3

Wikipedia – WW2 Casualties

Stephen Bourne *Fighting Proud: The Untold Story of the Gay Men Who Served in Two World Wars*

London Review of Books, Richard Hornsey – *Queer London: Perils & Pleasures in the Sexual Metropolis 1918-57*, by Matt Houlbrook, p.34

The Independent – Obituary: Dudley Cave, Peter Tatchell, May 1999

BBC – WW2 People's War: A Gay Soldier's Story, Peter Tatchell, Jun 2004

Wikipedia – Quentin Crisp

Quentin Crisp *The Naked Civil Servant*; Uncle Sam quote p.103

Tommy Dickinson Curing Queers: Mental Nurses & Their Paitents, 1935-74; Charles Anderson quote p.44; Himmler quote p.46

Richard Platt *The Pink Triangle: The Nazi War Against Homosexuals*; Himmler quote p.99

History Revealed – On the Same Side: Homosexuals During the Second World War, Emma Mason, Jan 2014

BBC Timewatch: Sex and War, Sep 1998

Rictor Norton – Gay History & Literature: I'll Be With You Tonight, The Gay Love Letters of Ralph Hall to Montagu Glover, 1998

Ian Gleed *Arise to Conquer*

Wikipedia – Ian Gleed

Hatfield-Herts – Wing Commander Ian Richard Gleed

Gay Star News – How Gay Was the Battle of Britain? Kevin Charles, Aug 2015

Gay Dad – Homosexuals in the RAF

The Queer Story File – Flying Figaro

Jonathan Reeve *Battle of Britain Voices: 37 Fighter Pilots Tell Their Extraordinary Stories*

Williams, Thomas, Myers, Macauley, by Rachel Williams – Squadron Leader Christopher Llewellyn Gotch, 1923-2002; incl. YouTube BBC2 Programme It's Not Unusual: Programme 1: The Age of Innocence 1920-1951

Chapter 9

Kinsey Institute – Historical Report: Diversity if Sexual Orientation; also – The Kinsey Scale

Wikipedia – Kinsey Reports, Alfred Kinsey

ONS – Sexual Identity, UK 2016

Equality & Human Rights Commission: Estimating the Size & Composition of the LGB Population in Britain, Peter J Aspinall, University of Kent, 2009

The Guardian – One in Fifty People in UK Now Say They Are LGB, Haroon Siddique, Oct 2017

The Telegraph – 6% of Population Are Gay or Lesbian According to Whitehall Figures, Fiona Govan, Dec 2005

The Royal Society – Evidence for Maternally Inherited Factors Favouring Male Homosexuality & Promoting Female Fecundity, Andrea Camperio-Ciani, Francesca Corna & Claudio Capiluppi, Oct 2014

New Scientist – Survival of Genetic Homosexual Traits Explained, Andy Coghan, Oct 2004

Nature – Epigenetic Tags Linked to Homosexuality in Men, Sara Reardon, Oct 2015

BBC News Magazine – The Evolutionary Puzzle of Homosexuality, William Kremer, Feb 2014

Desi Speaks – Homosexuality; Evolutionary Necessity; incl. TedTalk video Homosexuality: It's About Survival Not Sex by Dr James O'Keefe, Nov 2016

Chapter 10

Wikipedia – Wilhelm von Gloeden

Bird in Flight – What It Was Like: First Porn, Julia Chuzha, May 2015

Wikiwand – *A Free Ride*

Wikipedia – *Le Coucher de la Mariée, Le Ménage Moderne de Madam Butterfly, The Surprise of A Knight*

Wikipedia – Gay Pornography

Closet Professor – History of Gay Porn, Sep 2011

Al Di Lauro & Gerald Rabkin *Dirty Movies: An Illustrated History of the Stag Film 1915-1970* (Three Comrades) p.102

Wikipedia – *Boys In The Sand*, Joey Stefano, Jeff Stryker

The Independent – Danny Wylde; Former Porn Star, on Pay, the Stigma of Doing Gay & Straight Scenes & Why He Left The Industry, Olivia Blair, Mar 2017

Wikipedia – Priapism

Campaign Live – With Innovation, Porn Beats Tech to the Punch, I-Hsien Sherwood, Mar 2017

Chapter 11

History.com – Stonewall Riots

The Atlantic – An Amazing 1969 Account of the Stonewall Uprising, (Dick Leitsch quote) Garance Franke-Ruta, Jan 2013

Wikipedia – Dick Leitsch

Wikipedia – Paragraph 175

Archer Magazine – Homosexuality & Aboriginal Culture: A Lore Unto Themselves, Steven Lindsay Ross, Oct 2014

BuzzFeed – Here's What It's Like to Grow Up Gay & Indigenous in Australia (Gregory Phillips) Allan Clarke, Dec 2015

Unfit For Publication – NSW Supreme Court, Quarter Sessions & Police Court, Bestiality, Buggery, Sodomy & Other Sex Offences Trials 1727-1930: 1828 Alexander Brown & Edward Curtiss

The Conversation- Debauchery On the Fatal Shore: The Sex Lives of Australia's Convicts, Graham Willet, University of Melbourne, Dec 2017

Wayne R Dyres, Encyclopaedia of Homosexuality Vol 1, (Australia), p.93

SBS – Gold: Impact of Gold on Australia: High Cost of Labour, Tim Scott

UIDAHO Edu – Australian Aboriginal: Initiation & Mourning Rites of Passage

NCBI National Library of Medicine – Ritual Mutilation, Subincision of the Penis Among Australian Aborigines, D J Pounder, 1983

Anthro Source Online Library – The Australian Subincision Ceremony Reconsidered: Vaginal Envy or Kangaroo Bifid Penis Envy, Phillip Singer, 1966

Wikipedia – Penile Subincision

Bob Hay – Boy Wives of the Aranda: Homosexuality Among the Aranda

Quartz – The History of the Tango is Actually Kind of Gay, Olivia Goldhill, Aug 2016

Dance of the Heart – History of the Argentine Tango, Deb Sclar, Jun 2013

Chapter 12

BBC News – HIV/AIDS: Why Were the Campaigns Successful in the West? Jon Kelly, Nov 2011

YouTube – AIDS Don't Die of Ignorance (1987 TV Ad)

Avert: Global Information & Education on HIV & AIDS – Origin of HIV & AIDS, Jan 2017

NCBI US National Library of Medicine – The Early Spread & Epidemic Ignition of HIV-1 in Human Populations, Oct 2014

Smithsonian – Why Kinshasa in the 1920's Was the Perfect Place for HIV to Go Global, Marissa Fessenden, Oct 2014

CDC MMWR Weekly – Current Trends Update on Acquired Deficiency Syndrome (AIDS), United States, Sep 1982

BBC News – HIV Myths Endure From the 1980's, Dec 2016

HIV.Gov – How Is HIV Transmitted? May 2017

Healio Infectious Disease News – HIV/AIDS the Discovery of an Unknown Deadly Virus, Jun 2006

Avert Global Information & Education on HIV & AIDS – History of HIV & AIDS Overview, Jan 2017

BBC News – The 1980's AIDS Campaign, Oct 2005

BBC News – How Princess Diana Changed Attitudes to AIDS, Apr 2017

LGBT History Month – Section 28

Independent – Section 28: What Was Margaret Thatcher's Controversial Law & How Did It Affect the Lives of LGBT+ People? Joe Sommerland, May 2018

Wikipedia – Section 28

BBC News – HIV UN Meets Goal to Treat 15 Million, Michelle Roberts, Jul 2015

Prevention Access – Consensus Statement, Jul 2016

I-Base – The Evidence for U=U (Undetectable = Untransmittable): Why Negligible Risk Is Zero Risk, Simon Collins, Oct 2017

The Lancet HIV – U=U Taking Off in 2017, Nov 2017

Pozitive Hope – U Equals U Consensus Statement, (Dr Anthony Fauci quote), Dec 2016

HIV.Gov – Pre-Exposure Prophylaxis

UNAIDS – 90-90-90 Treatment For All

Chapter 13

Wikipedia – LGBT Rights by Country & Territory

The Guardian – Gay Relationships Are Still Criminalised in 72 Countries, Pamela Duncan, Jul 2017

The Independent – LGBT Relationships Are Illegal in 74 Countries, Siobhan Fenton, May 2016

Stop homophobia.com – Where Is It Illegal to be LGBT+?

Pink News – UN Passes Gay Rights Resolution, Jessica Geen, 2011

OHCHR – United Nations Resolutions: & Gender Identity

Wikipedia – Same-sex Marriage

CNN – Nigeria Bans Same-Sex Marriage, Anna Maja Rappard & Nana Karikari-apau, Jan 2014

The Diplomat – India Reinstates 153-year-old Law Criminalising Gay Sex, J. T. Quigley, Dec 2013

ILGA Europe

Chapter 14

Lucy Delap The Transformation of Male Homosexuality in Modern Britain, Mar 2014

British Social Attitudes: Personal Relationships – Homosexuality

Wikipedia – Timeline of LGBT History in the United Kingdom

Stonewall – LGBT Timeline

The Telegraph – Turing's Law: Oscar Wilde among 50,000 Convicted Gay Men Granted Posthumous Pardons, Kate McCann, Jan 2017

T and F Online – The Influence of Media Role Models on Gay, Lesbian & Bisexual Identity, Sarah C Gomillion, Traci A Giuliano, Feb 2011

Pride Power List 2017

Stonewall Scotland – Role Models: Being Yourself: LGBT Lives in Scotland

Psychology Today – I Could Do That: Why Role Models Matter, Nancy Darling, May 2012

Cayenne Consulting – The Seven Traits of a Role Model

Oxford Dictionary – Role Model definition

The Prince's Trust – Macquarie Youth Index 2017 Annual Report

Diversity Role Models

Part 2. Chapter 15

The Buggery Act 1533 – The British Library Collection

Wikipedia – The Buggery Act

Rictor Norton – The Medieval Basis of Modern Law

Paul Johnson & Robert Vanderbeck *Law, Religion and Homosexuality* p32-p34.

Chapter 16

Rictor Norton – Homosexuality in Nineteenth Century England: The Last Men Executed for Sodomy in England, 1835

Chapter 17

Wikipedia – Offences Against the Person Act 1828

Wikipedia – Robert Peel

BBC History – Sir Robert Peel (1788-1850)

Wikipedia – Offences Against the Person Act 1861

LGBT Archive – Offences Against the Person Act 1861 Section 61

British Library Collection Items – The Criminal Law Amendment Act 1885

Wikipedia – Henry Labouchére

UKPOL – Henry Labouchére – 1885 Speech on Homosexuality

Parliament – 1885 Labouchére Amendment

Famous Trials – Sentencing Statement of Justice Wills

Chapter 18

Rictor Norton – A Critique of Social Constructionism & Postmodern Queer Theory: The Term Homosexual

LGBT History Project – How Male Same-Sex Desire Became 'Homosexuality', May 2012

Lloyd Duhaime – Law Hall of Fame: Karl Heinrich Ulrichs

Hubert Kennedy – Karl Heinrich Ulrichs, First Theorist of Homosexuality

BBC Future – The Invention of Heterosexuality, Brandon Ambrosino, Mar 2017

Academia.edu – The Double Life of Kertbeny, Judit Takacs

Out History.org – Constructing the Hetero, Homo, Bi System:1868 Karl-Maria Kertbeny, Nov 2016

Chapter 19

Wikipedia – Oscar Wilde

Neil McKenna *The Secret Life of Oscar Wilde*

Oscar Wilde *Profundis*

Lord Alfred Douglas *Two Loves*

Chapter 20

Wikipedia – George Cecil Ives

Harry Ransom Center, The University of Texas at Austin – George Cecil Ives, An Inventory of His Papers at the Harry Ransom Center

Mancunian Matters – The Order of Chaeronea, Sian Broderick, Oct 2014

Neil McKenna *The Secret Life of Oscar Wilde*, p.18 'heady mix of art, idealism and politics', p.269, 270, 435 & 480 for 'Chaeronea'

Wikipedia – Sacred Band of Thebes

History Buffed – The Sacred Band of Thebes: The Other 300 Greeks, May 2017

Today I Found Out – The Sacred Band of Thebes Entirely Made Up of Male Lovers, May 2014

Oxford Index – George Ledwell Taylor

Wikipedia – George Ledwell Taylor

Lesely A Hall *A New Psychological Society, F W Stella Browne, International Journal of Ethics, Vol 28 1917-18*

Harry Ransom Center, The University of Texas at Austin – British Sexological Society: An Inventory of Its Records at the Harry Ransom Center

Chapter 21

University Cambridge – How Human Sexuality is Documented: What Can We Learn from Questionnaires and Life Writing, Ina Linge

Scielo Review – Conceptualization and Measurement of Homosexuality in Sex Surveys: A Critical Review: Early

History of Sex Surveys, Stuart Michaels, Birgitte Lhomond, Jul 2006

Florence Tamagne *A History of Homosexuality in Europe, Vol I & II*, p.85

Wikipedia – Louis-Charles Royer, Chevalier d'Eon

Kantar TNS Study – The Man Box: A Study on Being a Young Man in the US, UK and Mexico: Key Findings, B Heilman, G Barker, A Harrison, 2017

Chapter 22

Cinema UCLA Film & Television Archive, *Anders als die Andern* (Different from The Others) A Restoration in Progress (1919), Jan-Christopher Horak

J Clark Media, Jim's Review – *Anders als die Andern* (Different from The Others)

Wikipedia – Different from The Others

Wikipedia – Paragraph 175

The New York Times – A Daring Film Silenced No More, Robert Ito, Nov 2013

Chapter 23

Wikipedia – Scientific-Humanitarian Committee

Wikipedia – Adolf Brand, Der Eigene

Huffpost – Was the First Gay Rights Movement Run by Nazis? James Peron, Oct 2016

USHMM – 1933 Book Burnings

Wikipedia – Nazi Book Burnings, The Night of the Long Knives

Wikipedia – The Pink Triangle, Richard Plant

Richard Plant *The Pink Triangle: The Nazi War Against Homosexuals*

Digital Commons, Eastern Michigan University – The Persecution of Homosexuals During the, Jennifer Rokakis, 2013

Chapter 24

Encyclopaedia USHMM – Persecution of Homosexuals in the Third Reich

Wikipedia – Paragraph 175

Stop Homophobia – The Gay Holocaust, Kevin O'Neil

Wikipedia – Carl Vaernet

Andrej Koymasky – The Gay Holocaust: Nazi Criminals: 6.2.2 Dr Carl Peter Vaernet, Mar 2004

Wikipedia – Bent (play) by Martin Sherman

Wikipedia – Persecution of Homosexuals in Nazi Germany & the Hoolocaust

Keele University – Remembering the Gay Victims of the Holocaust

Chapter 25

Revolvy – Wolfenden Report

Wikipedia – LGBT Rights in the United Kingdom

Palgrave SocSciMatters – Knight & Wilson on the LGBT Community & the Criminal Justice System Part 1

The Guardian – Coming Out of the Dark Ages, Geraldine Bedell, Jun 2007

NCBI, US National Library of Medicine – Treatments of Homosexuality in Britain Since the 1950's: An Oral History, The Experience of Patients, Annie Bartlett, Michael King, Feb 2004

LGBT Archive – Antony Grey

Wikipedia – Alan Turing

History of Information – Alan Turing's Ambiguous Suicide, Jeremy Norman, Aug 2018

Wikipedia – John Gielgud

Wikipedia – The Lavender Scare

YouTube – Trailer for The Lavender Scare, a film by Josh Howard, Jul 2011

Wikipedia – Edward Douglas-Scott-Montagu, 3rd Baron Montagu of Beaulieu, Peter Wildeblood, Michael Pitt-Rivers

The Guardian – The Wildeblood Scandal: The Trial That Rocked 1950's Britain & Changed Gay Rights, Adam Mars-Jones, Jul 2017

National Archives – Before & After the Wolfenden Report

Wikipedia – Wolfenden Report

Parliament UK – Wolfenden Report

Chapter 26

The Guardian – Don't Fall For The Myth That It's 50 Years Since We Decriminalised Homosexuality, Peter Tatchell, May 2017

Wikipedia – Homosexual Law Reform Society

The Guardian – Coming Out of the Dark Ages, Geraldine Bedell, Jun 2007

Parliament UK – Homosexual Law Reform Society Letter

The National Archives – The Passing of the 1967 Sexual Offences Act, Vicky Iglikowski, Jul 2017

Legislation Gov UK – Sexual Offences Act 1967

BBC Man Alive: Consenting Adults:1 The Men, Jun 1967

Chapter 27
Dylan Jones *David Bowie: A Life*, p.89, p.107
The Guardian – Flashback: 22 January 1972, Michael Watts, Jan 2006
Wikipedia – Kinsey Scale
The Guardian – How Performing Starman on Top of the Pops Sent Bowie into the Stratosphere, David Hepworth, Jan 2016
Chapter 28
Independent – The Gay Captain Who Made Waves, David Randall, Nov 2002
Independent – Sacking Gay Sailors Would Have Scuppered Fleet, Chris Gray, Oct 2002
Wikipedia – Hector MacDonald, T. E. Lawrence
BiteBack Publishing – James Wharton
Oxford University Public Interest Law Submission – The Legal Treatment of Homosexuals in the Armed Forces of Europe ('incompatible' quote) p.9
The Guardian – The Military's Rainbow Revolution: From Dishonourable Discharge to Model Employer, Eleanor Tucker, Jun 2015
Eugene R Fidell, Elizabeth L Hillman, Dwight H Sullivan Military Justice: Cases & Materials: Lustig Prean & Beckett v United Kingdom: European Court of Human Rights, 1999 (1994 Armed Forces Policy & Guidelines on Homosexuality) ('close physical conditions' quote)
Wikipedia – Sexual Orientation & Gender Identity in Military Service: United Kingdom
BBC News – MoD Says Sorry to Gay Personnel, Jun 2007
The Guardian – Defence Ministry Apologises for Gay Discrimination, (Wing Cdr Sagar quote), Fred Attewill, Jun 2007
Paul Johnson *Going to Strasbourg: An Oral History of Sexual Orientation Discrimination & the European Convention on Human Rights* Rank Outsiders and Robert Ely p.109
Wikipedia – Stonewall Charity
The Guardian – UK Armed Forces Recruits to be Asked if They Are Gay, Jan 2015
The Telegraph – What Its Like To Be Gay in the Armed Forces, Theo Merz, Jan 2015
Army LGBT Forum – Forum Patron: A Message From Lieutenant General Patrick Sanders, 2017

Gay Dad – Commander Douggie Ward: Role Model
Pink News – This Is What It's Like To Be Out in the Royal
Navy, Hadley Stewart, Jun 2018

Epilogue

The Holy Male – Queer Men, Myths & Reincarnation, Toby
Johnson, Apr 2018
Gilles Herrada *The Missing Myth: A New Vision of Same-Sex
Love*
YouTube – Jordan Bach: A New Vision of Same-Sex Love with
Gilles Herrada, Oct 2013

Index

263

Acknowledgements

I'd like to thank my editor, Chris Newton (www.chrisnewton.co.uk) and cover designer Jessica Bell (www.jessicabelldesign.com). Contributors, Cdr. Douggie Ward and Linda Riley.

Without the brave men who have struggled, fought and survived against all the odds to live their lives with authenticity and truth, who have, in innumerable ways, big and small, changed societal views and punitive state regulations; this book, *This Forbidden Fruit*, and the lives of so many LGBT+ people today, me included, would not be possible or half as rich. I thank you all, both past and present, with all my heart.

If you have enjoyed *This Forbidden Fruit*, please use the link below to leave a review. A simple kind word or two is all that is needed and can help someone who is looking, to make the decision to read this book. By spreading the word, we can change the mythos.

Thank you, David Ledain.

www.amazon.co.uk/thisforbiddenfruit/createareview

David Ledain is on Facebook & Twitter @davidledain and at www.gaydad.co.uk

26874778R00153

Printed in Great Britain
by Amazon